FEED YOUR PEOPLE

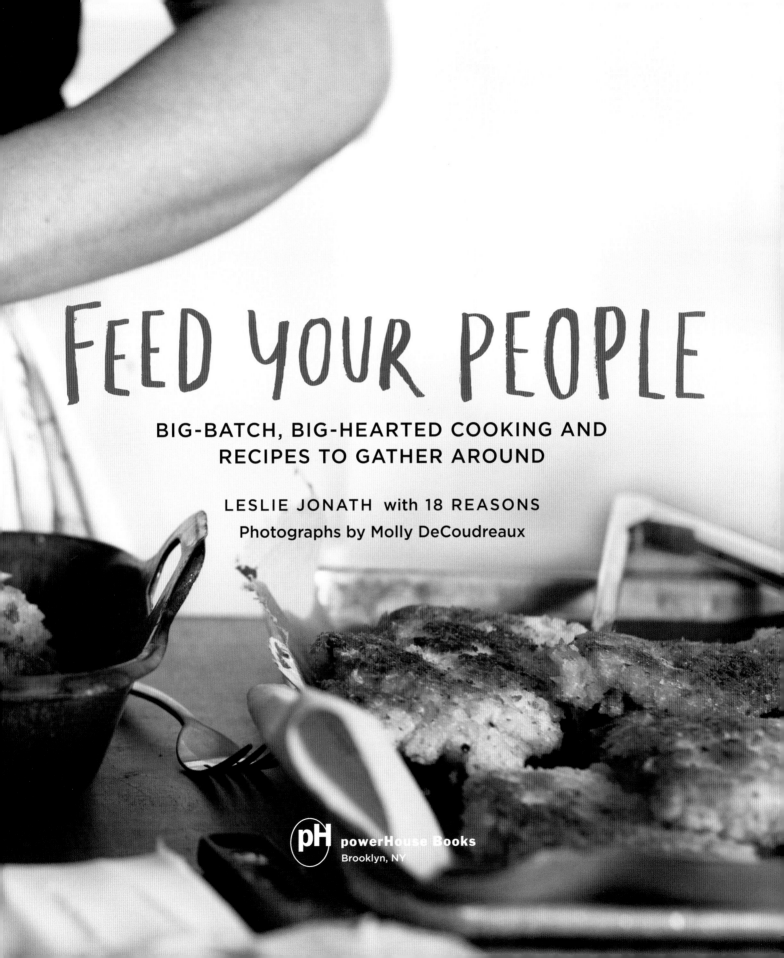

FEED YOUR PEOPLE

BIG-BATCH, BIG-HEARTED COOKING AND RECIPES TO GATHER AROUND

LESLIE JONATH with 18 REASONS

Photographs by Molly DeCoudreaux

pH powerHouse Books
Brooklyn, NY

CONTENTS

foreword

Why would a cooking school open its doors once a month to serve a $10 dinner to eighty people? The 18 Reasons Community Dinner began when our students, friends, and neighbors asked to spend more time in our beautiful classroom, not taking cooking classes but simply connecting with one another. We decided that a $10 dinner, changing every month according to who was cooking it and what we wanted to celebrate (red beans and rice for Mardi Gras, barbecued ribs in July), would be a fun way to bring people in. Community Dinner is now our most popular offering; as I write, it is regularly sold out for months in advance.

At 18 Reasons, we aim to inspire home cooks to learn new skills, maximize the knowledge and resources they already have, and spend more time cooking and sharing food with family and friends. As corporations promise to take care of us in every way, from driving us to work to feeding us a hot meal at the end of the day, reclaiming the simple act of cooking gives us an incomparable awareness of ourselves as human beings in control of our own lives. Cooking reminds us that we are capable of taking care of ourselves and others, and that this care makes our communities and families stronger and more connected.

Each month, we teach as many as seventy-five free cooking classes to low-income adults, teens, kids, and families, partnering with more than one hundred schools, clinics, community centers, and shelters each year. We teach another twenty-four paid classes in our classroom every month, on topics that vary from Basic Knife Skills to Flavors of the Malaysian Coast. At the end of each class, free or paid, we gather together to eat what we have made, to talk about what we have learned, and to enjoy one another's company. For immigrant moms, struggling low-wage workers, kids who rely on free school meals to keep their bellies full, and busy professionals alike, the act of sitting together and eating brings a sense of joy, empowerment, and community.

I am known within our little organization for always enthusiastically saying "yes!" to new ideas and projects, and when Leslie approached me to ask if 18 Reasons would partner with her to create this book, I knew immediately that *Feed Your People* aligned perfectly with what we do every day.

Whether you are making the Buttermilk Chess Slab Pie for a barbecue or inviting your friends over for a dumpling-making party, I encourage you to use this book as a starting place for food gatherings large and small. I'm sure you will be inspired not only to cook the delicious recipes you'll find in these pages, but also to take some of your own favorite recipes and figure out how to scale them for your community.

One of my favorite moments at any Community Dinner is when newcomers check in with me, look nervously at the rows of communal tables, and ask, "What do I do now?"

"Dinner is on its way," I tell them—with two seatings an hour apart, we serve our guests as soon as they arrive. "Go ahead, sit down, and make new friends!" At first they hesitate, but once eight people are squeezed around a table for a delicious dinner, they find that friendship comes naturally. I hope you feel the same way as you get to know the chefs and recipes in these pages, and that you are inspired to bring your community together for many fantastic meals to come.

Sarah Nelson
Executive Director, 18 Reasons

introduction

Every year my family throws a "latke-and-vodka" party. Well ahead of the event, my mom makes and fries batches of latkes and freezes them. After about a month of on-and-off cooking, she'll have made as many as two hundred potato pancakes. She and my father then pack them up in a cooler and deliver them to my house. At the party, she reheats them in the oven, while my dad leads the crowd in vodka shots with pickle chasers. Friends bring desserts and wine. What started as a small gathering has now grown to eighty people: friendships have been forged and even a romance or two have blossomed. For our family and friends, latkes and vodka are a beloved yearly ritual. But as much as people love latkes, the party's main appeal is that it brings everyone together.

Family food traditions are often centered around holidays. But people regularly cook for others in all kinds of ways—at cooking clubs, cook-offs, harvest gatherings, bake sales and other fund-raisers, and, of course, family celebrations that range from weddings and birthdays to memorials. Creating community through food is what this book is about. Two questions inspired it: how do we gather and what are the foods we gather around?

After hosting and cooking for many large parties on my own, I noticed that the best events were those that featured a spectacular main course. Once there was a main dish, it was simple to ask my friends to bring things like small bites, side dishes, beverages, and desserts to round out the meal. If someone was at a loss for an idea or even a recipe, it was easy to provide one. Even if we didn't all cook the meal in the same kitchen, it was still a wonderful group effort.

Building a party around one incredible dish can be cause for celebration. Just saying you are serving paella will draw a crowd, as will a promise of platters of tender carnitas and warm tortillas for a neighborhood taco feast. Racks of ribs star at backyard barbecues, a big pot of soup feeds a community dinner easily and inexpensively, a bumper crop of peaches inspires a block-long jam can, a huge batch of meatballs becomes a local fund-raiser, a pan of brownies can be shared at a cookie exchange or toted to a bake sale—all of them great candidates for a get-together.

Sharing a meal is a powerful way to build community. One night, facing an empty refrigerator, I decided to attend the monthly neighborhood dinner at 18 Reasons, a Bay Area nonprofit in San Francisco's Mission District. I had long known about this wonderful organization that brings people together for community dinners and for classes on cooking traditions from around the world, from Peru and El Salvador to Thailand and beyond. It also offers Cooking Matters classes to low-income families all over the Bay Area.

On the night I went to the community supper, which was served family-style on long wooden tables, I was a little nervous as a single diner, but my apprehension melted when so many nice people greeted me. Plate loaded with food, I sat down near a family who immediately invited me into their conversation. The experience confirmed my feeling that there is no easier way to meet and connect with people than at the table, an idea that anchors the community philosophy on which 18 Reasons is built. That first dinner led to the wonderful partnership that has created this book. Together, we organized meals to test the recipes and feed the community at the same time.

As a cookbook editor for many years, I have met many cooks and chefs for whom cooking for a large group of friends is easy and joyful. Perhaps you know someone like this—a person who seems relaxed in the kitchen and constantly pulls people together to eat, drink, and enjoy the moment. In that spirit, we approached a number of these "feeders" who generously shared their crowd-pleasing dishes.

Some cooks shared their all-time-great showstoppers, beloved (yet time-intensive) dishes that you would only make for a crowd. You can't make a timpano (the baked pasta dish made famous in the film *Big Night*) for less than fifteen people, a trifle by its very nature will feed at least twenty, and there is no such thing as small-batch porchetta.

Some cooks provided go-to recipes that are simple to scale. Above all we wanted to include a range of dishes that people would enjoy gathering around. With some savvy planning, this collection of great recipes (and a few fellow cooks by your side), we hope this book will encourage you to host big-hearted gatherings for your family and friends.

Leslie Jonath

1.
how to feed your people

IF YOU WANT to throw a party but are feeling overwhelmed, here is the best tip for cooking for a crowd: don't go it alone.

When you feed your people, the best part is *being with* your people. When I first started throwing parties, I would do all of the shopping and prepping by myself and then cook all day and night. I was so tired by the time the guests arrived that I wanted to say "Feed *yourselves*, people!" and then climb into bed.

Now, when I'm cooking for a crowd, I have at least two or three friends—and hopefully my mother—working in the kitchen with me. That makes preparing for the party as much fun as the party itself. Although many of us might aspire to be the type of host who can do it all, most guests actually like to make themselves useful. Cooking together is also a terrific way to make new friends, as any feeling of shyness or awkwardness is quickly overcome by common purpose.

Some recipes benefit from many hands in the kitchen. Foods like empanadas, dumplings, and tamales are best made in groups where people can fold, wrap, and/or roll while talking and enjoying one another's company As the saying goes, many hands make light (and delicious) work.

Forgo perfection in favor of connection. Of course, you want great food, but most people will remember the feeling of festivity as much as what they ate. Enlisting your family and friends in the cooking process has advantages beyond getting the meal on the table.

If you want to throw a party but fear you'll be overwhelmed, remember to share the effort. There is strength and fun in numbers.

7

HOW TO USE THIS BOOK

Menu cookbooks can seem intimidating, with multiple courses and elaborate timelines. This book encourages you to build the meal around one central dish and then invite others to provide any additional elements. Did you spend the day making lasagna? Serve a simple green salad and have a guest or two bring dessert. Is baking your specialty? Invite friends over for dessert and coffee and ask them to bring after-dinner drinks. Want to host an ice cream social but don't have an ice cream maker? Ask the guests to bring their favorite store-bought ice cream and you provide stellar homemade sauces and other toppings.

Building a meal centered on one big dish simplifies the process and creates excitement around the meal itself.

The dishes included here embrace many different cuisines and levels of cooking difficulty. Most recipes yield about ten servings with tips and ingredient lists for a double batch. If you need more food, you can add the two lists together or you can double the larger batch. Before you decide to go too big, however, keep in mind how much food can reasonably be prepared in your kitchen.

Each recipe provides information for various steps and components, assembling them in these categories:

MAKE-AHEAD provides guidelines for what can be prepared in advance and how to store it, to reduce the amount of the work on the day of the get-together.

EQUIPMENT outlines any larger-than-average cooking pots and pans, special tools, and other kitchen gear you'll need.

BIG BATCH NOTES share tricks that will come in handy for making the food in crowd-friendly batches.

SERVING presents advice on how to dish up the meal, with reminders for condiments and possible side dishes, special tableware, and other details.

INGREDIENT NOTES give helpful basic information about foods that are unusual and may be difficult to source.

Many recipes list all of these categories, while others offer only those that apply. Recipes for some favorite side dishes have been included, should you want to flesh out the meal on your own or offer them to guests to make.

If you are assigning recipes, keep in mind how much room you have in the oven or microwave for reheating. To avoid an overstuffed oven, rely on room-temperature dishes, salads, and appetizers or sides that don't need to be cooked.

MAKING IT HAPPEN

The secret to hosting a party for a crowd: Make Lists. Create lists for invitations; shopping; the menu, including all of the items that will be supplied by your guests; prepping; tableware; and anything else you can think of.

SHOPPING TIPS

○ In addition to adding fun to the adventure, consider bringing a friend or two with you for shopping to help check off items on the list, gather the ingredients, carry the bags, and (perhaps most important) unload your purchases at home. When you have a really big list, divide and conquer. Send your friend to one part of the store while you concentrate on another department. You can also assign shopping tasks, especially if multiple stops—butcher, baker, florist, farmers' market, liquor store—are required.

○ The most efficient way to organize the ingredients list is by category of ingredient. For example, write down all of the baking goods (flour, sugar, baking powder, and so on) on one section of your list. Put all of the produce together in a separate section and separate the herbs from the "storage" vegetables (like potatoes, onions, and garlic).

○ If you are a super-good planner, consider purchasing nonperishables a week or two ahead of time. Things like paper goods, most beverages, candles, and canned goods can be scratched off the list well before the event.

COOKING FOR A CROWD

Making food for a large group can be done most efficiently if you assess your kitchen and its limitations. If you have a six-burner stove with a double oven and an extra refrigerator, you are in great shape. But most of us deal with a less spacious and well-equipped cooking environment.

○ Make sure you have the right kitchen appliances to make your dish. Most of the recipes were designed with the home kitchen in mind, but there are instances when specialized equipment (noted in each recipe) will make the process much easier.

○ Clear out the refrigerator. If you are cooking for a big group, the first thing to do is to remove anything extraneous (and not perishable) from your fridge. Because of their acid content, condiments like ketchup, mustard, hot sauce, and pickles can be stored at room temperature for a day or two. If you are cooking for a very large crowd, and don't have access to a second refrigerator, coolers with ice cubes or dry ice will work as backup.

○ Make sure you have enough space to cook. Put away every appliance that is not absolutely necessary. If you don't have much countertop space, you can use folding tables.

THE DOUBLE BATCH APPROACH

In a few recipes, we advocate for making two single batches to yield a double batch. This is because it is easier, more time efficient, and the results are more consistent to cook these recipes in smaller batches. We don't expect readers to have access to a professional kitchen (and the huge stockpots, high BTU stoves, or double ovens that come with them), so we improvised to make these recipes achievable in any home kitchen. We've provided solutions for all of the recipes to yield a double batch, and called out when it is practical to make a double batch in one swift go, and when it is necessary to cook the batch in halves. There are also plenty of recipes that are naturally big batch, and don't require any doubling to feed a crowd: trifles, porchetta, lasagna, and paella, to name a few.

DOUBLE BATCH SEASONING

Doubling a recipe means increasing the amount of seasoning. When you see "season to taste," this is a cue that the food may require more seasoning than you expect. Taste the food before you serve it, and don't be afraid to add more salt.

STORING YOUR FOOD

Always cool hot food to lukewarm before storage. If you put a lot of hot food into the refrigerator it can raise the interior temperature to a level that can compromise foods already being stored. Devise ways to cool the food quickly so it doesn't stand at room temperature for longer than 2 hours. Here are some tips:

MAKE IT TO TAKE IT

Make a double batch and give one away. If you know a family with a new baby or have a sick friend, almost nothing is more welcome than the gift of homemade food. Allow the dish to cool before transporting and pack it in disposable containers so the recipient doesn't have to worry about returning your vessel. (Use an ovenproof container if the dish needs reheating.) Be sure to tuck the reheating or cooking instructions into the package.

o   Pick up a few bags of ice and store them in a cooler so you have plenty on hand to chill food quickly for storage.

o   For quicker cooling, transfer the food from its cooking vessel to a cold bowl or bowls. Nestle the bowl in an ice-filled sink or cooler. Stir the food a few times to distribute the cooler areas in the bowl. If the ice melts, add more.

o   Transfer cooled food to a specific storage container for refrigeration or freezing. Use disposable plastic lidded containers (the ones common at delicatessens, sold at restaurant supply stores in 1-, 2-, and 4-cup sizes) or zippered plastic freezer bags. The freezer bags are sturdier than the regular ones and are more versatile. Look for 2-gallon bags for storing some big batches. Once filled and tightly closed, freezer bags can be stored standing up or stacked horizontally to save space.

o   Large, wide rolls of aluminum foil and plastic wrap, sold at big-box stores and restaurant suppliers, are indispensable for large-batch cooking. Their added width allows you to cover large surfaces with the flick of a wrist. Heavy-duty aluminum foil is best because it doesn't tear or puncture as easily as standard foil when wrapped around food.

o   To label your stored items so you can easily distinguish them, use an indelible marking pen and waterproof masking tape.

ORGANIZING THE SERVING

Plan your serving strategy in advance.

o   Map out where everyone will stand or sit. Do you need to rent a table or borrow a few chairs?

o   Evaluate your tableware and dishes. If you need more dishes, go for a mismatched strategy, borrowing from friends. If you have the budget, consider renting (which is nice because it saves on cleanup; rented dishes and glassware can be returned dirty or simply rinsed off). Also consider using supplies or tableware that can be recycled or composted, like plates made of bamboo. Platters, big bowls, and serving spoons and forks should be checked, too, as well as table linens (tablecloths and napkins).

o   If you are serving buffet-style, be sure you have enough room for everything, including the plates, napkins, eating utensils, breads, condiments, centerpiece, and other miscellany. It's a good idea to set the table with the empty platters and bowls and additional items before the party, so you have time to move things as needed.

o   To set up a buffet table: Put plates at the beginning of the line and eating utensils and napkins at the end. That way, guests need to hold only the plate as they serve themselves. Roll or wrap the silverware in a napkin as a single package. Plan the order of the food on the buffet. When considering the placement of the food, arrange it logically according to how it falls on the menu.

○ If you have a very large group, assign servers to help dish up the food. Allow room around the serving table against a wall. Service will go more quickly if people can approach the food from both sides of the table.

○ Feed the elders. Make a plate for each and deliver it to them. Think of other people in the group who might appreciate this extra help, too.

CLEANING UP

If people offer to help, perhaps the most useful thing someone can do is to hang around after the meal to chat and clean up. Put on some good music, pour a glass of wine, and make the process part of the after-party.

○ Before the party, empty your recycling and have sufficient garbage bags ready. Then, as the party gets going, keep an eye on the beverage bottles and cans and dispose of the empties as needed. You may want to enlist a friend or two to help you periodically whisk them away.

EQUIPMENT

Always check that you have the necessary pots, pans, and the like before you start cooking. The recipes are geared for the home cook and most use readily available equipment. If you need to purchase special items or want to track down larger pots and other vessels for big batch cooking, restaurant supply stores are a great source. Most are open to the general public, and the prices are relatively inexpensive. While each recipe specifies any necessary equipment, some general pieces of equipment are particularly useful for big batch cooking.

Keep in mind that professional cookware often requires a professional stove. For example, in a restaurant kitchen, a *rondeau* (a wide, squat pot) is a common cooking vessel, but you rarely see one in a home kitchen.

This is because the wide base heats more efficiently on the wide, hot burner on a restaurant-grade stove.

SHEET PANS. The full sheet pan, made from sturdy aluminum and measuring about 13 by 36 inches, is designed to fit in a huge professional oven. The half sheet pan is half the size (13 by 18 inches) of the full sheet, making it much more practical for home use. The smaller quarter sheet pan, which measures 9 by 13 inches, has its own set of uses. Half and quarter sheet pans are sometimes sold with lids to cover sheet cakes, big batches of baked brownies, and the like.

Once considered professional equipment, half sheet pans are now sold at reasonable prices at nearly every kitchenware store. They can be stacked, either flat or on their sides, to accommodate your storage space.

Half sheet pans will hold large numbers of cookies and vegetables, multiple roasts, whole fish, whole and cut-up poultry, and more when baking or roasting. They are also perfect for prepping, acting as a kind of staging area for gnocchi, empanadas, dumplings, and the like before they are cooked. Half sheet pans can be used to set up your *mise en place* (the recipe ingredients prepared for cooking), or they can act as a large tray for transporting foods across the room or even across town.

HOTEL PANS. This deep, wide metal container is sold in many sizes and depths, with lids and without. The largest size is about 12 by 20 inches and between 2 and 6 inches deep. Hotel pans are used mainly to braise foods in the oven and are not for the stove top. If the pan you have is the right size, it can be inserted into a chafing dish as a serving vessel. If you decide to purchase a hotel pan, be sure to measure your oven before you do, then choose one that allows 3 inches of clearance between the pan and the oven sides, back, and door. Pans without lids can be covered with aluminum foil for oven use and storage.

CHAFING DISHES AND WARMING EQUIPMENT. Chafing dishes (rectangular or round), which are heated by canned fuel, are the classic warming vessels. Very often, hotel pans are sized to fit into the dishes, which are also known as chafers. An 8-quart rectangular pan or a 5-quart round pan is a convenient size. Get a second (or even a third) pan to hold extra batches, which can go right from the oven to the chafer. Be sure to have sufficient fuel to last the length of your serving period.

Electric hot plates are another way to go. A range of attractive warmers in a variety of sizes is available.

Slow cookers are useful to hold many different kinds of foods: soups, stews, warm dessert toppings, and more. Multicookers, which have a temperature range of high to low, can also be used for keeping hot food hot.

PLASTIC STORAGE CONTAINERS. These essential receptacles often go by the name of their best-known manufacturer, Cambro. This food-safe, white or clear plastic container, which ranges in size from 1 pint to 5 gallons, is sold with and without a lid, but the lids are a good investment, especially if you have to transport the food. Cambros are fantastic for storing anything from soups to grain salads and for mixing up large batches of dough. They do take up a lot of room in a home refrigerator, however, so buy sizes that make sense for your purposes. Square containers are more space efficient than round ones.

BIG POTS. A Dutch oven of enameled cast iron is probably one of the most versatile of all cooking vessels because it can go from stove to oven. There are many conflicting theories as to how the Dutch oven got its name, but one thing is known for sure: the original design held hot coals in a slightly concave lid so food could cook from a top and bottom heat source simultaneously. This heat penetration is still true today because the heavy metal lid absorbs the heat, which then rebounds down onto the cooking food.

Cast-iron Dutch ovens are designed to brown the food (for example, beef for chili) right in the pot. When cooking for a crowd, however, it is often better to brown some of the food in a separate skillet to save time. Also, if you try to brown the full amount of meat in the Dutch oven, the resulting glaze (called a *fond*) tends to build up on the pot bottom and burn.

For cooking a big batch, a 6-quart Dutch oven is a middle-of-the-road size. Keep in mind that Dutch ovens are heavy, and that a pot filled with food will be even heavier, so select one that you can handle.

If you need a specialized big pot (like a huge seafood cooker or an extra-wide paella pan), consider buying it with other people from your community and dubbing it the community pot. Then, when anyone needs the pot, he or she borrows it and returns it when the party is over.

BIG BOWLS. Stainless-steel bowls can be used for more than mixing ingredients. For example, because they are heat-resistant, they can be turned into double boilers by fitting them over pots of simmering water. Also, even if they aren't pretty, they are useful for serving salads and more. A set of nested bowls is indispensable for handling just about every size of mixing task. If you do a lot of cooking for a crowd, buy a super-size bowl (the largest you can store easily) for mixing up extra-large amounts of salads and the like.

KITCHEN SCALE. Most of the recipes in this book are in standard measurements, however, there are times when you need to know the weight of a food item. Although many supermarkets these days print out the weight of produce on the sales receipt, you may shop at a farmers' market without the resource of the receipt. Digital, battery-operated kitchen scales are inexpensive. Many bakers note the importance of weighing flour and certain other ingredients for baking. In this book, with so many contributors, it proved impossible to get a consensus on specific weights and a method for scaling, so no weights are provided unless they were provided by the individual cook.

STAND MIXER. If you can afford one, a heavy-duty stand mixer is useful for mixing batters, kneading dough, whipping up large batches of whipped cream, and similar tasks. A stand mixer has two main attributes: First, it can easily handle large batches of dough, batter, and more. Second, it frees up your hands to do other jobs while the dough is being kneaded or the batter is being beaten for several minutes. The best-known mixers also have useful attachments for other jobs, such as juicing or rolling out pasta dough. The standard mixer has a bowl with a capacity of 4½ to 5 quarts, but if you are committed to turning out large batches, look for a 6- or even 7-quart model. It is extremely helpful to have two bowls because sometimes you need to put a second bowl into action when the first one is already in use. This especially happens with cakes when it comes time to whip egg whites for a batter. Some mixer brands have timers that can be set for the mixing period, which is a particularly helpful feature.

An electric handheld mixer is useful for preparing smaller amounts of food that don't need a big-capacity bowl, like whipping a cup or two of cream or just a few eggs.

FOOD PROCESSORS. The food processor is useful for many jobs, from making pastry dough to shredding vegetables to pureeing soup. For big parties, use a model with an 11-cup or greater capacity bowl.

STACKED STEAMER. For large batches, a stacked steamer with multiple tiers will hold many more items, so you don't have to keep refilling as you would with a single basket.

There are two basic models: inexpensive bamboo and slightly pricier metal. Unless you are using a metal

FEED YOUR PEOPLE: FEED THE WORLD

When you feed people, you feed yourself both literally and spiritually. Most of the contributors in this book volunteer for events and organizations that nourish people in need. Please think about joining an organization that feeds the hungry or provides food for those who are struggling. Consider holding a fund-raiser, even something small, such as a bake sale, a soup swap, or a pop-up dinner. By joining with other people and organizations, whether local, national, or international, you will help not only to make an impact but also to create community, which can lead to meaningful connections. By feeding your people, you can feed the world.

steamer set, which includes the pan, tiers, and lid, choose a large saucepan that will snugly hold the stacked tiers on top. First, add water to a depth of 2 to 3 inches to the pan, cover the pan tightly, and bring the water to a boil over high heat. Now remove the lid and put the filled and stacked tiers on top. Cover the top tier, reduce the heat to low to keep a good of head of steam going, and cook the food as directed. Always keep in mind that the steam is hot, so use pot holders and avert your face when removing the tiers from the pot.

2.
small bites,
big parties

DUMPLINGS, EMPANADAS, TAMALES, onigiri—some of the world's most popular foods come in small packages. These hand-held bites are fun foods to make and benefit from having many hands in the kitchen to speed the work of shaping, filling, wrapping, and cooking.

Inviting friends to participate in assembling these foods gives the get-together purpose and makes it more enjoyable. If you are making filled foods, you can streamline the process by preparing the fillings ahead of time and then inviting friends to help wrap them. Because this is big-batch cooking, I recommend that you use store-bought wrappers as many good ones are sold and they're time savers. That way you can spend more time chatting, cooking, and eating together.

Serve these tasty bites as snacks or surround them with side dishes to make them the centerpiece of a big meal. Most of them can be made in advance and frozen (you may need to borrow space in a friend's freezer to accommodate them all). You can even put together two celebrations: host an "assembly day" and then invite guests to come for the party on another date.

empanadas

EMPANADAS ARE A way of life in Latin America, and different versions are found in nearly every country. The name comes from the Spanish *empanar*, "to encase in bread," and these handheld dough pockets are stuffed with a wonderful array of fillings, including various meats, vegetables, cheeses, and fruits. The dough is typically made with wheat flour, though cornmeal and sometimes even cassava, plantain, or sweet potato is used. Some empanadas are baked and others are encased in flaky pastry and fried. All of them are especially fun to make with family and friends. Sandra A. Gutierrez, author of *Empanadas: The Hand-Held Pies of Latin America*, likes to make them with her daughters because "conversation flows so easily while our fingers are distracted crafting, filling, and crimping."

Sandra grew up eating empanadas in all sorts of social settings, from casual picnics to elegant bridal showers, rustic *churrascos* (barbecues) to fancy birthday parties. Their portability and their flexible serving temperature—hot, warm, or room temperature—make them an ideal party, picnic, or potluck choice. They are easy to eat out of hand, too, especially if you opt to skip the sauces, which means no silverware and plates. That said, a delicious sauce or dip is worth a little messiness on the trip from hand to mouth.

It's a good idea to offer two different fillings—with meat and without—when you are serving a crowd. Here, Sandra provides the classic Cuban beef filling, followed by a bean, cheese, and poblano chile filling. Although empanadas are more often fried than baked, the logistics of frying so many pieces of food makes baking a better choice for some cooks, so both options are included here.

To save time, Sandra recommends using store-bought wrappers. You'll find prepackaged empanada disks in the freezer section of Latino markets and many well-stocked grocery stores. Goya and LaFe are two popular brands. The vegetarian filling calls for canned refried beans—another time-saver—though you can make your own, of course. If you decide on store-bought, make sure the label on the can clearly indicates it is vegetarian.

Single Batch **Makes 30 empanadas**
Double Batch **Makes 60 empanadas**

MAKE AHEAD

The beef filling can be refrigerated for up to 1 day. The Chimichurri can be stored at room temperature for up to 2 hours. The Pico de Gallo is best if served right away, though it can be refrigerated for up to 1 day. The uncooked empanadas can be frozen for up to 3 months. To freeze, arrange them in a single layer on the parchment paper–lined sheet pans as directed, then place in the freezer until frozen solid, 1 to 2 hours. Transfer to large ziplock plastic freezer bags and place in the freezer. They can be fried or baked directly from the freezer, adding 2 to 3 minutes to the cooking time. The fried empanadas can be kept warm in a low oven for up to 2 hours.

Two or three half sheet pans for holding the folded empanadas; one large, deep skillet, two or three half sheet pans with cooling racks, and a deep-frying thermometer if frying the empanadas; two or three half sheet pans if baking the empanadas.

BIG BATCH NOTES

Make plenty of space in the refrigerator to hold the folded empanadas on the sheet pans, as they should be chilled before baking. The empanadas can be fried or baked; baking is easier, as it is more hands-off. For baking, transfer the cold empanadas to freshly lined sheet pans and be sure to cool the pans between batches.

SERVING

Plan on two or three empanadas per person. Both types of empanada can be eaten plain, but the sauces are fairly quick to make and add lots of flavor. Or if pressed for time, you can buy the sauces from a high-quality source. Round out the menu with a green salad, dulce de leche ice cream, and sangria and Mexican beers.

EMPANADAS

INGREDIENTS	SINGLE BATCH	DOUBLE BATCH
Beef filling (page 22) or Vegetarian, Cheese, Bean, and Poblano filling (page 23)	1 recipe	2 recipes
Store-bought empanada disks, 5 inches in diameter	30	60
Canola oil, if frying		
Large eggs, if baking	2	3
Water, if baking	2 tsp	1 Tbsp
Chimichurri and/or Pico de Gallo, for serving (see facing page)		

Have ready the beef and/or vegetarian filling.

Assemble the empanadas: Line two or three half sheet pans with parchment paper. Line up a few empanada disks on a work surface.

If using the beef filling, working with 1 empanada disk at a time, spoon 2 tablespoons of the filling evenly onto the bottom half of each disk, leaving about a ¼-inch border uncovered. Fold the uncovered half of the disk over the filling to form a half-moon, then press the edges together with your fingertips. Use the tines of a fork to crimp the edges to seal securely, then transfer the empanada to a prepared sheet pan. Repeat until all of the empanadas are formed. As you work, keep the finished empanadas covered with a dry kitchen towel.

If using the vegetarian filling, working with 1 empanada disk at a time, spoon about 1½ heaping tablespoons of the beans onto the bottom half of each disk, leaving about a ¼-inch border uncovered. Top the beans with two pepper strips and about 1½ heaping tablespoons cheese. Fold the uncovered half of the disk over the filling to form a half-moon, then press the edges together with your fingertips. Use the tines of a fork to crimp the edges to seal securely and transfer the empanada to a prepared pan. Repeat until all of the empanadas are formed. As you work, keep the finished empanadas covered with a dry kitchen towel.

To fry the empanadas: Pour the oil to a depth of 1 to 1½ inches into a large, deep skillet or Dutch oven and heat to 375°F on a deep-frying thermometer. Place wire cooling racks on two or three half sheet pans and set the pans near the stove. Preheat the oven to 250°F if not serving right away.

Working in batches, carefully slide the empanadas into the hot oil and fry, turning them over halfway through cooking and lowering the heat if they are browning too

CHIMICHURRI

Makes about 2 cups

2 cups coarsely chopped fresh flat-
    leaf parsley
⅔ cup finely chopped white onion
8 garlic cloves, minced
3 Tbsp red wine vinegar
1 tsp fine sea salt
½ tsp red pepper flakes
½ tsp freshly ground black pepper
1 cup extra-virgin olive oil

In a bowl, stir together the parsley,
onion, garlic, vinegar, salt, red
pepper flakes, and black pepper, mixing well. Whisk in the oil.
Alternatively, for a condiment that
is easy to drizzle, combine all of
the ingredients in a food processor
and pulse until almost smooth.
Transfer to a serving bowl, cover,
and let stand for at least 30 minutes before serving.

PICO DE GALLO

Makes about 2 cups

1½ cups seeded and chopped plum
    tomatoes
½ cup finely chopped white onion
1 serrano chile, seeded (if you want
    less heat) and minced
½ cup finely chopped fresh cilantro
Fresh lime juice, for seasoning
Salt

In a bowl, stir together the tomatoes, onion, chile, and cilantro,
mixing well. Season to taste with
the lime juice and salt. This salsa is
best if served right away.

quickly, until golden brown and crisp, 3 to 4 minutes. Using a slotted spoon or wire skimmer, transfer to a cooling rack to drain for 1 to 2 minutes. Serve immediately or at room temperature.

To bake the empanadas: Position racks in the top third and center of the oven and preheat the oven to 400°F.

Whisk together the eggs and water in a small bowl until foamy. Just before baking, brush the top of each empanada lightly with the egg mixture. Bake the empana-das, switching the pans between the racks and rotating them front to back halfway through the baking, until golden, 8 to 12 minutes.

Serve the empanadas hot, warm, or at room temperature, accompanied with the sauces.

Ajicito dulce, also known as ají dulce or cachuca, is a variety of small sweet chile. Although it looks like the crinkly, multicolored Scotch bonnet chile (which, in turn resembles the habanero), it is both much milder, with hardly any heat at all, and smaller. You'll find these sweet chiles at Latin markets with a Central American and Caribbean clientele. Just make sure you are not buying one of the hotter chiles. If you cannot find them, substitute an equal amount of sweet red bell pepper (the ajicito dulce is typically 1 to 2 inches long and 1 to 1¼ inches wide) and add a bit of jalapeño or serrano for a little heat.

If purchasing canned refried beans, make sure the label indicates the contents is vegetarian. Can sizes can vary from 14 to 16 ounces. You will need 24 ounces for the single batch or 48 ounces for the double batch.

BEEF FILLING

INGREDIENTS	SINGLE BATCH	DOUBLE BATCH
Extra-virgin olive oil	2 Tbsp	¼ cup
White onion(s), finely chopped	1	2
Small green bell pepper(s), seeded and finely chopped	1	2
Ajicitos dulces, seeded and minced (optional; see *Ingredient Notes*)	4	8
Garlic cloves, minced	4	8
Lean ground beef	1 lb	2 lb
Tomato paste	2 Tbsp	¼ cup
Dried oregano	1 tsp	2 tsp
Ground cumin	1 tsp	2 tsp
Fine sea salt	1 tsp	2 tsp
Freshly ground black pepper	½ tsp	1 tsp

Heat the oil in a large skillet over medium-high heat. Add the onion, bell pepper, and ajicitos dulces (if using) and cook, stirring occasionally, until softened, about 4 minutes. Add the garlic and continue to cook for 1 minute. Add the beef and cook, stirring occasionally and breaking up any clumps with a wooden spoon, until no longer pink, 4 to 5 minutes.

Add the tomato paste, oregano, cumin, salt, and pepper and cook, stirring, for 1 minute. Reduce the heat to low and cook, stirring, for 2 minutes more. Taste and adjust the seasoning with salt and pepper if needed, then transfer to a bowl and let cool to room temperature. Cover with plastic wrap and refrigerate until cold, about 30 minutes.

VEGETARIAN CHEESE, BEAN, AND POBLANO FILLING

INGREDIENTS	SINGLE BATCH	DOUBLE BATCH
Poblano chiles	8	16
Vegetarian refried beans (see *Ingredient Notes*)	3 cups	6 cups
Crumbled queso fresco	3 cups	6 cups

Preheat the broiler. Line a sheet pan with aluminum foil. Place the poblanos on the prepared pan, slip the pan under the broiler, and broil, turning the chiles occasionally, until they are almost completely charred and blistered on all sides, 6 to 10 minutes.

Transfer the chiles to a glass bowl and cover the bowl with plastic wrap, or place in a brown paper bag and seal tightly. Let stand until cool enough to handle, about 10 minutes. Peel, seed, and devein the poblanos, then cut them lengthwise into narrow strips. You will need a total of 60 strips if making a single batch or 120 strips if making a double batch (2 strips for each empanada). Let the strips cool completely.

Ready the refried beans and queso fresco and set alongside the poblano strips.

ALICIA VILLANUEVA
alicia's tamales

IN MEXICO, TAMALES are an essential part of the Christmas menu, and getting together to make them, at parties known as *tamaladas*, is part of the country's holiday tradition. "Making tamales together means spending time with friends and family, sharing stories, and carrying on traditions," says Alicia Villaneuva, who started Alicia's Tamales Los Mayas, a tamale cart business, with the help of La Cocina, a nonprofit food-business incubator in San Francisco's Mission District. When Alicia arrived in the United States from Mexico, she started selling tamales door to door, sometimes making up to five hundred a week. Now, her business sells close to five thousand tamales weekly.

Tamales, like empanadas (page 19), boast many different fillings and wrappers depending on their country of origin. Every holiday season, Alicia teams up with other cooks from La Cocina and teaches a class that showcases the different versions. She shared her recipes for chicken tamales and a vegetarian version here but points out that tamales are adaptable and can be stuffed with whatever you have on hand, from leftover Thanksgiving turkey to cheese to carnitas (page 145). If you are hosting a big crowd, you may want to make a batch of tamales with meat and a batch without.

Although tamaladas are most common during the Christmas holidays, tamales are a wonderful dish for almost every occasion, from a festive Sunday brunch to a big summer picnic.

Single Batch
Makes 25 to 30 tamales
Double Batch
Makes 50 to 60 tamales

MAKE AHEAD

The masa can be made up to 2 hours ahead and left at room temperature. Both fillings can be refrigerated for up to 2 days. The corn husks can be soaked for up to 2 hours, but do not drain and dry until ready to use. The tamales should be steamed within about 1 hour of folding them. They can then be cooled, slipped into large ziplock plastic bags, and refrigerated for up to 2 days, then steamed over boiling water for 15 to 20 minutes just before serving. The uncooked tamales can also be frozen for up to 2 months. To freeze, place the sheet pans of wrapped tamales in the freezer until the tamales are frozen solid, about 2 hours, then transfer them to large ziplock plastic freezer bags and place in the freezer. They can be steamed directly from the freezer, adding 15 to 20 minutes to the cooking time.

TAMALES

INGREDIENTS	SINGLE BATCH	DOUBLE BATCH
Chicken Filling or Vegetarian Bean and Nopalito Filling (pages 28 and 29)	1 recipe	2 recipes
Dried corn husks	30	60

continued on following page

Two very large bowls for soaking the corn husks and making the masa; one or two large bowls for mixing the filling; half sheet pans for holding the folded tamales; steamer setup for cooking the tamales.

BIG BATCH NOTES

Invite a few friends over and set up an assembly line to make the tamales. Soak the corn husks before the helpers arrive, but drain and dry just before using. A 1 pound bag of corn husks usually includes 80 to 100 husks. This will be more than you need, however they aren't expensive and some may be torn or otherwise unusable. Have plenty of large plastic storage bags ready for storing the dough and the tamales. When making the dough for a big batch, make two single batches and combine them.

SERVING

Plan on two tamales per person, and set out bowls for disposing of the empty husks. Accompany with margaritas (easy to make in large batches and serve from pitchers), black beans and rice, chopped jicama and orange salad, a couple of salsas store-bought or homemade (see tomatillo salsa, page 147), and Mexican chocolate ice cream.

INGREDIENTS	SINGLE BATCH	DOUBLE BATCH
Masa Dough		
Instant corn masa mix, preferably Maseca brand	2½ lb (9½ cups)	5 lb (19 cups)
Baking powder	1 tsp	2 tsp
Kosher salt	2 Tbsp	4 Tbsp
Lard, at room temperature, or vegetable oil	3¼ cups	6½ cups
Cooled chicken cooking liquid or water	3½ cups	7 cups

Make one or both fillings and refrigerate until needed. Put the corn husks in a very large bowl and add hot tap water to cover. They will be soft and pliable within 30 minutes or so, but they can sit in the water for up to 2 hours.

Make the masa dough: If you are making a double batch of dough, make two single batches for ease, then combine them. Put the masa in a large bowl and whisk in the baking powder and salt. Add the lard/vegetable oil, the chicken cooking liquid if using the chicken filling or the water if using the vegetarian filling; using your hands or a wooden spoon, mix until a spongy dough forms. Cover the bowl and set aside for up to 2 hours.

Assemble the tamales: Drain the soaked corn husks and pat them dry with kitchen or paper towels. Lay a corn husk vertically, with the narrow end pointing away from you, on a clean work surface. Using your hands or a rubber spatula, spread a generous ⅓ cup of the prepared masa on the middle of the corn husk, covering about two-thirds of the husk with a layer of masa about ½ inch thick. Leave a 1-inch border at the bottom of the husk and a roughly 3-inch border at the top (narrow end). Top the masa with about 3 tablespoons of the filling.

Gently fold the left side of the husk over the filling, making sure the masa fully covers the filling. Fold over the right side of the husk, overlapping slightly. Now, fold the tamale away from you, toward the narrow end, creating a small package. Place the folded tamale, folded side down, on a half sheet pan. Repeat with the remaining husks, masa, and filling.

Cook the tamales: Set up your steamer. Pour water into the steamer pot to reach just below the rack and set over high heat. Remove the rack from the pot and place the tamales, folded side down, in the rack. Do not pack them too tightly, as they will expand during cooking. Return the rack to the pot over the boiling water. Cover, reduce the heat so the water is simmering, and steam until the tamales have firmed up and the filling is hot, 40 to 45 minutes.

Using tongs, transfer the tamales to platters and serve right away.

Tomatillos are sold at Latin groceries and many supermarkets. Before
using, remove and discard their
papery husks and rinse with cold
water to remove the natural sticky
coating. If you cannot find them
fresh, canned whole tomatillos can
be substituted. Drain and rinse well
before chopping. You will need
about 2 cups chopped for a single
batch or 4 cups chopped for a
double batch.

Mexican oregano has a different, more savory flavor than the
common Mediterranean variety. If
you cannot find it, Mediterranean
oregano can be substituted.

Nopalitos, or edible cactus
paddles, are available fresh and
canned. Here, canned nopalitos
have been used for ease. Look for
them in Latin markets and well-
stocked supermarkets. They taste
very much like green beans, which
can be substituted in a pinch.

CHICKEN FILLING

INGREDIENTS	SINGLE BATCH	DOUBLE BATCH
Sofrito		
Small yellow onion, roughly chopped	½ (1 cup)	1 (2 cups)
Garlic cloves	2	4
Canned diced, fire-roasted green chiles	½ cup	1 cup
Cilantro, leaves only	½ bunch	1 bunch
Celery, coarsely chopped	½ rib	1 rib
Tomatillos, husks removed, rinsed, and chopped (see *Ingredient Notes*)	8 oz	1 lb
7-oz skin-on, bone-in chicken breast halves	2	4
Dried oregano, preferably Mexican (see *Ingredient Notes*)	1½ tsp	1 Tbsp
Kosher salt	1 tsp	2 tsp
Canola oil	1 Tbsp	2 Tbsp
Yellow onion, roughly chopped	¼	½
Garlic cloves, chopped	3	6
Kosher salt		

To make the sofrito, combine the onion, garlic, chiles, cilantro, celery, and tomatillos
in a food processor. Pulse until the vegetables are finely chopped but not pureed.
Set aside.

Place the chicken breasts in a saucepan and add cold water to cover by 1 inch. Add the
oregano and salt, place over high heat, and bring to a boil, skimming off any foam that
forms on the surface. Reduce the heat to a simmer, cover, and let the chicken cook.
Begin checking after 8 minutes; it is done when it is just opaque in the center. It will
typically cook in 10 to 14 minutes, depending on the thickness.

When the chicken is done, remove it from the poaching liquid, let it cool until it can
be handled, then remove and discard the skin and bones and shred the meat with
your fingers or two forks. Let the liquid cool, then use for making the masa dough.

Heat the oil in a Dutch oven over medium heat. Add the onion and cook, stirring
often, until beginning to soften, 2 to 3 minutes. Add the garlic and cook, stirring
often, until the garlic just starts to take on color, 2 to 3 minutes. Stir in the sofrito
and the shredded chicken, reduce the heat to low, and cook, stirring occasionally, for
about 20 minutes to blend the flavors. Season to taste with salt.

Remove from the heat, let cool, cover, and refrigerate until ready to use.

VEGETARIAN BEAN AND NOPALITO FILLING

INGREDIENTS	SINGLE BATCH	DOUBLE BATCH
Sofrito		
Small yellow onion, roughly chopped	½ (1 cup)	1 (2 cups)
Drained, coarsely chopped canned ripe (black) olives	½ cup	1 cup
Canned crushed tomatoes	½ cup	1 cup
Green bell pepper, seeded and roughly chopped	½ (⅔ cup)	1 (1⅓ cups)
Garlic cloves	2	4
Dried oregano, preferably Mexican (see *Ingredient Notes*)	1½ tsp	1 Tbsp
Kosher salt		
Canola oil	2 Tbsp	¼ cup
Small yellow onion, cut into ½-inch dice	½ (1 cup)	1 (2 cups)
Assorted bell peppers (red, yellow, and/or orange), seeded and cut into ½-inch dice	2½ (1⅔ cups)	5 (3⅓ cups)
Garlic cloves, chopped	3	6
15-oz can(s) garbanzo beans (chickpeas), drained and rinsed	1	2
Drained, rinsed, and chopped canned nopalitos, in ½-inch pieces (see *Ingredient Notes*)	1½ cups	3 cups
Chopped green beans, in ½-inch pieces	1 cup	2 cups
Kosher salt		

To make the sofrito, combine the onion, olives, tomatoes, bell pepper, garlic, and oregano in a food processor. Pulse until the vegetables are finely chopped but not pureed. Season to taste with salt.

Heat the oil in a Dutch oven over medium heat. Add the onion and cook, stirring often, until softened and just beginning to brown, 2 to 3 minutes. Add the bell peppers and garlic and cook, stirring often, until the peppers begin to soften, 2 to 3 minutes more. Stir in the garbanzo beans, nopalitos, and green beans and cook, stirring occasionally, for 3 to 4 minutes. Stir in the sofrito and cook, stirring occasionally, until the green beans are tender, 8 to 10 minutes. Season to taste with salt.

Remove from the heat, let cool, cover, and refrigerate until ready to use.

ANDREA NGUYEN

chinese dumplings

COOKBOOK AUTHOR, WRITER, and teacher Andrea Nguyen is known to her family and friends as their in-house dumpling expert. "People come over to my house, and they get dumplings. I go to parties or potlucks, and I take dumplings." The author of many books, including *Asian Dumplings, Into the Vietnamese Kitchen, The Banh Mi Handbook,* and *The Pho Cookbook,* Andrea teaches dumpling-making classes that sell out every time—partly, she believes, because the hands-on classes feel like family gatherings, where every pair of hands gets pressed into service and people share their stories. Her students start out strangers and end up friends.

Andrea's love of dumplings began when she was a young child. Her family often drove to Chinatown in Los Angeles, a three-hour round trip, for a dim sum breakfast and regularly made dumplings at home. Her mother would prepare the fillings and buy the wrappers and then hand things over to Andrea and her sisters. They made a lot—at least sixty every time—because they were a family of seven who adored dumplings.

The sisters even held dumpling-shaping contests to see who could make the best-looking ones or who could come up with a new shape. Mastering beautiful dumplings takes practice, so Andrea is quick to assure her students that dumplings taste good no matter what they look like.

Dumplings are at the center of many Asian celebrations, especially Chinese Lunar New Year, which begins on the first new moon that falls between January 21 and February 20 and then lasts for weeks. "It is like all of the major Western holidays rolled into one," says Andrea, "and is an important time for renewal, relaxation, and rebooting." It is also a good time to gather your people for a dumpling-making party, though dumpling time is really any day of the year.

Make the fillings, fill and shape the dumplings, and then cook them to share with friends. Here are two basic dumpling recipes, a steamed vegetable dumpling and a meat-and-chive pot sticker, that are shaped the same way but are cooked differently.

Single Batch **Makes 30 dumplings**
Double Batch **Makes 60 dumplings**

MAKE AHEAD

The fillings for the dumplings can be made up to 1 day ahead and refrigerated; bring to room temperature before assembling the dumplings. The uncooked dumplings can be covered with plastic wrap and refrigerated for up to a few hours before cooking. The dipping sauce can be made up to 6 hours in advance and kept at room temperature. To freeze the dumplings, slip the sheet pans, uncovered, into the freezer until the dumplings are hard, about 1 hour, then transfer the dumplings to large ziplock plastic freezer bags and freeze for up to 1 month. If making steamed dumplings, thaw completely on lined steamer trays before steaming. If making pot stickers, thaw partially, using your finger to smooth over any cracks that may have formed during freezing, before cooking.

Two or three half sheet pans; one
large pot and stacked steamer
trays for steamed dumplings; at
least two large nonstick skillets
(the larger the better) with lids for
fried pot stickers.

BIG BATCH NOTES

Supply each dumpling maker
with a bowl of filling and a stack
of dumpling wrappers to make
dumplings, one at a time, from
start to finish. This works better
than having some makers fill the
dumplings and others fold them.
Keep parchment-lined sheet pans
nearby for holding the finished
dumplings. You should be able to
fit about eight dumplings per rack
on the typical bamboo steamer,
more on wide metal steamers.

If you don't have enough space
on your steamer trays to steam
all of the dumplings at once, or if
you are not steaming them right
away, place the waiting dumplings,
sealed side up, on the sheet pans,
spacing them a good ½ inch apart.

SERVING

Plan on six to eight dumplings
per person. Serve the steamed
dumplings directly from their
steaming racks and serve the pot
stickers on platters. Outfit each
eater with chopsticks and with
a Chinese-style soup spoon or
rice bowl.

STEAMED SHIITAKE AND VEGETABLE DUMPLINGS

INGREDIENTS	SINGLE BATCH	DOUBLE BATCH
Filling		
Dried shiitake mushrooms	5	10
Lightly packed, coarsely chopped spinach	5 cups (about 10 oz)	10 cups (about 1¼ lb)
Asian sesame oil	2 Tbsp	¼ cup
Light soy sauce (see *Ingredient Notes*)	1½ Tbsp	3 Tbsp
Sugar	¾ tsp	1½ tsp
Non-iodized table salt	¼ tsp	½ tsp
Freshly ground white pepper	¼ tsp	½ tsp
Water	1 Tbsp	2 Tbsp
Cornstarch	2 tsp	4 tsp
Canola oil	2 Tbsp	¼ cup
Peeled and finely minced fresh ginger	1 Tbsp	2 Tbsp
Finely chopped or grated carrots	⅔ cup	1⅓ cups
Finely chopped store-bought marinated baked tofu (see *Ingredient Notes*, page 34)	⅔ cup (4 oz)	1⅓ cups (8 oz)
Finely chopped fresh Chinese chives (see *Ingredient Notes*, page 34) or green onions (white and green parts)	½ cup	1 cup
Assembly		
All-purpose flour, for dusting (if making ahead)		
Round dumpling wrappers (1 or 2 packages; see *Ingredient Notes*, page 34)	30	60
Tangy Soy Dipping Sauce (see facing page)	1 recipe	2 recipes

Make the filling: Put the shiitakes in a bowl with warm water to cover and let soak
until soft. Drain the mushrooms into a fine-mesh sieve placed over a bowl, capturing
the soaking water in the bowl. Trim off and discard the tough stems and chop the
caps. You should have a generous ½ cup if making a single batch or a generous 1 cup
if making a double batch. Set the mushrooms and soaking water aside separately.

While the mushrooms are soaking, put the spinach in a large, heatproof bowl. Bring a
kettle of water to a boil and pour a generous amount over the spinach. Let the spinach
wilt for about 30 seconds, then drain into a colander, rinse with cold water, and drain
again. To remove excess moisture, squeeze the spinach in your hands over the sink.
You should have about ½ cup firmly packed spinach if making a single batch and
1 cup if making a double batch.

Measure ¼ cup of the mushroom soaking water if making a single batch, or ½ cup of the water if making a double batch. In a small bowl, combine the measured soaking water, sesame oil, soy sauce, sugar, salt, and white pepper and stir until the sugar dissolves. Set this flavoring sauce aside. In a small bowl, stir together the water and cornstarch until the cornstarch dissolves and set aside.

In a wok or large skillet, heat the canola oil over medium heat. Add the ginger and stir-fry until aromatic, about 30 seconds. Add the spinach, mushrooms, carrots, and tofu, then pour in the flavoring sauce and stir to combine. At first all of the liquid will seem to have been absorbed, but after about 2 minutes, a little bubbling liquid will be visible in the pan. At this point, give the cornstarch mixture a final stir and then stir it into the filling. When the mixture thickens, turn off the heat and add the Chinese chives.

Transfer to a bowl and set aside to cool completely before assembling the dumplings. You should have about 2 cups filling for a single batch or 4 cups for a double batch.

Assemble the dumplings: Line steamer trays or two or three half sheet pans with parchment paper. (If you are making the dumplings in advance of either steaming or freezing, lightly dust the parchment-lined pans with flour to avoid sticking.) Ready a small bowl of water and place it and the dumpling wrappers within reach.

For each dumpling, hold a wrapper in a slightly cupped hand. Scoop up about 1 table-spoon of the filling and position it slightly off-center toward the upper half of the wrapper, pressing and shaping it into a flat mound and leaving a ½- to ¾-inch border on all sides. Lightly dampen the border of the wrapper with wet fingers to help seal the edges. Fold, pleat, and press to enclose the filling and create a half-moon shape. To make the dumpling sit up in the steamer tray, make a series of pleats from one side to the other. If you are steaming the dumplings right away, place the finished dumpling in a steamer tray, sealed side up. If using a metal steamer tray, position it 1 inch away from the edge. Keep the finished dumplings covered with a dry kitchen towel as you make the rest.

Cook the dumplings: Set up your steamer with water and bring the water to a boil. Steam the dumplings over the boiling water until slightly puffed and somewhat translucent, about 8 minutes.

To serve, remove the tray(s) from the pot and place atop a serving plate(s). Serve the dumplings immediately with the dipping sauce, either in a communal bowl with a spoon or portioned into individual bowls. As with all steamed dumplings, it is easiest to eat these with chopsticks in one hand and a soup spoon or rice bowl in the other, angling the bowl or spoon to catch any drips.

TANGY SOY DIPPING SAUCE

Makes about 1 cup

Here is a classic dipping sauce that includes chile oil for a touch of heat. For an interesting change, try the balsamic-garlic variation, or offer both versions.

⅔ cup light soy sauce (see *Ingredient Notes,* page 34)
⅓ cup unseasoned rice vinegar
2 teaspoons chile oil, or more to taste
⅛ teaspoon sugar
2 tablespoons peeled and finely shredded fresh ginger

In a bowl, whisk together the soy sauce, vinegar, chile oil, and sugar until the sugar dissolves. Cover and set aside at room temperature for up to 6 hours. Just before serving, stir in the ginger.

Balsamic-Vinegar Sauce: Substitute balsamic vinegar for the rice vinegar and 1 heaping tablespoon minced garlic for the ginger.

INGREDIENT NOTES

Marinated baked tofu is sold in clear plastic packages stocked in the refrigerated section.

Chinese chives, also known as garlic chives, are wider and flatter than ordinary chives and have a slight garlic flavor.

Soy sauce is sold in two main types, light and dark. The former is lighter, saltier, and thinner than the latter.

A traditional Chinese rice wine made in Zhejiang Province, Shaoxing has a distinctive fragrance and a lovely pale amber color. All of these foods can be found in most Asian markets and in some supermarkets. An Asian market is also the best place to look for round dumpling wrappers (they should be about 3½ inches wide).

MEAT AND CHINESE CHIVE POT STICKERS

INGREDIENTS	SINGLE BATCH	DOUBLE BATCH
Filling		
Ground beef chuck or ground lamb	10 oz	1⅓ lb
Finely chopped fresh Chinese chives (see *Ingredient Notes*) or green onions (white and green parts)	⅔ cup	1⅓ cups
Peeled and minced fresh ginger	1½ or 2 Tbsp	3 or 4 Tbsp
Chicken stock	⅓ cup	⅔ cup
Light soy sauce (see *Ingredient Notes*)	2 Tbsp	¼ cup
Canola oil	1½ Tbsp	3 Tbsp
Shaoxing wine (see *Ingredient Notes*) or dry sherry	1 Tbsp	2 Tbsp
Asian sesame oil	1½ Tbsp	3 Tbsp
Kosher salt	½ tsp	1 tsp
Freshly ground white pepper	½ tsp	1 tsp
Assembly		
All-purpose flour, for dusting (if making ahead)		
Round dumpling wrappers (1 or 2 packages)	30	60
Canola oil, for frying		
Tangy Soy Dipping Sauce (page 33)	1 recipe	2 recipes

Make the filling: In a bowl, combine the beef or lamb, chives, and the smaller amount of ginger if using beef and the larger amount if using lamb. Use a fork or rubber spatula to stir and lightly mash the ingredients together.

In a small bowl, stir together the stock, soy sauce, canola oil, wine, sesame oil, salt, and white pepper until the salt dissolves. Pour the stock mixture over the meat mixture, then stir and fold the ingredients together. Once you have broken up the large chunks of meat, stir briskly until a cohesive, thick mixture forms. Cover with plastic wrap and let stand at room temperature for 30 minutes to develop the flavors.

Assemble the dumplings: Line two or three half sheet pans with parchment paper. (If you are making the dumplings in advance of either frying or freezing, lightly dust the parchment-lined sheet pans with flour to avoid sticking.) Ready a small bowl of water and place it and the dumpling wrappers within reach.

For each dumpling, hold a wrapper in a slightly cupped hand. Scoop up about 1 tablespoon of the filling and position it slightly off-center toward the upper half of the wrapper, pressing and shaping it into a flat mound and leaving a ½- to ¾-inch border on all sides. Lightly dampen the border of the wrapper with wet fingers to help seal the edges. Fold, pleat, and press to enclose the filling and create a half-moon shape. To make the dumpling sit up in the skillet, make a series of pleats from one side to the other. As the dumplings are shaped, place them on the prepared sheet pans, spacing them a good ½ inch apart and keeping them covered with a dry kitchen towel as you make the rest.

Cook the dumplings: Heat 2 large nonstick skillets over medium-high heat and add 2 tablespoons oil to each skillet. (If you have only medium-size skillets, add 1½ tablespoons oil to each skillet.) Place the dumplings, one at a time and sealed side up, in a winding circle pattern in each pan. The dumplings can touch. (In general, large skillets will accommodate 16 to 18 dumplings and medium skillets will accommodate 12 to 14 dumplings.) Fry the dumplings until they are golden or light brown on the bottom, 1 to 2 minutes. Holding a skillet lid or a large piece of aluminum foil close to the skillet to lessen the dramatic effect of water hitting hot oil, and using a kettle or liquid measuring cup, pour water to a depth up roughly ¼ inch into each pan (plan on using about ⅓ cup water for each pan). The water will sputter and boil vigorously.

Immediately cover the skillets with their lids (you can use aluminum foil if you don't have lids), reduce the heat to medium, and let the water bubble away until it is mostly gone, 8 to 10 minutes. After 6 to 8 minutes, move the lid so it is slightly ajar to allow steam to shoot out from underneath. This lessens the drama of condensation dripping down onto the hot oil when you remove the lid. The moment you hear sizzling noises (a sign that most of the water is gone), remove the lid. Let the dumplings fry until the bottoms are beautifully browned and crisp, 1 to 2 minutes longer.

Turn off the heat and wait until the sizzling stops. Then, using a spatula, transfer the dumplings to platters. Make sure their bottoms are facing up so they remain crisp. Serve hot, with the dipping sauce in a communal bowl for people to help themselves or divided among individual small bowls. Eat the pot stickers with chopsticks in one hand and a Chinese soup spoon or rice bowl in the other to catch any drips of dipping sauce or of the juices that will spill out when you bite into a pot sticker.

nepalese momos

NEPALESE MOMOS—BITE-SIZE DUMPLINGS typically filled with spiced ground meat—may not be as well known as Shanghai soup dumplings or Chinese wontons, but entrepreneur and cook Binita "Bini" Pradhan is working to bring these Himalayan favorites to a wider audience through Bini's Kitchen, her San Francisco–based food business. Located between India and China, Nepal boasts a cuisine that is influenced by both of its big neighbors. These dumplings are an example of that culinary marriage.

Bini found the commercial kitchen space, business advice, and mentorship she needed at La Cocina, the same kitchen incubator program in San Francisco's Mission District geared toward assisting low-income immigrant women that helped Alicia Villanueva (page 25). Even more important, she found a supportive community of women from around the world, all working hard to build their lives and businesses by creating and selling delicious, affordable food. Bini turned to the dishes she had learned to prepare from her mother, who had cooked for the Nepalese royal family in the 1960s. Her momos quickly became popular, and over the years, she has sold thousands of her plump, flavor-packed dumplings at the annual La Cocina food festival.

Bini enjoys watching her customers' eyes light up when they bite into their first momo, especially when it's been swiped through her signature dipping sauce, a bright, flavorful blend of charred tomatoes, cilantro, garlic, and Sichuan peppercorns. She also believes that even novice dumpling makers can have fun mixing the fragrant spiced turkey stuffing, then filling, twisting to seal, and steaming the finished momos, so invite a few friends over to help you put together your own momo feast.

Single Batch
Makes about 40 momos

Double Batch
Makes about 80 momos

MAKE AHEAD

The sauce can be refrigerated for up to 3 days. The meat stuffing can be refrigerated for up to 1 day. The assembled momos can be covered with plastic wrap and refrigerated for up to 3 hours. You can also slip the half sheet pans, uncovered, into the freezer until the dumplings are frozen solid, about 2 hours, then transfer the dumplings to large ziplock plastic freezer bags and freeze for up to 2 months. They can be cooked directly from the freezer; add 2 to 3 minutes to the cooking time.

BIG BATCH NOTES

The onion and cilantro must be finely minced, so put your friends with the best knife skills to work on these tasks. Supply each dumpling maker with a bowl of filling and a stack of dumpling wrappers to make dumplings, one at a time, from start to finish. This works better than having some makers fill the dumplings and others fold them. You should be able to fit about eight dumplings per rack on the typical bamboo steamer, more on wide metal steamers.

SERVING

Plan on six to eight momos per person. Mango lassi, which can be purchased, is the perfect beverage with momos. Offer sliced tropical fruits for dessert.

INGREDIENT NOTES

Asafetida is a ground Indian spice that imparts a strong onion-garlic flavor. Look for it in South Asian markets and online. If you cannot find it, use equal parts onion and garlic powder.

MOMOS

INGREDIENTS	SINGLE BATCH	DOUBLE BATCH
Tomato-Cilantro Sauce		
Plum tomatoes, cored	2 lb	4 lb
Packed fresh cilantro leaves	3 cups	6 cups
Canola oil	2 Tbsp	¼ cup
Minced garlic	2 Tbsp	¼ cup
Sichuan peppercorns	1 Tbsp	2 Tbsp
Asafetida powder (see *Ingredient Notes*)	1½ tsp	1 Tbsp
Kosher salt		
Filling		
Coriander seeds	½ tsp	1 tsp
Cumin seeds	½ tsp	1 tsp
Black cardamom seeds	¼ tsp	½ tsp
Green cardamom seeds	¼ tsp	½ tsp
Bay leaves, crumbled	1	2
Ground cinnamon	¼ tsp	½ tsp
Freshly grated nutmeg	¼ tsp	½ tsp
Ground dark-meat turkey	1¼ lb	2½ lb
Minced yellow onion	1 cup	2 cups
Minced fresh cilantro	⅓ cup	⅔ cup
Canola oil	3 Tbsp	⅓ cup
Peeled and minced fresh ginger	1 Tbsp	2 Tbsp
Kosher salt	1½ tsp	1 Tbsp
Assembly		
All-purpose flour, for dusting (if making ahead)		
Round dumpling wrappers (1 or 2 packages)	40	80

Make the tomato-cilantro sauce: Heat a large, heavy skillet, preferably cast iron, over high heat for 5 minutes. Add the tomatoes in a single layer and cook, turning, until blackened on all sides, about 4 minutes.

Transfer the charred tomatoes to a food processor, add the cilantro, oil, garlic, Sichuan peppercorns, and asafetida, and process until smooth. Scrape the sauce into a bowl. Season to taste with salt. Cover and refrigerate until ready to serve. Remove from the refrigerator 1 hour before serving.

Make the filling: In a spice grinder, combine the coriander seeds, cumin seeds, black and green cardamom seeds, and bay leaf and grind finely. Transfer to a small bowl and stir in the cinnamon and nutmeg.

In a large bowl, combine the turkey, the ground spice mixture, the onion, cilantro, oil, ginger, and salt. Using your hands, mix until the meat is evenly seasoned. Cover and refrigerate for 1 hour to blend the flavors.

Assemble the dumplings: Line two or three half sheet pans with parchment paper. (If you are making the dumplings in advance of either frying or freezing, lightly dust the parchment-lined sheet pans with all-purpose flour to avoid sticking.) Ready a small bowl of water and place it and the dumpling wrappers within reach.

For each dumpling, hold a wrapper in a slightly cupped hand. Scoop up about 2 teaspoons of the filling and place in the center of the wrapper. Bring up the edges of the wrapper to meet over the filling, loosely pleat the edges, and then twist together into a topknot. Place the dumpling on its base on a prepared sheet pan. Repeat with the remaining ingredients, adding the dumplings to the pans and keeping them covered with a dry kitchen towel as you work.

Cook the dumplings: Set up your steamer with water and bring the water to a boil. Spray each steamer tray with nonstick cooking spray, then arrange the dumplings in the steamer trays, spacing them about 1 inch apart. Steam over boiling water until cooked through, about 5 minutes.

To serve, transfer the momos to platters. Spoon some of the tomato-cilantro sauce over the momos and serve them hot, with the remaining sauce on the side.

SONOKO SAKAI

onigiri party

WHEN A JAPANESE mom makes a bento box for her child's lunch, very often one of the items will be *onigiri*, basically cooked rice molded into a cute design. There are onigiri molds for kitty heads, flowers, pandas, and more, and the finished shapes can be decorated with nori (dried seaweed), various seeds, or whatever strikes the mom's—or the kid's—fancy. The similarity of onigiri to sushi is in their shared use of the same type of short-grain rice and some ingredients, but onigiri are much easier to make than most varieties of sushi. They are a fun appetizer or addition to picnics, potlucks, barbecues, or birthday parties, and because they are rice based, they are naturally gluten-free, which will appeal to many guests.

Plain and nori-wrapped versions are the most common, and the traditional shapes are a triangle, a cylinder, and a flattened ball. They can be stuffed with a tiny bit of filling—pickled vegetable or fruit, salt-cured salmon, bonito flakes mixed with soy—or left unfilled; sprinkled with sesame seeds, shiso leaf powder, *furikake* (savory sprinkles), or left plain; or the rice can be mixed with peas, furikake, toasted black sesame seeds, or other ingredients before shaping.

Onigiri expert Sonoko Sakai, author of *Rice Craft*, teaches onigiri classes for children, but the attending parents always seem to get involved, too. She provides them with plain cooked rice and an assortment of garnishes, shows them the basics, and then encourages them to let their imaginations run wild as they decorate their onigiri. Their creativity is inspiring and charming. It comes with a price at cleanup time, however, so check the Big Batch Notes (page 44) for strategizing.

Each guest will want to make about three onigiri. Plan on making one batch of rice for every seven to eight guests.

FOR EACH BATCH

Short-grain or medium-grain white or haiga rice (see *Ingredient Notes*, page 44)	5 cups
Fine sea salt (optional), plus more for molding	1 tsp
Water	5½ cups

continued on page 44

Makes about 20 onigiri

MAKE AHEAD

All of the individual onigiri decorations and garnishes can be put into individual bowls and plates and covered with plastic wrap up to 1 day in advance. Refrigerate the fresh ingredients. The rice can be cooked and the bowls of water and salt for shaping the onigiri can be readied up to 1 hour in advance.

One or two rice cookers or one Dutch oven; cutting board and small knife; and small bowls for water and salt for each guest; onigiri molds (optional).

BIG BATCH NOTES

Rice cookers are useful for making multiple batches of rice, and you can use them both to cook the rice and to keep it warm while you ready the other onigiri ingredients. Consider borrowing a rice cooker or two from friends.

During assembly, change the water bowls regularly, as they get dirty fast.

Rice is sticky, which means it will glue itself to floors, tabletops, and counters and can be difficult to clean up. Cover all of the work surfaces and floors with drop cloths, craft paper, or newspapers.

SERVING

Plan on about three onigiri per person. Have fruit juices for the kids and a selection of sake, Japanese beers, and hot and/or iced tea for the adults. Purchase an array of sweet and savory Japanese snacks, from rice crackers (available in a huge range of flavors and colors) to pickled vegetables.

ASSORTED DECORATIONS AND GARNISHES

Fresh herbs and flowers
Shiso leaves, curly and flat-leaf parsley, basil, sage, and oregano; pesticide-free edible flowers, such as chrysanthemums, borage, nasturtiums, and violas, and their leaves, such as nasturtium and borage

Sprouts
Radish, broccoli, alfalfa

Dried fruits
Cranberries, cherries, blueberries, raisins, currants, apricots

Fresh fruit zests
Lemon, lime, orange

Nuts and seeds
Walnuts, almonds, pistachios, pecans, pumpkin seeds, sunflower seeds, black and white sesame seeds, poppy seeds

Cooked legumes
Adzuki, pinto, navy, soybean, lentil, English pea

Dried seaweed and seasoning mixtures
Nori, furikake (brightly colored seasoning mixture), shichimi togarashi (seven-spice seasoning)

Cook the rice: For each batch of rice, rinse the rice in a colander or fine-mesh sieve under cool running water, using your hands to gently swish the grains for about 15 seconds. Drain well.

Put the drained rice, measured water, and salt (if using) into a Dutch oven or rice cooker and let soak for 30 minutes. If using a Dutch oven, bring to a rolling boil over medium-high heat. Cover and turn down the heat to the lowest possible setting and cook until the water is absorbed and the rice is tender, about 12 minutes. Turn off the heat and let stand for 10 minutes without opening the lid. If using a rice cooker, follow the manufacturer's instructions.

Assemble the onigiri: Scoop the rice into large bowls. Set up each guest with a cutting board and a small knife for cutting the garnishes. Put out the onigiri molds, if using, and the selection of garnishes—the more, the merrier. Fill small bowls or ramekins with fine sea salt and water, providing each guest with one of each.

Once all of the guests are outfitted with bowls of water and salt and all of the decorations and garnishes are set out, explain to everyone how to make each onigiri: Moisten your hands with the water to keep the rice from sticking to them. Then lightly dip the tips of your fingers into the bowl of water again and then into the bowl of salt. Rub the salt from both hands onto your palms. Be careful not to use too much salt. Scoop about ¾ cup of the rice into your hands. For a triangular shape, cup one hand to hold the rice ball. Press gently with your other hand to create the top corner of the triangle, using your salted fingers as a guide. Turn the ball and repeat a couple of more times to give the onigiri three corners. Or shape the rice into a ball, cylinder, square, or rectangle. (If using a mold, fill the mold with rice.) The onigiri should be about 1 inch thick, firm on the outside but soft and airy, like a pillow, on the inside. Decorate the onigiri however you like with the various decorations and garnishes. Put the finished onigiri on a platter.

Display the onigiri and eat them within an hour or so of making them.

INGREDIENT NOTES

Short-grain rice is used for making sushi and onigiri . Even though it is usually a domestic product, the packages typically carry Japanese names. Haiga rice is a partially milled short-grain rice—neither white nor brown—that retains more of the natural nutrients of the grain than white rice. Cooked short-grain rice is very tacky and holds together when pressed into shapes. Look for Japanese short-grain white rice and haiga rice at Japanese and other Asian markets, well-stocked supermarkets, and online. Do not confuse it with sweet rice, also known as glutinous or sticky rice. If using an older crop of rice (1 year old), increase the water to 5 ¾ cups.

potato latkes

EVERY YEAR, MY family celebrates Hanukkah with a "latke-and-vodka" party for eighty people. Well ahead of the event, my mother, Suzanne, fries all of the latkes, then the day of the get-together my friend Anya Fernald contributes her wine-braised brisket (page 133), and my dad leads everyone in taking vodka shots with pickle chasers.

As anyone who has ever fried a big batch of latkes can attest, it is a messy job. But it is also a herculean effort that is wildly appreciated by everyone who gets to sit down and eat the latkes. There is no such thing as too many potato pancakes, so good planning is critical. My mother's strategy is to set up a few cooking sessions during the weeks leading up to the party, making multiple batches of latkes and freezing them in ziplock plastic freezer bags. That way, they're easy to reheat and serve, and all of the messy work is done—and cleaned up—well before the event. It's also the only way to ensure that there'll be enough latkes for everyone.

As for the vodka ritual, it was taught to my family by one of my father's colleagues, a Russian man named Edward. Their friendship was perhaps an unlikely one, since they were both astrophysicists during the Cold War. One enduring takeaway from that long ago camaraderie was that Edward taught my dad how to sling back ice-cold shots of vodka followed by a pickle chaser. The trick? Exhale, take the shot, and then inhale while biting the pickle. Many of the Hanukkah party guests have come to look forward to this ritual, and now they are served a quick shot the minute they enter the house.

Single Batch
Makes about 25 pancakes

Double Batch
Makes about 50 pancakes

MAKE AHEAD

Suzanne is a strong advocate of the freeze-ahead method for latkes. She makes one fifty-latke batch at a time, freezes them, and then reheats them in the oven on the day of the party. To freeze the latkes, fry them as directed, let them cool completely on the sheet pans, and then transfer them to clean sheet pans in a single layer and freeze until solid, about 1 hour. Layer the frozen latkes, separating the layers with parchment or waxed paper, in large ziplock plastic freezer bags and freeze for up to 3 months. To reheat the frozen latkes for serving, preheat the oven to 450°F. Arrange the latkes in a single layer on half sheet pans and thaw at room temperature for about 15 minutes, then bake until sizzling and crisp, 5 to 10 minutes (or 15 to 20 minutes if you don't have time to thaw them).

INGREDIENTS	SINGLE BATCH	DOUBLE BATCH
Vitamin C (see *Ingredient Notes*, page 48)	1 tablet	2 tablets
Boiling water	2 Tbsp	¼ cup
Russet (baking) potatoes	2½ lb	5 lb
Yellow onion(s), cut into 2-inch pieces	1	2
Matzo meal	2 Tbsp	¼ cup
Large eggs, lightly beaten	2	4
Kosher salt	1 tsp	2 tsp

continued on following page

At least two large skillets for frying the latkes; two large bowls for mixing the latke mixture; at least four half sheet pans for draining the fried latkes and for keeping them warm in the oven until serving.

BIG BATCH NOTES

The best way to feed a crowd is to make multiple batches in advance and freeze them. You can invite a few guests to help peel the potatoes and shape and fry the latkes. Plan on defrosting the pre-made latkes at least an hour before the party.

SERVING

Plan on four to six latkes per person. Latkes, vodka, and pickles are a party on their own, but if you want a more substantial meal, make Wine-Braised Brisket (page 133) and serve mandarin oranges or Orange and Almond Cake (page 275) for dessert.

INGREDIENT NOTES

One of the issues with prepping any potato dish ahead of time is keeping oxidation (browning) at bay. The acid in the vitamin C takes care of this problem.

INGREDIENTS	SINGLE BATCH	DOUBLE BATCH
Baking powder	¼ tsp	½ tsp
Canola oil, for frying		
For serving		
Sour cream (optional)	2 cups	4 cups
Applesauce (optional)	2 cups	4 cups

Make the latkes: Crush the vitamin C tablet(s) to a powder in a mortar with a pestle, or on a cutting board with a heavy saucepan. Transfer to a small heatproof bowl and stir in the boiling water. Let cool.

Peel the potatoes and cut into 2-inch pieces. Fit your food processor with the shredding attachment and, working in batches, shred the potatoes. Remove the shredded potatoes from the processor bowl and fit the processor with the blade attachment. Again working in batches, return the shredded potatoes to the food processor and pulse until they are the size of rice grains. Transfer the finely chopped potatoes to a large bowl (or two bowls if making a double batch), add the vitamin C mixture, and toss to combine.

Let the potato mixture stand for about 10 minutes until some liquid is released and the starch has settled into a thick paste at the bottom. Drain off the liquid from the bowls, leaving behind the starch at the bottom. Stir the starch back into the potatoes, mixing well.

Fit the processor with the shredding attachment and shred the onions. Remove the onions from the processor bowl and fit the processor with the blade attachment. Return the shredded onions to the food processor and pulse until they are the size of rice grains. Add the onions to the potato mixture along with the matzo meal, eggs, salt, and baking powder and stir until incorporated.

Line two half sheet pans with a double thickness of paper towels. Position racks in the top third and center of the oven and preheat the oven to 200°F. Have two additional sheet pans ready for the oven.

Heat two large skillets over medium-high heat. Pour the oil into the skillets to a depth of ¼ to ½ inch and heat until hot but not shimmering. (Mom's trick for checking the temperature is to put the end of a wooden chopstick in the oil; if bubbles quickly form around the chopstick, the oil is ready.) Using a soup spoon, and allowing about 2 generous tablespoons per pancake, spoon the potato mixture into the hot oil. If when you scoop up the potato mixture, liquid is visible in the spoon, drain the liquid back into the bowl from the spoon before adding the potato mixture to the oil. Do not crowd the spoonfuls in the pan or the latkes will give off too much steam, inhibiting crisping. Flatten the latkes slightly with the back of the spoon, then fry, turning once, until golden brown, 2 to 3 minutes on each side. Using a spatula, transfer the latkes to a paper towel–lined sheet pan to drain for a couple of minutes, keeping them in a single layer. Then move the latkes to an unlined sheet pan and keep warm in the oven for up to 1 hour.

Repeat with the remaining potato mixture, replenishing the oil as needed to maintain the same depth throughout cooking and bringing the oil back up to temperature between batches. Use a wire skimmer or slotted spoon to remove any burned bits from the oil before adding a new batch.

Serve the latkes warm with the sour cream and applesauce (if using) on the side.

3.
one-bowl gatherings: soups and stews

SOUPS AND STEWS are the ultimate community comfort food and are among the most versatile of dishes. They can be made year-round with all kinds of ingredients, be humble or elegant, are typically easy to scale for a crowd, and tend to be forgiving on the stove top. Much of your time goes to getting the ingredients ready, and then once everything is in the pot, you need only stop by the stove every now and again to stir.

If you don't already have a 12- to 14-quart stockpot, investing in one for big-batch soups and stews is a good idea. In the absence of a single big pot, you can divide a recipe between two large saucepans or Dutch ovens. If your kitchen is big enough, it's nice to serve these soups and stews directly from their pots on the stove. When a buffet is a better choice, slow cookers are perfect for keeping them warm. Serve them in bowls, preferably with wide rims for easy handling, or if tables and chairs are limited, outfit guests with mugs and spoons.

For a large crowd, a soup swap or chili cook-off, with friends contributing their favorite recipes, works well. And because bread is so much a part of many soup and stew experiences, you'll find recipes for a couple of favorites here.

In an old folk tale known as stone soup, two travelers stop for a night in a village where the residents have little food. The visitors set an iron pot over a fire in the town square, fill it with water, and put a stone in the bottom. One by one, the villagers contribute food and flavorings until there is enough soup to feed the village. This chapter celebrates that natural impulse of people to come together and share what they have with others.

ALICE WATERS

minestrone

IN ITALIAN, THE word *minestrone* means "big soup." Like many rustic Italian dishes, minestrone has never been made according to a fixed recipe. Instead, local custom, improvisation, and the season have long determined what goes in the pot. That means minestrone might be a simple broth with lightly cooked spring vegetables, a hearty stew-like soup swirled with pesto, or a bread-thickened Tuscan ribollita.

Most traditional versions call for borlotti beans and their broth, as does this one from Alice Waters, chef-owner of the famed Chez Panisse restaurant in Berkeley, California. She describes minestrone as one of her favorite recipes because it is easy, inexpensive, and infinitely versatile.

It is also a favorite of everyone at the Edible Schoolyard, a program that Alice founded in 1995 in a vacant lot at the Martin Luther King Jr. Middle School in Berkeley. Her idea was to create and sustain an organic garden that involved students in the experience of growing, harvesting, preparing, and sharing food. Since then, the Edible Schoolyard has expanded to other cities and is now teaching not only the pleasures of growing and cooking food but also the values of stewardship of the land and nourishment of the community. Every early fall, when Berkeley experiences both its warmest days and its biggest harvest season of the year, the Edible Schoolyard students make this soup and enjoy the fruits of their labor together.

Single Batch
Makes 8 to 10 servings

Double Batch
Makes 16 to 20 servings

MAKE AHEAD

The dried beans must be soaked overnight before cooking. The cooked beans and their liquid can be refrigerated for up to 2 days or frozen for up to 2 months. Let the beans cool in their liquid as directed, then transfer them in their liquid to one or more airtight containers and refrigerate or freeze.

EQUIPMENT

One or two large bowls for soaking the beans; one or two large soup pots or Dutch ovens.

BIG BATCH NOTES

The double batch of soaked dried beans will swell to an impressive amount, so be sure to use two bowls or an oversize single bowl.

Because this recipe requires a lot of chopping, having a second set of hands to help is highly recommended.

For a double batch make sure you season with plenty of salt.

SERVING

Start with assorted salumi, Italian cheeses, and olives and serve the soup with crusty country bread. Pour a selection of Italian wines.

INGREDIENTS	SINGLE BATCH	DOUBLE BATCH
Dried borlotti or cannellini beans	2 cups	4 cups
Kosher salt		
Olive oil	⅓ cup	⅓ cup
Large yellow onions, chopped	2	4
Carrots, peeled and finely chopped	4	8
Garlic cloves, coarsely chopped	8	16
Fresh thyme sprigs	10	20
Bay leaves	2	4
Water	3 cups	6 cups
Small leeks, white part only, finely diced	2	4
Green beans, trimmed and cut into 1-inch lengths	1 lb	2 lb

continued on following page

53

PESTO

Makes about ¾ cup

"Pesto is my favorite sauce to make," says Alice Waters. "I love the sensory experience of pounding it and smelling it and tasting it as I go." She regards it as much more than a pasta sauce, too, describing it as "delicious on sliced tomatoes, as a dipping sauce for vegetables, on a pizza, or as a sauce for grilled chicken and vegetables." It is also wonderful swirled into bowls of her minestrone.

1 garlic clove
Kosher salt
¼ cup pine nuts, lightly toasted
¼ cup grated Parmesan cheese
1 bunch basil
½ cup extra-virgin olive oil

In a good-size mortar with a pestle, pound together the garlic and a pinch of salt to a paste. Add the pine nuts and pound until finely ground. Add the cheese, working it into the pine nut mixture. Transfer this mixture to a bowl.

Pick the leaves from the basil bunch. You should have about 1 lightly packed cup. Coarsely chop the basil leaves and put them in the mortar, then pound them to a paste. Return the pine nut mixture to the mortar and pound together with the basil until fully blended. Continue to pound as you gradually pour in the oil, mixing it in evenly. Taste and adjust with salt if needed.

VARIATIONS

• Substitute flat-leaf parsley or arugula for some or all of the basil.

• Substitute grated pecorino cheese for half or all of the Parmesan.

• Substitute walnuts for the pine nuts.

INGREDIENTS	SINGLE BATCH	DOUBLE BATCH
Tomatoes, peeled, seeded, and chopped	4	8
Zucchini, cut into small dice	4	8
Spinach leaves, coarsely chopped	1 lb	2 lb
Extra-virgin olive oil, for serving	⅔ cup	1⅓ cups
Grated Parmesan cheese, for serving	1 cup	2 cups
Pesto, for serving (see left)	1 recipe	2 recipes

Pour the beans into a large bowl (for the double batch, use two bowls) and cover with water, making sure no beans are poking out of the water. Soak the beans overnight, then drain.

Pour the beans into a large, heavy-bottomed pot and add fresh cold water to cover by 1 inch (or divide between two pots for a double batch). Bring to a boil over high heat, then reduce the heat to a simmer and cook until the beans are tender, about 2 hours, adding more hot water as needed to keep the beans covered. Remove five beans from the pot and taste them. If all of them are tender, the beans are done. Season with salt (the cooking liquid should taste just a bit salty) and remove from the heat.

Let the beans cool in their cooking liquid. (If the beans are drained right away, the skins will crack and they will look shaggy.) Drain the cooled beans into a colander placed over another pot or large bowl, reserving the beans and cooking liquid separately.

Heat the oil in a large, heavy-bottomed pot (or two pots if making a double batch) over medium heat. When the oil is hot, add the onions and carrots and cook, stirring occasionally, until tender, about 15 minutes. Add the garlic, thyme, bay leaves, and 2 teaspoons salt if making a single batch and 4 teaspoons if making a double batch. Cook, stirring occasionally, for about 5 minutes. Pour in the water and bring to a boil over medium-high heat. When the water is boiling, add the leeks, green beans, tomatoes, and zucchini and cook, stirring occasionally, for 15 minutes. Taste and adjust the seasoning with salt.

Add the cooked beans, 2 cups of the bean cooking liquid if making a single batch and 4 cups if making a double batch, and the spinach and cook for 5 minutes. If the soup is too thick, add more bean cooking liquid or water.

Remove and discard the bay leaves and thyme sprigs. Serve the soup hot, with the extra-virgin olive oil and the Parmesan and pesto on the side.

INGREDIENT NOTES

Fresh tomatoes are always preferred but high-quality canned tomatoes can be used, especially in winter when tomatoes are out of season. Use one 28-ounce can tomatoes for a single batch and two cans for a double batch.

MERRY "CORKY" WHITE

little cranberry chicken potpie

THE COMMUNITY ON Little Cranberry, a two-hundred-acre island off the coast of Maine, just southeast of Mount Desert Island, is a tight-knit one. With only seventy year-round residents (a number that balloons to three hundred in the summer), everyone knows one another, banding together in times of adversity and joy. One particularly joyful gathering is the annual Harvest Supper, which takes place on a crisp fall evening each October in the lovely harbor town of Islesford and draws visitors from the mainland.

The menu is constant. Using the same recipe, a cadre of local cooks each makes a chicken potpie—essentially chicken stew with a top crust—at home, which they then tote to the community center for the supper. Although they all are cooking from the same recipe, no two pies are alike. Residents and guests jockey for seats at the folding tables that hold the best-looking pies or hold those prepared by the most notoriously good cooks, all of whom can't help but add their own fillip to their pie.

Merry "Corky" White, a food anthropologist at Boston University, has been going to Islesford for decades to spend time with her brother, Henry, who owns a home on the island. White, a former caterer, literally wrote the book on cooking for gatherings: her cookbook, *Cooking for Crowds*, was first published in 1974 and reprinted in 2013. With decades of experience under her belt, she recognizes that Islesford's approach to the community potluck is a clever one. The folks who gather around the tables each year and spoon chicken potpie onto the plates of their neighbors and friends don't seem to have any complaints, either.

Single Batch **Makes 8 to 10 servings (one 9-by-13-inch pie)**

Double Batch **Makes 16 to 20 servings (two 9-by-13-inch pies)**

MAKE AHEAD

The pastry dough can be refrigerated for up to 1 day or frozen for up to 1 month; if frozen, thaw in the refrigerator overnight. The filling can be made up to 1 day ahead and refrigerated. The pie(s) can be made and refrigerated unbaked for up to 4 hours; add 10 to 15 minutes to the baking time.

BIG BATCH NOTES

If making two pies, make two single batches of dough, as a double batch will overwhelm a standard-size food processor. The filling can be made in a large Dutch oven, or it can be made in two large saucepans and then combined before dividing it between the baking dishes. A double batch of the filling and crust makes enough for two 9-by-13-inch baking dishes or three 9- or 10-inch deep-dish pie dishes.

If you wish, buy rotisserie chicken instead of cooking the chicken thighs. You'll need 4 cups chicken for the small batch and 8 cups chicken for the double batch.

SERVING

For a really big gathering, follow the island's lead and ask others to bring their version of this recipe. A citrusy salad with bitter greens and toasted nuts is a good accompaniment. For dessert, offer ice cream and fresh fruit.

INGREDIENT NOTES

Fresh pearl onions come in white, yellow, and red varieties, sometimes packaged together in a combination of all three colors. To peel them, drop them into a saucepan of boiling water over high heat and cook until the skins loosen, about 1 minute. Drain in a colander and rinse under cool running water until cold. Using a small, sharp knife, trim off a thin slice from the top and bottom of each onion, then make a shallow vertical incision in the skin and peel them.

To skip the peeling altogether, use thawed frozen pearl onions.

PASTRY CRUST

Since a food processor will only fit one batch of dough, you'll have to make one batch per pie.

INGREDIENTS	SINGLE CRUST
Unbleached all-purpose flour	3 cups
Kosher salt	1½ tsp
Baking powder	1 tsp
Cold solid vegetable shortening, cut into small cubes	½ cup
Cold unsalted butter, cut into small cubes	¼ cup
Ice water	½ to ⅔ cup

Make the pastry: For each pie, in a food processor, combine the flour, salt, and baking powder and pulse a few times until mixed. Scatter the shortening and butter over the flour mixture and mix quickly and lightly with your fingers until each piece is coated with flour. Pulse 10 times, until the fat is the size of peas. With the motor running, add just enough of the ice water to moisten the flour mixture and for the dough to come together in clumps.

Lightly flour a work surface and dump the dough out onto the floured surface. Quickly gather up the dough into a mass, knead briefly, and shape into a thick, flat rectangle. Wrap the dough in plastic wrap and refrigerate for at least 30 minutes or up to 1 hour. It is easiest to work with if it is chilled but not hard.

PIE FILLING

INGREDIENTS	SINGLE BATCH	DOUBLE BATCH
Skinless, boneless chicken thighs	2 lb	4 lb
Olive oil	3 Tbsp	6 Tbsp
Kosher salt and freshly ground black pepper		
Chicken stock	5 cups	10 cups
Unsalted butter	¾ cup	1½ cups
Yellow onions, chopped	2	4
Carrots, peeled and cut into ½-inch dice	2	4
Celery ribs, cut into ½-inch dice	2	4
Unbleached all-purpose flour	¾ cup	1½ cups
Heavy cream	¼ cup	½ cup

INGREDIENTS	SINGLE BATCH	DOUBLE BATCH
10-oz package(s) frozen peas, thawed	1	2
Pearl onions (see *Ingredient Notes*)	1½ cups	3 cups
Finely chopped fresh flat-leaf parsley	½ cup	1 cup
Egg Glaze		
Large egg	1	1
Water	1 Tbsp	1 Tbsp
Kosher salt and freshly ground black pepper		

Make the filling: Preheat the oven to 350°F. Place the chicken thighs on a sheet pan, drizzle evenly with the oil, and season with salt and pepper. Roast until the chicken is cooked through, 25 to 30 minutes. Set aside to cool, then cut into large dice.

Meanwhile, in a saucepan, bring the stock to a simmer over medium heat. Melt the butter in a large Dutch oven over medium-low heat. Add the yellow onions, carrots, and celery and cook, stirring occasionally, until the onions are translucent, 10 to 15 minutes. Stir in the flour, reduce the heat to low, and cook, stirring constantly and not allowing the flour to brown, for about 2 minutes. Gradually add the hot stock while stirring constantly, then cook, stirring, until the sauce thickens, about 1 minute. Stir in the cream.

Add the chicken, peas, pearl onions, and parsley and stir to mix well. Season with salt and pepper, then remove from the heat and let cool.

Assemble the pie(s): Increase the oven temperature to 375°F. If baking two pies, position racks in the top third and center of the oven. Transfer the filling to a 9-by-13-inch baking dish or divide the filling evenly between two dishes if making two pies.

On a floured work surface, roll out the dough into an 11-by-15-inch rectangle about ⅛ inch thick. If making two pies, roll out the second batch of dough. Center the dough over the dish(es) and press along the sides, decoratively crimping or fluting the edges.

Make the egg glaze: In a small bowl, whisk together the egg and water until blended. Lightly brush the dough with the glaze. Sprinkle the dough with salt and pepper. Cut three evenly spaced slits in the top to allow steam to escape.

Place the pie(s) on a sheet pan to catch any drips. Bake until the top is golden brown and the filling is bubbling hot, about 1 hour. Serve hot or warm.

NOAH BERNAMOFF AND RAE COHEN

mile end deli's matzo ball soup

GATHERING FRIENDS TOGETHER around steaming bowls of this homey matzo ball soup—soft, savory dumplings bobbing in golden chicken stock—is like group therapy. The recipe comes from Noah Bernamoff and Rae Cohen, owners of Mile End Deli, who have been serving globally inspired deli food in the highly competitive New York City deli scene since 2009.

Born in Montreal, Noah has fond memories of his late grandmother's chicken soup, especially the large, fluffy matzo balls that arrived in every bowl. The secrets he learned from his nana include adding schmaltz and baking powder to the matzo mixture and cooking the balls in stock rather than the usual salted water. Both the schmaltz and the stock contribute considerable flavor to the balls, and the baking powder ensures lightness. Dissenters who prize a clear broth point out that the matzo balls will make the liquid cloudy, and those who skip the baking powder (or seltzer, another way to guarantee a lighter finish) favor what matzo ball aficionados describe as "sinkers" over the "floaters" served at Mile End.

But Noah sticks by his nana's rules, including her advice always to use a light touch when mixing and forming the balls to prevent them from becoming too dense. Her stock is a great all-purpose recipe, too, which you can make for using in other dishes. If you opt to do that, you can skip the dill, if you like, or make only a half batch, if that's all you need.

This recipe works wonderfully as the first course of a meal. But if you are serving this soup as the main event, double the recipe so you have plenty of matzo balls on hand. A double batch will feed 10 as a main course and a doubled double batch will feed 20 as main course. This is a huge amount of stock, so be forewarned.

Not surprisingly, Mile End serves dozens of orders of this home-style soup every day. It is also a crucial part of the deli's annual Passover Seder, a community event that helps raise funds for Share Our Strength's No Kid Hungry campaign.

Single Batch **Makes 10 servings as a first course**

Double Batch **Makes 20 servings as a first course**

MAKE AHEAD

The matzo ball mixture can be refrigerated in a covered container (leave room for the mixture to expand by about one-fourth) for up to 1 day. The stock can be refrigerated for up to 2 days or frozen for up to 2 months. The cooked chicken for the soup can be refrigerated for up to 2 days.

One large stockpot; one or two large soup pots or Dutch ovens; two or three half sheet pans

BIG BATCH NOTES

If making a double batch, divide the stock and soup between two large pots as the balls will swell when poached. You will need to have lots of stock on hand, as the balls will soak it up.

SERVING

Plan on one or two matzo balls per person. This soup is typically served as a first course at Passover celebrations, but it is also a nice midwinter meal with Challah (page 243).

INGREDIENT NOTES

Schmaltz, or rendered chicken fat, is a staple at kosher butchers, and shelf-stable versions can be purchased online.

INGREDIENTS	SINGLE BATCH	DOUBLE BATCH
Chicken Stock		
Chickens, each about 3½ lb and cut into 8 pieces	2	4
Black peppercorns	10	20
Kosher salt	2 tsp	4 tsp
Large yellow onions, halved through the stem end	2	4
Parsnips, peeled	2	4
Carrots, peeled	2	4
Celery ribs	2	4
Fresh dill sprigs	3	6
Fresh flat-leaf parsley sprigs	3	6
Fresh thyme sprigs	3	6
Bay leaves	2	4
Matzo Balls		
Matzo meal	1½ cups	3 cups
Large eggs, lightly beaten	4	8
Schmaltz (see *Ingredient Notes*)	⅓ cup	⅔ cup
Baking powder (see *Ingredient Notes*)	1 Tbsp	2 Tbsp
Kosher salt	¼ tsp	½ tsp
Freshly ground black pepper	¼ tsp	½ tsp
Soup		
Large yellow onion(s), coarsely chopped	1	2
Parsnips, peeled and cut into 2- to 3-inch batons	2	4
Carrots, peeled and cut into 2- to 3-inch batons	2	4
Celery ribs, cut into 2- to 3-inch batons	2	4
Kosher salt and freshly ground black pepper		
Fresh dill for garnish		

Make the stock: In a large stockpot, combine the chicken pieces, peppercorns, and salt. (If making the double batch, divide the ingredients between two large pots.) Add water to cover the ingredients by about 2 inches, then bring to a simmer over medium heat. Reduce the heat to maintain a low simmer and continue cooking, uncovered, for about 1½ hours, occasionally skimming off any foam and fat that rise to the surface.

Using a slotted spoon or tongs, remove the breast and thigh sections and reserve them for the soup (or for another use, like chicken salad), leaving the drumsticks and wings in the pot. Add the onions, parsnips, carrots, and celery and continue to simmer for another 1½ hours, stirring and skimming occasionally.

Remove from the heat and add the dill, parsley, thyme, and bay leaves. Set aside to steep for 30 minutes.

Using a large slotted spoon or wire skimmer, scoop out and discard the large solids from the stock. Strain the stock through a large fine-mesh sieve set over another pot in the sink.

Let the stock the cool, then cover and refrigerate until needed.

If using the reserved chicken pieces for the soup, bone and skin them and cut into bite-size pieces. Cover and refrigerate until needed.

Make the matzo ball dough: At least 3 hours before serving, in a large bowl, stir together the matzo meal, eggs, schmaltz, baking powder, salt, and pepper until thoroughly mixed. It will look loose at this point but will firm up once it has rested. Be sure the bowl is large enough to allow for expansion of the dough. Cover and refrigerate for 2 hours.

Make the matzo balls: Line two or three half sheet pans with parchment paper. Allowing about 1 heaping tablespoon for each ball, shape the matzo mixture with your hands into balls a little smaller than a golf ball. They should be completely smooth on the outside, with no cracks. Set them aside on the prepared sheet pans. You should have about 10 balls if making a single batch and about 20 balls if making a double batch.

Make the soup: Return the strained stock to the pot and bring to a low simmer. Add the onions, parsnips, carrots, and celery, then carefully drop in the matzo balls. Simmer until the balls are light and cooked through, about 20 minutes. During the last 5 minutes of cooking, add the chicken meat, if you like.

Taste and adjust the seasoning with salt and pepper. Garnish with fresh dill and serve hot.

new england fish and clam chowder

Single Batch
Makes 10 to 12 servings

Double Batch
Makes 15 to 20 servings

MAKE AHEAD

The chowder can be made up to 1 day ahead and refrigerated. Reheat slowly over medium-low heat, stirring often, until piping hot. This chowder does not freeze well because of the dairy ingredients.

EQUIPMENT

One or two large soup pots or Dutch ovens.

BIG BATCH NOTES

If making a double batch, it's best to cook it in two pots rather than a single large one, as it makes it easier to prevent scorching and the chowder will cook more evenly.

If you are not good with a shucking knife, ask your fishmonger to shuck and shell the clams. Make sure he or she reserves all of the juices. If you are opening the clams at home, consider enlisting helping hands for the job. The same goes for peeling the potatoes.

SERVING

Oyster crackers are the traditional topping for chowder, but rustic bread or biscuits would also be welcome. Round out the meal with a green salad and a fruit crisp (see page 281).

IN HER 2016 book *Soup Swap,* Kathy Gunst, an award-winning food journalist and prolific cookbook author, tells a story about the "soup swap" parties she and a friend started many years ago to fight the midwinter blues among her Maine neighbors. The concept is simple: Each guest or couple brings a large pot of homemade soup that yields enough servings to feed each guest twice, one small serving to enjoy the night of the soup swap and one good-size serving to take home. You cook once but go home with a wide selection of tasty new soups and great recipes. The swaps are popular and fun, the soups are delicious, and—amazingly—no two guests have ever brought the same soup to the party.

This chowder is a New England classic, using a combination of freshly shucked clams, chunks of firm white fish like haddock or cod, and potatoes in a base of fish stock, clam juice, milk, and cream. Adjust the ratio of cream to milk to suit your own taste; more cream makes a richer chowder, while more milk (or stock) makes a lighter one. Depending on where you live and what seafood is available, you can try using mussels instead of clams, or substitute other firm white fish for the haddock or cod. If clams aren't available or you're allergic, substitute 1½ pounds smoked haddock or trout flaked into small pieces and increase the fish stock by 1½ cups.

INGREDIENTS	SINGLE BATCH	DOUBLE BATCH
Clams, shucked with juices reserved (see *Ingredient Notes*)	3 lb	6 lb
Country-style or thick-cut sliced bacon (see *Ingredient Notes*)	5 oz	10 oz
Olive oil	2 Tbsp	¼ cup
Finely chopped yellow onions	2	4
Kosher salt and freshly ground black pepper		
Chopped fresh thyme	2 Tbsp	4 Tbsp
Yukon Gold potatoes, peeled and cut into ½-inch cubes	2 lb	4 lb

INGREDIENTS	SINGLE BATCH	DOUBLE BATCH
Low-fat milk	2 cups	4 cups
Heavy cream	2 cups	4 cups
Skinned haddock, cod, or other firm-fleshed white fish fillets, cut into 1-inch cubes	2½ lb	5 lb
All-purpose flour	2 Tbsp	¼ cup
Fish stock	3 cups	6 cups
Finely chopped fresh flat-leaf parsley	½ cup	¾ cup
Cayenne pepper	Pinch	¼ tsp

Shuck and chop the clams and reserve the juices as directed in the *Ingredient Notes*. Set the chopped clam meats and juices aside. You should have 1 cup juices if making a single batch and 2 cups if making a double batch.

In a large soup pot (or in two pots if making a double batch), cook the bacon over medium heat, flipping it occasionally, until crisp, about 5 minutes. Transfer to paper towels to drain and cool, then crumble. Pour off all but 1 tablespoon of the fat (from each pot if making a double batch).

Add the oil to the fat remaining in the pot and reduce the heat to low. Add the onions and cook, stirring frequently, until soft and just beginning to turn golden, about 6 minutes. Add a pinch of salt (clams can be very briny, so go light on the salt at this point), a few grinds of pepper, and half the thyme and stir well. Add the potatoes and cook, stirring, for a minute or so to coat the potatoes thoroughly with the onion mixture.

Meanwhile, heat the milk and cream in a saucepan over medium heat just to a simmer. Add the haddock and the chopped clams to the potato mixture, sprinkle with the flour, and stir for about 1 minute, mixing evenly. Add the stock and strained clam juices, stir well, and cook for about 2 minutes. Add half of the crumbled bacon, the remaining thyme, and the warm milk mixture. Raise the heat to medium-high and bring to a simmer, stirring occasionally.

When the chowder begins to simmer, reduce the heat to low, add half of the parsley and all of the cayenne, and stir well. Cover and simmer gently until the potatoes are tender, 10 to 15 minutes.

Serve the chowder hot, with the remaining parsley and bacon on the side for guests to add as they like.

INGREDIENT NOTES

The number of clams to the pound will vary according to the type used. Plan on 24 cherrystones, 10 quahogs, or 30 littlenecks, steamer, or Mahogany clams for the single batch and twice that number for the double batch. If any raw clams do not close to the touch, discard them. Scrub the clams well under cold running water before shucking.

To shuck the clams, you will need a shucking knife and a thick glove or kitchen towel to protect the hand holding the clam. Working over a bowl, insert the tip of the knife between the shells of a clam (opposite the hinge), twist slightly to break the seal of the clam, and pry open the top shell, capturing the juices in the bowl. Scrape the raw clam meat from the shell into a second bowl and discard the shells.

Line a fine-mesh sieve with dampened cheesecloth or paper towels and set over a deep bowl. Strain the clam juices through the sieve to remove any grit. You should have 1 cup liquid if making a single batch and 2 cups liquid if making a double batch. On a cutting board, preferably with a carving well, chop the clam meat. Strain any juices from chopping through the sieve into the bowl.

You can omit the bacon if you like, substituting olive oil for the bacon fat when cooking the onions.

STREAMLINED NEW ENGLAND FISH AND CLAM CHOWDER

Nothing beats chowder made with just-opened clams and their juice. But for expediency's sake, you may want to use packaged fresh clams, available at many fishmongers, and bottled clam juice. Substitute 8 ounces chopped clams for the freshly shucked clams and 1 cup bottled clam juice for the juice in the single batch and 1 pound chopped clams and 2 cups bottled juice for the double batch.

black bean soup

CHEF, COOKING TEACHER, and writer Deborah Madison knows what it means to feed people. She started cooking for her community when she joined the Zen Center after college, on her way to becoming an ordained Buddhist priest and the founding chef of Greens, San Francisco's celebrated vegetarian restaurant. Since then, Deborah has authored many cookbooks, including her much-loved *Vegetarian Cooking for Everyone*. An avid gardener, she is also committed to community gardening. As she once wrote, "Connecting people to the food they eat, its source and its history, has long been my work, and writing is one way to reveal the deeper culture of food."

This black bean soup is based on the black bean chili Deborah used to make at Greens. When she first started offering it, black beans were considered exotic. Nowadays, there are many more varieties of beans to choose from, but she still loves the heartiness, rich flavor, and subtle sweetness of black beans. They also make this soup a filling—and inexpensive—dish for a crowd.

The key to perfecting this recipe is to follow your own taste: adjust the amounts of cilantro, smoked paprika, chipotles, and salt to suit your palate.

Single Batch **Makes 10 servings**

Double Batch **Makes 20 servings**

MAKE AHEAD

The soup can be refrigerated for up to 3 days or frozen for up to 3 months; if frozen, thaw in the refrigerator overnight. Reheat the soup over low heat, stirring often, to prevent scorching.

INGREDIENTS	SINGLE BATCH	DOUBLE BATCH
Dried black beans	1 lb	2 lb
Yellow onions, cut into ½-inch squares	1	2
Garlic cloves, finely chopped	2	4
15-oz can(s) diced tomatoes	1	2
Large bunch cilantro, chopped	½	1
Pureed chipotle chiles in adobo sauce	1 to 2 Tbsp	2 to 4 Tbsp
Smoked paprika, for seasoning		
Sea salt	2 tsp	4 tsp
Shredded Monterey Jack cheese, for serving		
Sour cream, for serving		

EQUIPMENT

One or two large soup pots or Dutch ovens.

BIG BATCH NOTES

If making a double batch, it's best to cook it in two pots rather than a single large one. The soup will cook more quickly and evenly, with less risk of scorching on the bottom. Cook the beans in a heavy-bottomed pot or use a heat diffuser.

SERVING

Tortillas, pickled onions, and shredded cabbage tossed with lime juice are all good accompaniments. Serve lime wedges on the side.

Sort through the beans and remove any debris, then rinse them well. Put the beans in a large, heavy-bottomed soup pot (or two pots if making a double batch) and add water to cover by 1 inch. Bring to a boil over medium-high heat. Boil for 10 minutes, skimming off and discarding any foam that collects on the surface.

Reduce the heat to low and stir in the onion(s) and garlic. Cover and cook until the onion(s) has softened, about 15 minutes. Add the tomatoes with their juices, half of the cilantro, half of the chipotle puree, and a pinch or more of smoked paprika. Cook, uncovered, for 1 hour.

Season with the salt and continue cooking until the beans are soft, about 30 minutes or so. As the soup cooks, check the level of the liquid occasionally and add hot water as needed if the soup becomes too thick. When the beans are ready, taste the soup and add more salt, chipotle puree, and/or smoked paprika if needed.

Just before serving, stir in the remaining cilantro. Deborah recommends that you taste the soup at this point and adjust the seasoning with more cilantro, chipotle puree, smoked paprika, and salt if needed. Serve hot, with the Monterey Jack, cilantro, and sour cream on the side for guests to top their servings as they like.

ROBB WALSH

el real's chili con carne

IN HIS WONDERFUL book, *The Chili Cookbook*, Texas food expert Robb Walsh delves into the five-hundred-year history of chili, with recipes from Texas, Mexico, New Mexico, the Midwest, and beyond. From three bean to four alarm, and from con carne to vegetarian, everyone has a favorite version.

This is Robb's go-to chili, the one he serves at his restaurant, El Real Tex-Mex Cafe in Houston. His homemade chili powder makes for a just-spicy-enough, full-flavored chili. Don't skip the step of dry roasting the cumin seeds. And as dictated by Texas tradition, Robb's chili does not contain beans. A pot of pinto beans is often served on the side.

Chili is the ultimate hearty one-pot meal and is so popular it has inspired countless cook-offs around the country. A chili cook-off is a fun way to get people to cook together and showcase a variety of different iterations (page 71), or you can dispense with the competition and just have a party.

INGREDIENTS	SINGLE BATCH	DOUBLE BATCH
Cumin seeds	3 Tbsp	6 Tbsp
Bacon slices, chopped	12 oz	1½ lb
Boneless beef chuck, cut into ¼-inch cubes	4½ lb	9 lb
Yellow onions, chopped	3	6
Vegetable or olive oil, if needed		
Homemade chili powder (page 70)	¼ cup	½ cup
Sweet paprika	1 Tbsp	2 Tbsp
Dried Mexican oregano (see *Ingredient Notes*, page 70)	1½ tsp	1 Tbsp
Freshly ground black pepper	1½ tsp	1 Tbsp
Dried thyme	¾ tsp	1½ tsp
Kosher salt	1 Tbsp	2 Tbsp
Large garlic cloves, finely chopped	6	12
Beef stock	2¼ cups	4½ cups
Water	1 cup	2 cups

continued on following page

Single Batch **Makes 10 servings**

Double Batch **Makes 20 servings**

MAKE AHEAD

You can make the chili powder up to 2 weeks in advance. Store it in an airtight container at room temperature. The chili can be refrigerated for up to 3 days or frozen for up to 3 months; if frozen, thaw in the refrigerator overnight. To reheat, transfer to a large, heavy-bottomed Dutch oven, place over low heat, cover partially, and heat gently until warmed through.

EQUIPMENT

One or two large Dutch ovens.

BIG BATCH NOTES

The most difficult part of the recipe is cutting the beef into small pieces. Recruit helpers for this, setting them up with cutting boards and big, sharp knives. The beef will be easier to cut if it is first cut into 1-inch cubes, arranged on sheet pans in a single layer, and slipped into the freezer until semifrozen, about 1 hour. Have the same crew help with chopping the onions and garlic.

It is best to split the double batch between two pots for ease of stirring and cooking. Once the chili is assembled, it can be transferred to one or two slow cookers, where it will cook unattended.

The traditional toppings for chili are chopped onions, shredded cheese, and saltines. The chili can also be spooned over rice or potatoes, transformed into a Frito pie, or combined with beans. Set out spiced nuts, a green salad, and plenty of beer. Finish the meal with Texas Sheet Cake (page 265).

INGREDIENT NOTES

Mexican oregano has a spicier, sharper aroma and flavor than its Mediterranean counterpart. You'll find the anchos and the oregano sold at Latin markets, well-stocked supermarkets, and online.

Ancho chiles are the dried version of fresh poblano chiles. They are somewhat sweet and fruity and not very hot.

HOMEMADE CHILI POWDER

Makes about ½ cup

5 ancho chiles (see *Ingredient Notes*)
1 tsp cumin seeds
1 tsp dried Mexican oregano (see *Ingredient Notes*)
½ teaspoon garlic powder

Stem and seed the chiles, then split lengthwise. Lay the chiles flat in a cast-iron skillet, place over medium heat, and toast lightly, flipping occasionally, untii brittle. Remove and let cool. Add the cumin seeds to the skillet over medium-high heat and toast, stirring and shaking the pan, just until fragrant, 1 to 2 minutes. If desired, toast some of the chile seeds along with the cumin for extra heat. Pour the seeds onto a plate to cool.

Using scissors, cut the chiles into small strips. Working in batches, grind the strips in a spice grinder to a coarse powder and transfer to a small bowl. Next, grind the cumin and chile seeds (if using) to a coarse powder and add to the bowl. Stir the oregano and garlic powder into the ground chile mixture. Then, in batches, grind the chile mixture until very finely ground, about 2 minutes per batch.

INGREDIENTS	SINGLE BATCH	DOUBLE BATCH
15-oz cans tomato puree	3	6
Ancho chiles (see *Ingredient Notes*), stemmed and seeded but left whole	3	6

Finely chopped yellow onion, for serving
Shredded cheese, for serving

Toast the cumin seeds in a skillet over medium-high heat until fragrant, 1 to 2 minutes. Transfer to a work surface and, using a smaller skillet or a metal or wooden tool with a flat surface, coarsely crush the seeds. Set aside.

Cook the bacon in a large Dutch oven (or two pots if making a double batch) over medium-high heat, stirring occasionally, until crisp. Using a slotted spoon, transfer the bacon to a large, rimmed plate or a half sheet pan.

Increase the heat to high and, working in batches, brown the beef. As each batch is ready, using a slotted spoon, transfer it to the plate or pan holding the bacon.

Reduce the heat to medium, add the onions, and cook, stirring occasionally, until translucent, 10 to 12 minutes. If the pan begins to look dry, add a few spoonfuls of oil.

Add the toasted cumin, chili powder, paprika, oregano, black pepper, thyme, salt, and garlic and cook, stirring occasionally, for 1 minute. Crumble the bacon and return it to the pot along with the beef, stock, water, tomato puree, and chiles. Bring to a boil, then reduce the heat to medium-low, cover partially, and simmer, stirring occasionally and adding hot water as needed to maintain the desired consistency, until the meat is very tender, about 2 hours. Alternatively, transfer to a slow cooker (or two slow cookers if making a double batch) set on low and cook for at least 6 hours or up to 8 hours.

Remove the ancho chiles, puree in a blender, and return half of the puree to the chili. Stir to combine, then taste the chili and adjust the seasoning with more ancho puree, chili powder, salt, or pepper.

Serve hot, with the onion and cheese on the side for guests to add as they like.

CHILI COOK-OFF

FOR DIE-HARD CHILI LOVERS, the ingredients and preparation of chili are as sacred as the tenets of a religion. Some swear by bean-heavy recipes, while others argue that a true chili is meat-only. Beef purists balk at the inclusion of poultry or pork, and masters of these varieties swear by their concoctions. Some insist chili must be red, others say green. The inclusion of toppings is another controversial element. The best way to settle the question of what makes a great chili? Throw a chili cook-off and let the people decide.

The first documented chili cook-off took place in 1967 in Terlingua, Texas. Two Texan journalists needed to settle a feud over who was the most knowledgeable chili connoisseur. Judges were arranged, proud chefs cooked fiery pots of chili, bowls were filled, a winner was proclaimed, and thus the great chili cook-off was born. Nowadays, chili cook-offs are popping up in unexpected places: at county fairs, supermarkets, fire stations, festivals, and more. There's even a day dedicated to the stuff: National Chili Day is the fourth Thursday in February.

Here are a few tips for how to throw your own chili cook-off:

○ **Pick a setting.** You can go low-key and invite a handful of friends for a cook-off in your home, or go all-out and rent a large public space, such as a local school cafeteria or the basement of a public office after hours, and get the whole community involved.

○ **Spread the word.** Pick a date and start telling people about the cook-off. If opting for a smaller, more intimate affair, an email invitation will suffice.

If you're opening the event to a larger community, hang fliers around town with details of the event and how to get involved. You'll need volunteers, judges, chili cooks, and tasters.

○ **Sort your chilis.** Make sure there are at least three chilis to be judged. The more variety, the better, so try to find participants who are experts in making vegetarian, meat-based, bean-based, poultry, red, and green chilis.

○ **Plan your toppings.** Participants can bring their own toppings, but it's also good to have some standard toppings on hand. All of these can be prepped the morning of the event: grated cheeses (one yellow, one white), tortilla chips, cornbread, saltines, sour cream, diced red onion, sliced green onion, sliced jalapeños, fresh cilantro, lime wedges, salsa fresca, and diced avocado.

○ **Get organized.** Try to plan the cook-off near a kitchen so large pots of chili can be kept warm. Alternatively, set up a serving table near electric outlets so slow cookers and electric warming pots can be plugged in. Or move the party outside and keep the chilis warm on a charcoal grill. You'll also need bowls, spoons, and napkins for all attendees, as well as ladles for serving. Don't forget prizes for the winner!

grandma salazar's chile verde

SAN FRANCISCO CHEF and restaurateur Traci Des Jardins has been enjoying this robust stew all of her life. A native Californian, she grew up with Spanish-speaking grandparents and calls dishes like this one her soul food. Her grandmother, a dedicated home cook who was born in Mexico, made this chile verde frequently for family gatherings and also taught her young granddaughter how to make it. It was just one of the many family recipes that has inspired Traci's lifelong passion for cooking and bringing people together around the table—in her restaurants, at home, and at countless events in support of food equity.

For this homey dish, Traci uses a pork butt, which is a delicious and relatively inexpensive way to feed a crowd of family and friends. She combines it with tomatillos, cilantro, chiles, and other staples of her traditional family pantry and then braises it slowly to yield a flavorful broth and lots of tender meat ideal for pairing with warm tortillas.

Single Batch **Makes 10 servings**

Double Batch **Makes 20 servings**

MAKE AHEAD

The stew can be refrigerated for up to 3 days or frozen for up to 1 month.

INGREDIENTS	SINGLE BATCH	DOUBLE BATCH
Boneless pork butt (shoulder)	4 lb	8 lb
Kosher salt	1½ Tbsp	3 Tbsp
Freshly ground black pepper		
All-purpose flour	2 Tbsp	¼ cup
Vegetable oil	2 Tbsp	¼ cup
Tomatillos, husks removed, rinsed, and quartered	3 lb	6 lb
Anaheim or poblano chiles, stemmed and cut into ½-inch pieces	1 lb	2 lb
Yellow onions, cut into ½-inch pieces	2	4
Garlic cloves, roughly chopped	6	12
Cilantro, leaves only, coarsely chopped	1 bunch	2 bunches
Ground cumin	1 tsp	2 tsp
Dried oregano	½ tsp	1 tsp
Chicken stock, or as needed	3 cups	6 cups

Two half sheet pans; one or two
large non-reactive (not cast iron)
soup pots or Dutch ovens.

BIG BATCH NOTES

Do not crowd the pork when
browning it or it will give off too
much steam, which will prevent it
from developing good color.

SERVING

Start with tortilla chips and guaca-
mole, set out one or more salsas, a
stack of warm tortillas, and a green
salad with the stew, and offer ice
cream with cajeta (page 268) for
dessert.

INGREDIENT NOTES

If you want to make this dish
gluten-free, it is fine to omit
the flour. Nothing is needed in
its place.

Trim the pork of excess fat and cut into 1½-inch chunks. Spread the pork on half sheet pans and season generously with the salt and several grinds of pepper. Sprinkle with the flour and toss until coated.

Heat a large Dutch oven(s) over medium-high heat. When the pan is hot, add the oil and, working in batches, fry the pork until golden brown on all sides. Using tongs, transfer to a sheet pan.

When all of the meat has been browned, add the tomatillos, chiles, onions, and garlic to the pot(s) and reduce the heat to low. Cook until the vegetables are soft, 10 to 15 minutes.

Return the meat to the pot and add the cilantro, cumin, and oregano. Pour in enough stock just to cover the meat, raise the heat to medium-high, and bring to a gentle boil.

Reduce the heat to a simmer, cover, and cook, stirring occasionally, until the pork is tender, about 2 hours. Serve hot.

PABLEAUX JOHNSON

new orleans
red beans and rice

IN NEW ORLEANS, red beans and rice is the traditional Monday-night dinner, a custom that dates to the nineteenth century. Back then, Monday was wash day, so cooks knew that they had to prepare something for dinner that could simmer slowly all day while they did the laundry. The dish, which was often flavored with a ham bone from Sunday night's supper (here, spicy andouille sausage is used), was an economical and nutritious meal.

Pableaux Johnson, a New Orleans–based photographer and writer, loves this tradition, so he took it on. In the beginning, he had Monday-night suppers at his house with family and close friends. He made the red beans and rice and served it with skillet cornbread, and his guests brought whatever they wanted to drink. He has since taken this show on the road—literally. Traveling under the aptly named "Red Beans Road Show," Pableaux journeys to different cities, prepares his red beans and rice with skillet cornbread, and a host chef contributes a starter and dessert. No phones are allowed and all tables seat eight people to encourage conversation. To date, the road show has toured dozens of cities, from San Diego to Boston, Chicago to Tampa, drawing big groups of people at every stop. Friendships are made and every dinner is typically followed by a celebratory shot of whiskey.

Red beans and rice is especially good for feeding a crowd because it is so easy. You'll spend most of your time chopping, and then once everything is in the pot, you and your guests can enjoy the savory aroma that fills your kitchen together.

Single Batch
Makes 10 to 12 servings

Double Batch
Makes 20 to 24 servings

MAKE AHEAD

The beans can be cooked up to the point at which you add the parsley and greens and refrigerated for up to 3 days or frozen for up to 2 months. If refrigerated, reheat gently over low heat, stirring often to prevent scorching, until hot, then stir in the parsley and green onions and taste and adjust the seasoning with salt. If frozen, thaw overnight in the refrigerator and reheat as directed for refrigerated beans. You can also skip the thawing and reheat the frozen beans over low heat, which can take up to 1 hour.

EQUIPMENT

One or two large Dutch ovens, one or two rice cookers.

BIG BATCH NOTES

The double batch of soaked dried beans will swell to an impressive amount, so be sure to use two large bowls or a single oversize bowl. The same is true for cooked beans, which means you will need to use two large pots or one very large pot to cook them.

Pableaux uses a rice cooker, but if you don't have one, we have included a classic stove top recipe (page 76).

INGREDIENTS	SINGLE BATCH	DOUBLE BATCH
Dried red (kidney) beans, preferably Camellia brand (see *Ingredient Notes*, page 76)	3 cups	6 cups
Olive oil	4 Tbsp	8 Tbsp
Andouille sausage, cut into ½-inch cubes	1 lb	2 lb
Yellow onions, finely chopped	2	4

continued on following page

75

This is a robust one-bowl dinner, but you can do as Pableaux does and ask guests to supply a starter and dessert.

INGREDIENT NOTES

In New Orleans, cooks traditionally reach for Camellia brand red kidney beans when making this dish. If you cannot find them in your local store, look for them online.

CLASSIC STEAMED RICE

If you don't have a rice cooker, you can make rice on the stove top in a heavy-bottomed 4- to 5-quart Dutch oven or saucepan.

Most types of rice work here: short grain, medium grain, or long grain. If using the brown variety of any of these, increase the cooking time to 45 minutes or so.

The proportion of water to rice is 2 parts water to 1 part rice. If using jasmine, use 1½ parts water to 1 part rice. The rice will triple in volume when cooked. So, 3½ cups uncooked rice yields about 10½ cups cooked rice, or 10–14 servings. A 4-quart (16-cup) Dutch oven will allow sufficient headroom and keep the rice from boiling over.

3½ cups short-grain, medium-grain, or long-grain rice
7 cups water (5¼ cups for jasmine)
1½ teaspoons kosher salt (optional)

Rinse rice under cold water until the water is clear. Drain rice well.

Combine the rice, water, and salt (if using) in 4- to 5-quart heavy-bottomed Dutch oven and bring to a boil over high heat. Reduce the heat to low and cover tightly. Cook until the rice is tender and has absorbed the water, about 17 minutes. Remove from the heat and let stand, covered, for 5 minutes. Fluff the rice with a fork and transfer to a serving dish.

INGREDIENTS	SINGLE BATCH	DOUBLE BATCH
Garlic cloves, minced	6	12
Large celery rib(s), finely diced	1	2
Green bell pepper(s), seeded and chopped	1	2
Hot-pepper sauce, such as Tabasco	1 Tbsp	1½ Tbsp
White wine vinegar	1 Tbsp	2 Tbsp
Kosher salt	1 Tbsp	2 Tbsp
Dried basil	2 tsp	4 tsp
Freshly ground black pepper	1½ tsp	1 Tbsp
Rubbed dried sage	¾ tsp	1½ tsp
Cayenne pepper	⅛ tsp	¼ tsp
Bay leaves	3	5
Finely chopped fresh flat-leaf parsley	1 cup	2 cups
Green onions, chopped	6	12
Classic steamed rice (see left), made with long-grain white rice	1 recipe (10 cups)	2 recipes (20 cups)

Sort through the beans, discarding grit or stones, then rinse them well in a colander under cold running water. Put the beans in a large bowl, add cold water to cover by 1 inch, and let soak for at least 4 hours or up to overnight.

If making a single batch, in a large, heavy Dutch oven, heat 1 tablespoon of the oil over medium-high heat. If using two pots for a double batch, put 1 tablespoon oil in each pot and then divide the remaining ingredients between them as you assemble the beans for cooking. Add the sausage and cook, stirring occasionally, until lightly browned and crisp, about 5 minutes. Add the remaining oil, the yellow onions, and the garlic, reduce the heat to medium, and cook, stirring occasionally, until the onions are translucent, about 6 minutes. Add the celery and bell pepper(s) and cook, stirring occasionally, until they soften, about 5 minutes.

Drain the beans and add them to the pot, then add water just to cover the ingredients. Increase the heat to medium-high and bring to a simmer. Add the hot-pepper sauce, vinegar, salt, basil, black pepper, sage, cayenne, and bay leaves and stir well. Reduce the heat to low and simmer, stirring occasionally, until the beans are almost tender, 1½ to 2 hours. Taste and adjust the seasoning.

Transfer 1 cup of the beans with their liquid if making a single batch or 2 cups if making a double batch to a bowl. Mash well with a fork and then stir them back into the pot to thicken the cooking liquid slightly. Stir in the parsley and green onions and continue to simmer over low heat until the beans are very tender, 15 to 30 minutes more. Serve the beans hot with the rice.

Single Batch
Makes 8 to 10 servings

Double Batch
Makes 18 to 20 servings

MAKE AHEAD

Cornbread always tastes best not long from the oven, but you can assemble the ingredients in advance. Mix together the dry ingredients a few hours before baking and have the buttermilk and eggs ready to go. Then just before you are ready to bake, mix the dry and wet ingredients together, heat the oil, add it to the batter, pour the batter into the hot pan(s), and bake as directed.

EQUIPMENT

One or two 10-inch cast-iron skillets. If you don't have a cast-iron skillet, use one or two 9-inch square or round baking pans, grease well with vegetable oil or unsalted butter, and place in the oven while it preheats. Heat the oil for the batter in a small skillet or saucepan on the stove top until very hot, mix it into the batter, add the batter to the hot greased pan(s), place in the oven, and bake as directed.

CORNBREAD

If you're looking for a traditional side dish that qualifies as a modern-day magic trick, cook up a batch of this skillet cornbread. This buttermilk-based recipe, which Pableaux learned from his grandfather (A.Leon Hebert, his mama's daddy), has a little bit of flour for lightness and just a hint of sugar to sweeten the batter. Guests always love the "sizzle and flip" method, which takes some time to master, but adds an interesting bit of last-minute kitchen theater to the evening.

INGREDIENTS	SINGLE BATCH	DOUBLE BATCH
White or yellow cornmeal	2 cups	4 cups
All-purpose flour	¼ cup	½ cup
Sugar	2 Tbsp	¼ cup
Baking powder	1½ tsp	1 Tbsp
Salt	1 tsp	2 tsp
Large eggs	2	4
Buttermilk, or as needed	1⅓ cups	2⅔ cups
Vegetable oil	¼ cup	½ cup

Preheat the oven to 400°F. Put a 10-inch cast-iron-skillet on the stove top. If making a double batch, put two 10-inch skillets on the stove top.

In a large bowl, whisk or stir together the cornmeal, flour, sugar, baking powder, and salt, mixing well. In a medium bowl, combine the eggs and buttermilk, stir with a fork to break up the egg yolks, then mix the eggs with the buttermilk until blended.

Turn the heat on under the skillet(s) to medium-high and heat until very hot. Meanwhile, add the egg-buttermilk mixture to the cornmeal mixture and, using a whisk or a large spoon, stir just until a good soft batter forms. It should be wet and medium soupy. If it seems too dry, add a little more buttermilk.

Add the oil to the hot skillet, or divide it evenly between the skillets if making a double batch, and let the oil heat until it is smoking. With a hot pad, quickly pour the hot oil into the cornmeal batter and return the hot skillet(s) to the stove top, still over medium-high heat.

Move quickly now. Stir the hot oil into the batter and then pour the batter into the hot skillet, or divide it evenly between the skillets if making a double batch. Let the batter heat until the sides are bubbling and sizzling, a minute or two. Turn off the burner(s) and transfer the skillet(s) to the hot oven.

Bake until the cornbread has risen, is dry on top, and is beginning to crack, about 20 minutes. Remove the pan(s) from the oven and turn the bread over, top side down. If you are up to it, do this step the way Pableaux does: shake the skillet slightly to make sure the cornbread moves freely, then, with a hot pad, grab the handle with both hands and, working quickly and confidently, flip the cornbread into the air, catching it top side down in the pan. If you prefer to be more cautious, use a wide spatula to flip the cornbread. Return the skillet(s) to the oven to brown the top side on the hot bottom surface of the pan, 4 to 5 minutes longer.

Remove the skillet(s) from the oven and flip the cornbread one more time onto a serving plate. Serve warm.

You should be able to fit two skillets or baking pans on the same rack in the oven. If not, preheat the oven with the racks in the top third and center of the oven. Switch the pans halfway through baking.

SERVING

Offer this cornbread as is, or do as Pableaux suggests and accompany it with butter and Steen's pure cane syrup from Louisiana.

mom's guju chili

Single Batch **Makes 10 servings**

Double Batch **Makes 20 servings**

MAKE AHEAD

The beans must be soaked overnight. The chili can refrigerated for up to 2 days or frozen for up to 3 months; if frozen, thaw in the refrigerator overnight.

EQUIPMENT

One or two large Dutch ovens.

BIG BATCH NOTES

The double batch of soaked dried beans will swell to an impressive amount, so be sure to use two bowls or an oversized single bowl. The double batch can be cooked in a large stockpot, but the beans may take 30 minutes or longer to cook to tenderness, so two big pots are a better choice.

SERVING

Set out papadams and chutneys. Put the yogurt in a plastic squeeze bottle for easy serving. Accompany with rice (page 76) or an Indian bread, Chai-Spiced Melt-Away Cookies (page 257), and beer.

GROWING UP IN the Midwest, Preeti Mistry frequently ate this version of her mother's moong dal—a spicy, fragrant, bean-based vegetarian soup—at home. Her mom had a general food schedule she followed during the week, and Wednesday was moong dal night, at which the family ate the dal as part of a traditional Gujarati dinner with rice, usually two vegetable dishes, whole wheat roti (flat bread), and raita.

Years later, after training in high-end restaurants in London and starting a pop-up restaurant, Preeti opened her own brick-and-mortar spaces, Juhu Beach Club (now closed) and Navi Kitchen. She served her versions of the street food she'd enjoyed on family trips back to Mumbai, including her mom's moong dal, which she dubbed Mom's Guju Chili in honor of her Gujarati Indian heritage. The popularity of dishes like this one and so many others at her restaurants inspired Preeti to write her own cookbook, *The Juhu Beach Club Cookbook*.

INGREDIENTS	SINGLE BATCH	DOUBLE BATCH
Dried mung beans	2 cups	4 cups
Cumin seeds	5 Tbsp	10 Tbsp
Coriander seeds	¾ cup	1½ cups
Rice bran oil	¼ cup	½ cup
Yellow onions, thinly sliced	2	3
Kosher salt		
Minced garlic	½ cup	1 cup
Peeled and minced fresh ginger	½ cup	1 cup
Seeded and minced serrano chiles	½ cup	1 cup
Tomato paste (see *Ingredient Notes*)	2 cups	4 cups
Pureed canned plum tomatoes, preferably San Marzano (see *Ingredient Notes*)	6 cups	12 cups
Water, or as needed	4 cups	8 cups
Lemons, juiced, or as needed	2	3
Citrus pickled onions (see facing page)	½ recipe	1 recipe
Fresh cilantro, chopped, for garnish		
Plain yogurt, for serving		

The night before making the chili, sort through the beans, discarding any grit or stones, then rinse them well in a colander under cold running water. Put the beans in a large bowl, add cold water to cover by 1 inch, and let soak overnight.

Set aside 1 tablespoon of the cumin seeds if making a single batch or 2 tablespoons if making a double batch. Working in batches, grind the remaining cumin seeds and all of the coriander seeds in a spice grinder or with a mortar and pestle until finely ground.

Heat the oil in large Dutch oven over medium-high heat. (If using two pots for a double batch, put ¼ cup oil in each pot and then divide the remaining ingredients between them as you assemble the chili.) Add the whole cumin seeds and let sizzle, stirring as needed to prevent burning, until fragrant and toasted, about 30 seconds. Add the onions, season with a few pinches of salt, and cook, stirring, until the onions are soft, about 6 minutes.

Add the garlic, ginger, and chiles and continue cooking over medium-high heat, stirring often, for about 3 minutes. Add the ground cumin and coriander and cook, stirring, until fragrant, about 1 minute. Stir in the tomato paste and pureed tomatoes, bring to a boil, and cook, stirring occasionally, for 5 minutes. Add the water and 1½ tablespoons salt if making a single batch or 3 tablespoons if making a double batch.

Drain the mung beans and add them to the pot(s). Add more water if needed to cover the beans fully. Adjust the heat to a simmer and cook uncovered, stirring occasionally to prevent sticking, until the beans are soft and beginning to fall apart, 40 to 45 minutes.

Remove from the heat and let cool slightly. Using an immersion blender, or in batches in a stand blender (be sure the lid is ajar to allow steam to escape), puree until smooth, adding more water if the dal is too thick. Stir in the lemon juice, then taste and adjust the seasoning with salt and more lemon juice if needed.

Serve hot, garnished with the pickled onions and cilantro and with the yogurt on the side for guests to add as they like.

INGREDIENT NOTES

For the tomato paste, you will need to purchase three 6-ounce cans or one 18-ounce can for the single batch or double the number of cans for the double batch. For the pureed tomatoes, you will need to purchase two 28-ounce cans for the single batch or double the number of cans for the double batch.

A market specializing in South Asian foods is the best place to find fresh ginger, dried mung beans, and cumin and coriander seeds in bulk (you need a lot for this recipe) in a single stop. Using whole spices, rather than ground ones, will impart brighter, more vivid flavors to the finished dish. Preeti adds that any leftover guju chili is especially good with a grilled cheese sandwich for a quick lunch.

CITRUS PICKLED ONIONS

Makes 1 quart

These quick pickled onions are made with the addition of black salt which gives them a classic Indian street food flavor and fragrance. The rock salt is black but turns pink when ground. Black salt, also known as *kala namak*, is available in Indian grocery stores. This recipe will provide more than you need for a double batch and will keep refrigerated in an airtight container for up to 1 month.

3 large red onions, julienned
2 lemons, juiced
2 limes, juiced
1 tablespoon salt
2 tablespoons black salt

Toss the onions with the citrus juices and salts. Set aside in a sealed plastic container in the refrigerator for at least 6 hours. Shake the container every couple of hours to keep the juice well distributed throughout the mix. The onions will turn bright red and taste slightly milder than raw.

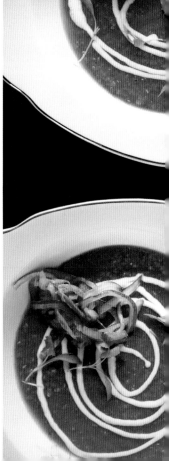

DANA VELDEN

chickpea curry soup
aka the hippie curry

FOR MANY YEARS, Dana Velden and her neighbors have hosted an Empty Bowls party in their beautiful Oakland, California, courtyard. Empty Bowls is an international grassroots organization whose mission is to fight hunger and raise awareness around hunger and food insecurity. The premise is simple: Potters donate their handmade bowls and people are invited to a gathering where, for a donation, they choose a bowl and are served soup to fill it. They sit down with others in their community, share in the soup and company, and then take their bowls home with them when they are done. Over the years, Empty Bowls Oakland has donated tens of thousands of dollars to the local Alameda County Community Food Bank.

"We make sure that everything we use is donated," says Dana, "so that all of the proceeds raised go directly to the food bank, which in turn will multiply our dollar amount by six to provide food for hundreds of people. A local restaurant provides the bread, extra spoons, and glasses; neighbors lend their spare tables and chairs; and a yard sale is held a few months beforehand to raise money for incidentals such as butter and garnishes." A dozen or more big pots of soups are usually served, and over 150 people typically attend. Dana rewarms all of the soups on her stove and serves them to the crowd, who trickle in all afternoon. "We serve two pots of soup at a time, one vegetarian and one meat. People often come back so they can try as many as possible."

This recipe came to Dana's family over twenty-five years ago from Green Gulch, a Zen farm in Marin County, California. "We call it The Hippie Curry because it is far from authentic—more of a mishmash of Indian, Thai, and Northern California commune styles," says Dana. You can use an authentic curry paste, but Dana prefers the bright yellow generic grocery store curry powder (labeled "Madras") for nostalgia's sake. The soup is simple and satisfying, as well as a pennywise way to serve a crowd.

Single Batch **Makes 10 servings**

Double Batch **Makes 20 servings**

MAKE AHEAD

The soup can be made up to 3 days in advance and refrigerated. Reheat it gently over medium-low to low heat, allowing an hour or more and stirring often to prevent scorching. If it is too thick when reheated, thin with stock or water. The nuts and coconut can be readied up to 1 day ahead, put into bowls for serving, covered, and kept at room temperature.

One or two large soup pots or Dutch ovens.

BIG BATCH NOTES

It is best to make two single batches instead of a double batch in a single pot. As the soup cooks and thickens, it needs to be stirred regularly to prevent it from sticking on the bottom.

SERVING

This is a thick soup. If you prefer a brothier version, thin it with stock or water as suggested in the recipe method, then taste and adjust the seasoning.

Accompany with Indian breads, such as naan and roti and/or with white or brown rice, a salad of tomatoes or cucumbers, fresh fruit, and rice pudding.

INGREDIENT NOTES

To turn this curry soup into a vegan dish, substitute additional soy sauce for the fish sauce and use vegetable stock rather than chicken stock.

INGREDIENTS	SINGLE BATCH	DOUBLE BATCH
Black peppercorns	2 tsp	4 tsp
Coriander seeds	2 tsp	4 tsp
Large garlic cloves	2	4
Peanut or grapeseed oil	¼ cup	½ cup
Mild curry powder	3 Tbsp	6 Tbsp
14-oz cans coconut milk	3	6
Cubed Yukon Gold potatoes, unpeeled, in ½-inch cubes	4 cups	8 cups
Sliced carrots, in ¼-inch-thick coins	4 cups	8 cups
Bite-size cauliflower florets	4 cups	8 cups
Large tomatoes, chopped	3	6
14-oz cans chickpeas (garbanzo beans), drained and rinsed	3	6
Soy sauce, plus more as needed	6 Tbsp	¾ cup
Asian fish sauce (see *Ingredient Notes*)	3 Tbsp	6 Tbsp
Honey or agave nectar, plus more as needed	3 Tbsp	6 Tbsp
Chicken or vegetable stock (see *Ingredient Notes*), if needed	1 to 2 cups	2 to 4 cups
Thinly sliced fresh basil leaves, plus small whole leaves for serving	1 cup	2 cups
Hot chile paste, for seasoning and serving		
Chopped roasted cashews or peanuts, for serving		
Toasted unsweetened shredded dried coconut, for serving		

In a mortar, coarsely crush the peppercorns and coriander with a pestle, then add the garlic and grind to a paste.

Heat the oil in a large, heavy-bottomed soup pot (or two pots if making a double batch) over medium heat. Add the garlic mixture and fry, stirring often, until fragrant, 1 to 2 minutes. Stir in the curry powder and fry for 1 minute or so until it releases its aroma. Add the coconut milk, potatoes, and carrots, bring to a gentle simmer, and simmer for about 5 minutes. Add the cauliflower, tomatoes, chickpeas, soy sauce, fish sauce, and honey and return to a gentle simmer. Cook, stirring occasionally, until the vegetables are tender and the sauce has begun to thicken, 10 to 15 minutes. If the soup seems too thick at any point, add the stock as needed.

Remove from the heat and stir in the sliced basil. Taste and adjust the seasoning with soy sauce and honey if needed. If your curry powder was not spicy enough, you may want to stir in some chile paste. Serve hot, with the cashews, coconut, whole basil leaves, and chile paste on the side for guests to add to their bowls as they like.

whole-loaf garlic cheese bread

THIS GARLICKY CHEESE bread from Elisabeth Prueitt, co-owner of Tartine Bakery and Tartine Manufactory in San Francisco, can be placed in the middle of the table as an edible centerpiece. The cross-hatched loaf is brushed with butter, strewn with cheese, and baked atop boiled marble potatoes, which act as an edible cooking rack. It is so easy to put together that you can make a number of loaves quickly. Serve it hot from the oven and invite guests to tear off sections with their fingers (have lots of napkins on hand). Soup and bread is a classic combination, which is why we have included one of our favorite breads in this chapter.

Single Batch **Makes 1 loaf**

Double Batch **Makes 2 loaves**

MAKE AHEAD

The boiled potatoes can be cooked up to 1 day in advance. The bread can be fully assembled and kept at room temperature, uncovered, for up to 2 hours. The bread is best eaten hot from the oven, so bake it just before you plan to serve it.

INGREDIENTS	SINGLE BATCH	DOUBLE BATCH
Marble-size potatoes	6	12
Large round or oval country-style bread(s)	1	2
Unsalted butter	¾ cup	1½ cups
Garlic cloves, finely chopped	4	8
Sea salt and freshly ground black pepper		
Chopped fresh flat-leaf parsley	2 Tbsp	¼ cup
Chopped fresh thyme	1 tsp	2 tsp
Chopped fresh rosemary	½ tsp	1 tsp
Cheddar or Gruyère cheese, grated	6 oz	12 oz

Preheat the oven to 350°F.

Put the potatoes in a saucepan and add water to cover. Bring to a boil over high heat and boil until the potatoes are tender. Drain and set aside.

With a serrated knife, cut the loaf of bread in a crosshatch pattern, cutting all of the way through the bread but stopping just before the bottom crust.

EQUIPMENT

One half sheet pan.

BIG BATCH NOTES

If you are making a double batch, you should be able to fit both loaves on a single half sheet pan.

SERVING

Serve this bread as a center-piece in the middle of the table to go with soups. You can also serve it as a side dish for pastas, roasted meats, or salads to round out a meal.

Place the potatoes in the center of a half sheet pan and lay the bread on top of them so it lies in a convex shape, revealing the interior of the loaf. If making two loaves, you can bake them side by side on the same sheet pan.

Melt the butter in a small saucepan over medium heat and add the garlic. Swirl the pan over the heat to cook the garlic gently without letting it brown, about 2 minutes. Season with salt and pepper and add the parsley, thyme, and rosemary. Remove from the heat.

Brush the flavored butter into all of the crevices and on top of the bread. Sprinkle with the cheese, making sure some gets into the cuts as well as on top.

Bake until the cheese has melted and the bread is warmed through, about 20 minutes. Serve the bread immediately, with the potatoes in a bowl alongside.

4.
pasta, noodles, and rice

ENJOYED ALL OVER the world, pasta, noodle, and rice dishes are easily expandable and can be a frugal way to feed a crowd, which makes them ideal for both fund-raisers and family meals. For many cultures, these starchy bases serve as a canvas for sauces and toppings, from humble to fancy, simple to complex.

Although most of these dishes aren't difficult, a few of them, like the timpano and the lasagna, have multiple components that take time and planning. The good news is that these sauces and toppings, like the Bolognese sauce and the *besciamella* (aka béchamel) for the lasagna, are useful building blocks for any cook's repertoire. In the way you might assign dishes to friends at a potluck, consider assigning a couple of components of a dish to two guests that they can make ahead of time. Then, the day of the event, assemble the dish together, and as with many dishes in this book, the cooking becomes the gathering.

le polpette della mama
mama's meatballs

WHO GLUES YOUR community together through food? In San Francisco's North Beach, the answer is Francis Ford Coppola. Some years back, Francis, founder of the film company American Zoetrope, started the North Beach Citizen's Alliance to help the needy in the area. Every year he gathers the community together in the basement of a local church for a family-style meatball and spaghetti feast that raises money to support the services the group provides. This recipe came from Francis's mother.

For this event, Francis's Kitchen makes one thousand meatballs to feed five hundred people. Each batch makes sixty meatballs which will serve thirty people. The crew prepares the meatball mixture in seventeen batches, with each batch using the following proportions: 5 pounds ground beef, 3½ pounds ground pork, 2 pounds onions, 2 ounces garlic, 1½ pounds bread crumbs, 10 eggs, and 3 ounces Parmesan cheese, plus plenty of seasoning. Here, you will find the directions for making a single batch of Francis's mom's meatballs, and the sauce to go with them, that you can scale up or scale down to feed your own crowd.

The sauce is made in one big pot. According to Francis, the secret to the sauce is to use great tomatoes—Francis favors DiNapoli brand—and excellent extra-virgin olive oil.

INGREDIENTS

Meatballs

Lean ground beef	5 lb
Lean ground pork	3½ lb
Yellow onions, finely diced	2 lb
Minced garlic	¼ cup
Fine dried bread crumbs	6 cups (about 1½ lb)
Large eggs, lightly beaten	10
Chopped fresh flat-leaf parsley	2 cups

continued on following page

Makes 60 meatballs (20 servings)

MAKE AHEAD

The sauce can be refrigerated for up to 3 days. The meatball mixture can be made and the meatballs shaped up to 2 days in advance. Arrange the meatballs in a single layer on half sheet pans, cover with plastic wrap, and refrigerate until ready to brown. The meatballs can be browned and then simmered in the sauce up to 1 day in advance. Let cool to room temperature, cover, and refrigerate, then reheat gently over low heat, stirring often, until the sauce is hot and the meatballs are heated through.

The meatballs and sauce can also be prepared and frozen separately. After browning the meatballs, let cool, then arrange on a single layer on sheet pans and freeze. Transfer the frozen meatballs to ziplock plastic freezer bags and freeze for up to 3 months. The sauce can also be frozen in airtight containers for up to 3 months. When ready to use, reheat the sauce over low heat in a large, heavy-bottomed pot. When the sauce defrosts and begins to warm, add the frozen meatballs and continue cooking over gentle heat, stirring occasionally, until warmed through.

BIG BATCH NOTES

If possible, put two sauté pans to work browning the meatballs and enlist a friend to help you shape the balls and brown them.

SERVING

This is a hearty supper that needs nothing more than a simple green salad, crusty bread such as Garlic Bread (page 87), and lots of wine to round out the menu.

INGREDIENTS

Grated Parmesan cheese	1 cup
Kosher salt	3 Tbsp
Red pepper flakes	1 Tbsp
Freshly ground black pepper	2 tsp
Extra-virgin olive oil, for frying	

Tomato Sauce

28-oz cans whole plum tomatoes, preferably DiNapoli brand	8
Extra-virgin olive oil	1½ cups
Large yellow onions, chopped	4
Fresh basil sprigs, leaves only	8
Red pepper flakes	4 tsp
Kosher salt and freshly ground black pepper	
Red wine	4 cups
Bone-in thin pork chops (about 8 oz each)	4
Sugar	½ cup
Tomato paste	1 cup

Spaghetti or other long pasta tubes or ribbons	4 lb
Grated Parmesan cheese, for serving	2½ cups
Fresh basil, chopped, for garnish	

Make the meatballs: In a large bowl, mix together the beef and pork. Add the onions, garlic, and bread crumbs and mix to distribute evenly. Add the eggs, parsley, Parmesan, salt, red pepper flakes, and black pepper and, using your hands, mix together all of the ingredients until evenly combined.

Use about 3 ounces of the meat mixture to form each meatball, using your hands to shape them. You want them to be big—slightly larger than a golf ball. You should have sixty meatballs.

Heat the oil in a large sauté pan over very high heat. You do not need a lot of oil; it should be about ¼ inch deep. Fry about ten meatballs at a time (or as many as will fit comfortably), turning them as needed to brown well on all sides. They do not need to be cooked through at this point, as you will be putting them into the sauce to continue cooking. You do want them to be nicely browned, however. Transfer them to large platters or sheet pans as they finish browning.

Make the sauce: Open the cans of tomatoes and use your hands to smoosh the tomatoes a bit. Place a large sieve over a big bowl and, working in batches, drain the crushed tomatoes, catching the juice in the bowl. Reserve the crushed tomatoes and juice separately.

Heat the oil in a large pot over medium heat. Add the onions and cook, stirring with a wooden spoon, until translucent, about 8 minutes. Add the basil and red pepper flakes, season with salt and pepper, and stir well. Delicately add the red wine and crushed tomatoes to the mixture, bring to a boil, and boil for 15 minutes, stirring constantly. Add the meatballs and pork chops, reduce the heat to low, and simmer for about 40 minutes, stirring occasionally but gently to prevent the sauce from scorching on the pan bottom. At this point, the meatballs and pork chops will be cooked through.

Using a slotted spoon, transfer the meatballs and pork chops to big platters or trays and set aside. Stir the sugar and tomato paste into the sauce and simmer, stirring occasionally until thickened, about 30 minutes. Adjust the consistency of the sauce as needed with the reserved juice. Taste and adjust the seasoning if needed.

While the sauce simmers, bring two large pots of salted water to a rolling boil.

Return the meatballs and pork chops to the sauce and heat until warmed through, about 10 minutes. Add the pasta to the boiling water and cook until al dente, according to the package directions, then drain.

To serve, divide the pasta among individual bowls, ladle the sauce over the pasta, and top with meatballs (and some pork chop, if desired). Sprinkle with the Parmesan and basil and serve.

JOYCE GOLDSTEIN

lasagna al forno

Single Batch
Makes 10 to 12 servings

Double Batch
Makes 20 to 24 servings

MAKE AHEAD

The ragù can be refrigerated for up to 4 days or frozen for up to 3 months; if frozen, thaw in the refrigerator overnight. The sauce can be reheated in large saucepans over low heat. The uncooked pasta can be tossed generously in semolina flour or fine-ground yellow cornmeal (to prevent sticking), covered, and refrigerated for up to 1 day.

The entire lasagna can be made, covered, and refrigerated for up to two to three days. If the ragù has not previously been frozen, the lasagna can be covered with a double thickness of aluminum foil and frozen for up to 3 months. To bake the frozen lasagna, do not thaw. Bake, covered with the foil, for 45 to 60 minutes or until heated. Remove the foil and continue baking until the lasagna is heated through and bubbling at the edges, 10 to 15 minutes longer.

THIS RECIPE FOR lasagna by Joyce Goldstein—chef, mentor, philanthropist, and cookbook author—is what she makes for special occasions for her family and friends and for the dinner parties she throws as fund-raisers for her favorite charities.

Unlike the typical American lasagna, which is laden with cheese, Joyce makes a classic Italian version, with layers of fresh pasta, a meaty Bolognese sauce, and a creamy besciamella (Italian béchamel). This recipe takes time to make, but it can be prepared in stages, as the *Make Ahead* instructions explain. Joyce always makes her own lasagna noodles, though store-bought fresh lasagna noodles, available in the refrigerated section of better supermarkets and at Italian delicatessens and pasta shops, can be used.

One of the beautiful things about this recipe is the wonderful Bolognese sauce. Of course, this deeply flavored ragù is the classic pasta meat sauce and used not only in lasagna. Keep the recipe on hand for when you want the ultimate version of this essential sauce of Italian cooking.

INGREDIENTS	SINGLE BATCH	DOUBLE BATCH
Ragù alla Bolognese		
Unsalted butter	6 Tbsp	¾ cup
Olive oil	¼ cup	½ cup
Celery ribs, finely diced	2	4
Carrots, peeled and finely diced	2	4
Medium yellow onions, finely chopped	2 (about 3 cups)	4 (about 6 cups)
Ground beef or chuck (85 percent lean)	1 lb	2 lb
Ground pork	1 lb	2 lb
Tomato paste	2 Tbsp	4 Tbsp
Hot water	1 cup	2 cups
Tomato puree (optional, see *Ingredient Notes*)	½ cup	1 cup
750-ml bottle(s) dry red wine	1	2

INGREDIENTS	SINGLE BATCH	DOUBLE BATCH
Whole milk (see *Ingredient Notes*)	1 cup	2 cups
Fine sea salt and freshly ground black pepper		
Beef broth	2 to 3 cups	2 to 3 cups
Fresh Pasta, store bought or homemade (page 99)	1 pound	2 pounds
Besciamella		
Unsalted butter	½ cup	1 cup
All-purpose flour	½ cup	1 cup
Whole milk, heated	4 cups	8 cups
Fine sea salt and freshly ground black pepper		
Freshly grated nutmeg		
Assembly		
Grated Parmigiano-Reggiano cheese	1 cup	2 cups
Unsalted butter, cut into small cubes, at room temperature	3 Tbsp	6 Tbsp

Make the ragù: Melt the butter with the oil in a large Dutch oven over medium heat. Add the celery, carrots, and onions and cook, stirring often, until the vegetables are soft and the onions are lightly golden, about 15 minutes. Using a slotted spoon, transfer the vegetable mixture to a bowl, leaving the fat in the pot.

Add the beef and pork and cook, stirring often and breaking up any chunks with a wooden spoon, until browned. Return the vegetable mixture to the pot.

Dilute the tomato paste in the hot water, then add to the pot with the tomato puree (if using) and wine and milk, if using, and stir well. Bring to a boil, then reduce the heat to low, cover, and simmer, stirring occasionally, for 1 hour. Uncover and continue to simmer for about 30 minutes longer. The sauce should be very thick and richly condensed after the long simmering. If it looks dry, continue to simmer until it thickens. If it begins to be dry, add the beef broth 1 cup at a time, but do not shorten the simmering time. Season with salt and pepper. You should have about 6 cups sauce if making a single batch or 12 cups if making a double batch.

Make the pasta: If you are making fresh pasta (page 99), prepare the dough, then roll out and cut the lasagna noodles as directed.

EQUIPMENT

Large Dutch oven for the ragù; large saucepan for the besciamella; one or two deep lasagna pans, about 9 by 13 by 3 inches; pasta machine; stockpot for cooking the pasta.

BIG BATCH NOTES

When making the pasta dough for a double batch, make two batches (3 cups flour for each batch). Mixing a 6-cup batch of dough can be too much for your arms (or your food processor) to handle. The old-fashioned hand-cranked pasta machine is inexpensive and does a great job (as any Italian *nonna* will tell you), but the electric pasta roller attachment available for some stand mixers allows you to roll out the dough in record time. It is an excellent investment for people serious about pasta.

SERVING

Pour a good Italian wine, accompany the lasagna with a salad of bitter greens, and cap off the meal with a favorite gelato.

INGREDIENT NOTES

A traditional bolognese does not have tomato puree, although many American adaptations do include tomato puree.

Adding whole milk to the bolognese acts as a tenderizer for the meat and takes the bite out of the broth.

Butter a lasagna pan about 9 by 13 inches and 3 inches deep (or butter two pans if making a double batch).

Cook the noodles: Bring a large pot of salted water to a boil over high heat. Prepare a large bowl of cold water, and lay dish towels out on a nearby work surface. Working in batches, slip the noodles into the boiling water and cook until just tender, 2 to 3 minutes. Using a wire skimmer, carefully scoop out the noodles and immerse them in cold water to halt the cooking. Once they are cold, transfer them to the dish towels, laying them flat.

Reheat the ragù over low heat, stirring often.

Make the besciamella: In a saucepan, melt the butter over low heat. Add the flour and cook, stirring constantly, until well incorporated with the butter, about 3 minutes. Do not allow the mixture to color. Gradually whisk in the hot milk, increase the heat to medium, and cook, whisking often to avoid scorching, until the sauce almost comes to a boil. Reduce the heat to low and cook, stirring often, until the sauce is quite thick and the flour has lost all of its raw taste, 6 to 8 minutes. Remove from the heat and season with salt, pepper, and nutmeg. You should have about 4 cups if making a single batch or 8 cups if making a double batch.

Assemble the lasagna: Preheat oven to 350°F. Spread a thin layer of the ragù on the bottom of the prepared pan. Add a layer of noodles, overlapping them slightly. Top with another layer of ragù, followed by a layer of besciamella. Sprinkle with 2 or 3 tablespoons of the cheese. Repeat the layers until you have used all of both of the sauces, the noodles, and the cheese, ending with a layer of noodles. Dot the top with the butter.

Bake until heated through and bubbling at the edges, 45 to 60 minutes. Remove from the oven and let rest for 10 minutes, then cut into squares and serve.

FRESH PASTA

Here is Joyce's recipe for fresh pasta dough, which makes lasagna noodles that are light, silky, and tender, with a lovely soft-yellow color. This same dough can be rolled out as directed and then cut into linguine, pappardelle, fettuccine, or other shapes, either with the cutter on the pasta machine or by hand, depending on the pasta. This recipe yields 1½ pounds, although you will only need 1 pound for the recipe. Having a little extra dough will be helpful, as some pasta might tear while rolling or cutting. For a richer dough, use 3 large whole eggs plus 3 large egg yolks in place of the 4 whole eggs.

Makes about 1½ pounds

3 to 3¼ cups unbleached all-purpose flour
1 tsp kosher salt
4 large eggs, lightly beaten (see *Ingredient Notes*, page 97)
3 to 4 Tbsp water, if needed
Semolina flour or fine-ground yellow cornmeal, for dusting

To make the dough by hand: In a large bowl, stir together 3 cups of the flour and the salt. Make a well in the center and add the eggs. With a fork, gradually pull the flour into the well until all of the flour is incorporated into the eggs and a rough, shaggy dough forms. If it seems too dry, add a bit of the water, 1 tablespoon at a time. If it is too wet, add more flour, 1 tablespoon at a time.

To make the dough in a food processor: Put 3 cups of the flour and the salt into a food processor and pulse briefly to combine. Add the eggs and pulse until the dough comes together in a rough ball; it will be crumbly. If it seems too dry, add a bit of the water, 1 tablespoon at a time. (Resist the temptation to add too much water,

or the dough will be too soft and sticky after it rests.) If it is too wet, add more flour, 1 tablespoon at a time.

Transfer the dough to a lightly floured work surface and knead until smooth and supple, 10 to 15 minutes. Divide the dough in half and flatten each half into a thick disk. Slip the disks into a plastic bag and allow the dough to rest at room temperature for 30 to 60 minutes to give the gluten in the flour time to relax.

Roll out the dough: Set up the pasta machine and adjust the rollers to the widest setting. Cut each disk into two or three pieces and return them to the bag. Working with one piece at a time, lightly dust the dough with flour and flatten it into a rectangle about the width of the rollers and thin enough to fit through the rollers. Pass the dough rectangle through the rollers. Fold the dough into thirds, like folding a business letter, and then starting at the short end, roll it through the rollers two more times. Fold it into thirds again and roll it through one more time. Now proceed to roll it through each succeeding setting on the machine one or two times, making it thinner with each pass and dusting it lightly with flour as needed to prevent sticking, until you have rolled it to the narrowest setting without having the dough wrinkle or resist. Every pasta machine is different, so this could be the second or third to last setting.

To cut lasagna noodles, lay the pasta sheet on a lightly floured work surface and, using a pastry wheel, cut it into strips 3 inches wide and about 13 inches long. To prevent sticking, toss the noodles with the semolina, then place on a half sheet and cover loosely with plastic wrap or a large plastic bag. Repeat with the remaining dough until all of the dough has been rolled out and cut.

big night timpano

A TIMPANO, OR timballo, as it was called in the bustling kitchen of Viola Buitoni's childhood home in Perugia, Italy, is a drum-shaped feat of culinary bravura, a peerless pasta dish in which noodles, sauce, cheese, and tiny meatballs are layered in a dough-lined bowl and then baked until the pastry is golden and flaky.

Most Americans know this dish from its star turn in the movie *Big Night*, though versions of it graced the aristocratic tables of southern Italy long before its 1996 film debut. There are many versions of timpanos, each one shaped and changed by the lexicon of family, place, culture, and season. Viola, a direct descendant of the famed Buitoni pasta and chocolate family, makes this showstopper to mark very special occasions.

A timpano is not hard to prepare, but because its components must be prepared and cooked separately, it is time-intensive. Fortunately, the pasta frolla, mushroom sauce, and meatballs can be prepared in advance of assembly and serving. Should you decide to make your timpano all in one go, the steps in the recipe are arranged in the most efficient order to make the most of your time in the kitchen.

Your efforts will be amply rewarded. When the finished dish is turned out of its mold (with all of the drama that accompanies it), your guests will be astounded!

INGREDIENTS

Mushroom Sauce

Dried porcini mushrooms	½ oz (½ cup)
Hot water	2 cups
Assorted fresh mushrooms, sliced	1½ lb
Sea salt and freshly ground black pepper	
Extra-virgin olive oil	2 Tbsp
Fresh thyme sprigs	3
Bay leaves	2
Prosciutto, finely diced	4 oz
Finely diced yellow onion	½ cup
Small carrot, peeled and finely diced	1

continued on following page

Makes 15 to 20 servings

MAKE AHEAD

The pasta frolla can be refrigerated for up to 3 days or frozen for up to 1 month. The mushroom sauce can be refrigerated for up to 4 days or frozen for up to 1 month. The cooked meatballs can be refrigerated for up to 3 days or frozen for up to 2 weeks. Thaw the frozen components overnight in the refrigerator before using.

The mushroom sauce may be a bit thin after thawing. Bring it to a simmer over low heat and cook, whisking often, until it thickens, about 15 minutes, taking care it does not burn.

Large skillet for the mushroom
sauce and meatbals; one stainless steel bowl, 12 to 14 inches in
diameter and 4 to 6 inches deep
(5- to 6-quart capacity), or one
large angel food cake pan, 10 to
12 inches in diameter, for assembling the timpano; two half sheet
pans for the meatballs; half sheet
pan and large cutting board for the
pastry rounds (at least 16 inches
square).

BIG BATCH NOTES

To save time, make the meatballs
while the sauce cooks.

SERVING

Start with a simple antipasto plate
and breadsticks, accompany the
timpano with a green salad, and
finish the meal with granita or
sorbetto.

INGREDIENTS

Small celery rib, finely diced	1
Cold water	¼ cup
28-oz can whole plum tomatoes, preferably San Marzano	1
Tomato paste	2 Tbsp

Meatballs

Ground beef (85 percent lean)	1 lb
Ground pork	1 lb
Sea salt	2 to 3 tsp
Freshly ground black pepper	½ tsp
Grated Parmigiano-Reggiano cheese	½ cup
Finely chopped fresh flat-leaf parsley leaves	1 cup
Large egg, lightly beaten	1
Finely grated orange zest	1½ tsp
Ground cinnamon or nutmeg	½ tsp
All-purpose flour	1 cup
Extra-virgin olive oil, plus more as needed	¼ cup

Pasta frolla

All-purpose flour	4⅓ cups (540 g)
Sugar	¼ cup
Sea salt	½ tsp
Unsalted butter, cut into Tbsp, at room temperature	1 cup plus 2 Tbsp
Large egg yolks	8

Assembly

Rigatoni, penne, or other tubular pasta	¾ lb
Heavy cream	2 cups
Grated Parmigiano-Reggiano cheese (about 8 oz)	2 cups
Large eggs, separated	4
Sea salt and freshly ground black pepper	
Unsalted butter, at room temperature, for the bowl	2 Tbsp
Fine dried bread crumbs	½ cup
Thinly sliced (but not paper-thin) prosciutto	6 oz
Fresh mozzarella cheese, thinly sliced, or whole-milk ricotta cheese	1 lb
Shredded fresh Montasio or Asiago cheese (about 8 oz) (see *Ingredient Notes*)	2 cups
Cold unsalted butter, cut into small cubes	6 Tbsp

Grated Parmigiano-Reggiano cheese, for serving

Make the mushroom sauce: Combine the dried mushrooms and hot water in a small bowl and set aside while you are preparing the other ingredients.

Put the fresh mushrooms in a large skillet, sprinkle with 2 teaspoons salt, cover, and place over medium-high heat. Cook, stirring occasionally, until they have released their liquid, about 5 minutes. Uncover and cook, stirring occasionally, until the liquid has reduced and the mushrooms are tender, 7 to 10 minutes. (The water content of different mushroom varieties varies, so if the mushrooms are not releasing enough liquid and are beginning to stick, add a few tablespoons of water to aid the cooking.) Transfer the mushrooms to a bowl, then wipe the skillet clean with paper towels.

Add the oil, thyme, and bay leaves to the skillet and place over medium-high heat until the oil begins to shimmer slightly. Add the prosciutto and cook, stirring, until it begins to brown, 3 to 4 minutes. Add the onion, carrot, celery, and a generous pinch of salt, reduce the heat to medium-low, and cook, stirring often, until the vegetables turn golden, 10 to 15 minutes. Add the cold water and continue cooking, stirring often, until the mixture is tender, aromatic, and slightly caramelized, 10 to 15 minutes longer. You are making a serious *soffritto* (traditional aromatic mix of finely cut vegetables), which takes time, so do not rush this step.

Meanwhile, lift the porcini from their soaking water and coarsely chop them. Strain the soaking water through a fine-mesh sieve (or a coffee filter), leaving the grit behind in the bowl. Add the mushrooms and the strained soaking water to the bowl holding the cooked fresh mushrooms. Pour the tomatoes and their juice into a separate bowl and crush them with your hands.

When the soffritto is ready, add the mushroom mixture and increase the heat to medium. When the liquid begins to simmer, stir in the crushed tomatoes and their juice and the tomato paste and season with salt and pepper. Bring to a boil, then reduce the heat to a gentle simmer and cook, stirring often to prevent sticking, until the sauce is thick and has turned a maroon red, about 1 hour. Season with salt and pepper, then remove from the heat and let cool completely.

Make the meatballs: In a large bowl, combine the beef, pork, salt, and pepper and mix well. Add the cheese, parsley, egg, orange zest, and cinnamon and mix until all of the ingredients are evenly distributed.

Line two half sheet pans with parchment paper and sprinkle half of the flour over each lined pan. Dampen your hands with water, then roll the meat mixture between your palms into tiny meatballs, each about the size of your thumbnail. As each ball is

shaped, transfer it to a floured pan. Keep your hands damp as you work to prevent the meat from sticking to them.

When all of the meatballs have been formed and are on the pans, tilt the pans back and forth and from side to side so the flour lightly coats the meatballs on all sides. The flour will aid the browning and absorb excess moisture.

In a large skillet, heat the oil over medium-high heat until it begins to shimmer but is not yet smoking. Working in batches, add the meatballs to the pan, forming a loose layer, and fry them until golden, 4 to 5 minutes. As the meatballs cook, shake and tilt the pan often so the whole surface of each meatball is evenly browned. Using a slotted spoon, transfer the meatballs to a clean sheet pan, platter, or baking dish. Repeat until all of the meatballs have been fried, adding more oil to the pan as needed to prevent sticking. Let the meatballs cool to room temperature.

Make the pasta frolla: In a large bowl, whisk together the flour, sugar, and salt. Add the butter and egg yolks and, using a pastry cutter or your fingers, cut and crumble the butter into the dry ingredients until the dough gathers into a mass. The dough will start to appear powdery and then crumbly. As you keep working the dough, the crumbs will become larger. Press the dough into a rough ball, then transfer to a lightly floured work surface. Knead the dough (it will be crumbly at first but will come together as you work) just enough that it holds together and is smooth and homogeneous. Form the dough into a thick disk, wrap it tightly in plastic wrap, and refrigerate for at least 30 minutes.

Assemble the timpano: Bring a large pot of salted water to a boil over high heat. Add the pasta and cook until very al dente, about 4 minutes. (Remember, the pasta is going to cook more when it is baked, so it should be only barely cooked here.) Drain, rinse under cold running water to halt the cooking, then drain again. Transfer to a large bowl and add 1½ cups of the cream, 1 cup of the Parmigiano, the egg yolks, and two-thirds (about 2½ cups) of the mushroom sauce and stir to mix well. Season with salt and pepper.

Preheat the oven to 375°F. Generously butter a stainless-steel bowl 12 to 14 inches in diameter and 4 to 6 inches deep (5- to 6-quart capacity), then coat evenly with the bread crumbs. Turn the bowl upside down over the sink and tap the side to shake off the excess bread crumbs. Alternatively, have ready a large angel food cake pan, 10 to 12 inches in diameter.

Line a half sheet pan with parchment paper. Have ready a second sheet of parchment paper. Cut off one-fourth of the dough, shape it into a disk, rewrap in plastic wrap,

INGREDIENT NOTES

Montasio and Asiago are cow's milk cheeses from northeastern Italy. They are sold both fresh (young) and aged. For this recipe, be sure to purchase young cheeses, which are smooth, moist, and have a mild, creamy flavor. If you can't find the varieties listed, try Fontina, cometé, Gruyère, or a good-quality Swiss cheese.

and return to the refrigerator. On a lightly floured work surface, shape the larger piece of dough into a disk. Using a lightly floured rolling pin, roll it out into a circle about 16 inches in diameter and ⅛ inch thick. Carefully transfer the dough round, folding it as needed to fit, to the lined sheet pan. Clean the work surface, dust again lightly with flour, and then roll out the smaller piece of dough into a circle 12 inches in diameter and ⅛ inch thick. Transfer it to the sheet of parchment and stack it on top of the first circle of dough. Transfer to the refrigerator and refrigerate for about 15 minutes.

Meanwhile, in a stand mixer fitted with the whip attachment (or in a large bowl with a handheld mixer), beat the egg whites on high speed until stiff peaks form. Whisk one-fourth of the whipped whites into the pasta mixture to loosen it, then gently fold in the remaining whites, working from the top to the bottom of the bowl in a circling motion and being mindful not to deflate the whites.

Remove the pasta frolla from the refrigerator. Lift off the parchment with the smaller circle and return it to the refrigerator. If using the crumb-coated bowl as a mold, with a sharp knife, cut the larger circle into wide triangles (like you would cut a pizza). Arrange the triangles in a single layer in the bowl, with the points meeting in the center of the bottom and the wide ends overhanging the rim of the bowl. Pinch the edges of the triangles together to create a seamless lining. If using the angel food cake pan, drape the uncut large circle in the pan, gently pressing it against the sides, the bottom, and the center tube and allowing the excess to overhang the rim. Trim away the dough covering the top of the tube.

Line the bottom and sides of the dough layer with a layer of prosciutto (see image, page 106). Add a 1-inch-deep layer of the pasta mixture to the bottom of the bowl. Top the pasta with a layer of mozzarella, followed by a layer of meatballs, a layer of the Montasio, one-third of the remaining Parmigiano, and a few butter cubes.

Lift the mold about 2 inches off the work surface and then drop it onto the surface. Repeat this three or four times, which will help compact the ingredients and help the timpano hold together when sliced.

Continue layering the prosciutto, pasta mixture, mozzarella, meatballs, Montasio, Parmigiano, and butter, compacting the timpano after each set of layers and ending with a layer of prosciutto (You should get two or three sets of layers, depending on the depth of the mold you are using. Adjust the amount of the ingredients used for each layer as needed.)

Trim away any excess dough from around the edge of the mold, leaving a small, even overhang, then brush the overhang with a little water. Remove the smaller dough circle from the refrigerator and place it on top of the timpano, tucking the edges into the rim and then folding over the overhang and pinching or fluting the edges together to seal. (If using an angel food cake pan, trim around the tube as needed.) Place the mold on a half sheet pan.

Bake until the crust is golden and flaky, 1 to 1¼ hours. Remove from the oven and let rest for 5 minutes. If using a bowl as the mold, invert a round serving platter on top of the timpano. Wearing oven mitts, and holding the bowl and the platter securely, invert them together in one swift motion and then carefully lift off the bowl. If using an angel food cake pan, use the tube to lift the timpano out of the pan, then invert the timpano onto a platter and gently lift the tube and base to remove it. Let the timpano rest for 10 minutes.

Just before serving, in a small saucepan, combine the reserved mushroom sauce with the remaining ½ cup cream and bring to a simmer over medium heat, stirring often. Transfer to a serving bowl.

Slice the timpano into wedges and top each serving with a spoonful of the sauce. Serve immediately, with grated Parmigiano-Reggiano on the side.

ANGELO GARRO

potato gnocchi with pesto

Single Batch
Makes 8 to 10 servings

Double Batch
Makes 20 to 25 servings

MAKE AHEAD

The tomato pesto can be refrigerated for up to 3 days; bring to room temperature and stir well, incorporating the oil topping, before using.

The gnocchi are best when formed, cooked, and eaten right away. They can be made up to 4 hours ahead, however. Cover the semolina-dusted pan with plastic wrap and refrigerate until ready to cook. Their color may change slightly, as the potatoes will oxidize as they sit in the refrigerator. To freeze the gnocchi, arrange them, not touching, in a single layer on a parchment paper–lined sheet pan and freeze until firm. When frozen solid, transfer to large ziplock plastic freezer bags. The frozen gnocchi can go straight from the freezer to the cooking water.

If making panfried gnocchi, the boiled gnocchi can be cooled, covered with plastic wrap, and refrigerated for up to 4 hours before frying.

ANGELO GARRO MAKES architectural wrought iron for a living, but Renaissance Forge, his live-work space in San Francisco, is where he gathers friends and family to cook together. Filled with eclectic objects, pots, pans, and salts and spices from Omnivore, his own line of artisanal seasonings and condiments, his kitchen is an essential part of his life philosophy of big-hearted generosity. He lives by the seasons, pursuing wild boar, urban fennel, ocean eel, and wild mushrooms with a passion for life that was detailed in Michael Pollan's *The Omnivore's Dilemma*. All year long, Angelo brings people together around Italian seasonal food rituals, from spit-roasted pigs and herb-laced porchetta to stuffing sausages and rolling fresh pasta.

For decades, Angelo cooked mainly for people he knew, but now he offers hands-on classes that teach students how to find food in nature and cook by the seasons, the way his family did in Sicily when he was a boy. This recipe for gnocchi is one of the dishes he makes regularly with his students because it is fun to do together, delicious, and goes beautifully with his homemade wine.

The word *gnocchi* is thought to come from *nocca*, which means "knuckles," or from the Lombard word *knohha*, which means "knot" (such as the knots found in wood). Both words point to the shape of the gnocchi we know today. Potato gnocchi are thought to date back to the sixteenth or seventeenth century, after Spanish explorers carried potatoes from South America to Europe, where they were soon introduced to Italian kitchens.

Gnocchi are delicate, and success comes from developing a "feel" for the dough. Each batch can vary depending on the moisture in the potatoes and other factors, so practice is helpful. Start with a smaller batch. Angelo boils the gnocchi and serves them dressed with pesto, or he boils them and then lightly panfries them and finishes them with big flakes of Parmigiano-Reggiano cheese.

Angelo typically serves gnocchi as part of a 3-course meal, with an antipasto plate and including a meat course, such as porchetta (page 135 or 138). Here, we've suggested portions that are suitable for the gnocchi to serve as the main course. If you're serving the gnocchi within multiple courses, a single batch will make about 20 small portions.

INGREDIENTS	SINGLE BATCH	DOUBLE BATCH
Russet potatoes, unpeeled	4 lb	8 lb
Water, plus more if needed	1¼ cups	2½ cups
All-purpose flour, plus more as needed	3 cups	6 cups
Semolina flour, plus more for dusting	2 cups	4 cups
Kosher salt	1 Tbsp	2 Tbsp
Baking soda	½ tsp	1 tsp
Large eggs	4	8
Extra-virgin olive oil, if panfrying the gnocchi		
Tomato-Almond Pesto (see page 113), if serving boiled gnocchi	1 recipe	2 recipes
Parmigiano-Reggiano cheese, grated if serving boiled gnocchi or shaved if serving panfried gnocchi	1 cup	2 cups

Preheat the oven to 400°F.

Arrange the potatoes in a single layer in a large baking pan. Add 1 cup of the water if making a single batch and 2 cups if making a double batch. Cover the pan tightly with aluminum foil, and bake the potatoes until they can be easily pierced with a fork, about 1 hour.

Remove the potatoes from the pan and let them cool until they are almost at room temperature. Peel them and then pass them through a ricer onto a clean work surface.

Bring two large pots of lightly salted water to a boil over high heat. Line two or three half sheet pans with parchment paper for holding the uncooked gnocchi.

On the same work surface, mix together the all-purpose and semolina flours, salt, and baking soda. Create a well in the flour mixture and crack the eggs into the well. Pour the remaining ¼ cup water if making a single batch or ½ cup water if making a double batch into the well. Using your hands, mix together the flour mixture, potatoes, eggs, and water until the dough begins to come together in a soft, sticky ball. Do not overwork the dough, or the gnocchi will be tough. If the dough seems dry, add more water, up to ¼ cup water for a single batch or ½ cup for a double batch. If the dough seems wet, mix in a little more all-purpose flour.

EQUIPMENT

A potato ricer is the best tool for readying the cooked potatoes. There are inexpensive models, but if you like homemade gnocchi, invest in a large professional model, sold online and at restaurant supply stores. You will also need a large baking pan for baking the potatoes, two or three half sheet pans for holding the gnocchi, two large pots for cooking the gnocchi, and a wide skimmer or slotted spoon for scooping the gnocchi from the cooking water. If panfrying the gnocchi, you will need two large skillets, preferably nonstick.

BIG BATCH NOTES

Have plenty of hands (and vegetable peelers) to peel the potatoes and shape the gnocchi. Boil the gnocchi in batches to ensure they all cook properly. If panfrying the gnocchi, use two large skillets and keep the gnocchi warm in a low oven until all of them are ready.

SERVING

Angelo serves the gnocchi with a Sicilian pesto, but they can be tossed with a classic basil pesto (page 54), with browned butter and fried sage leaves, or with a favorite tomato sauce. Serve a plate of salumi to start the meal, grilled vegetables with the gnocchi, and gelato to finish.

Clean the work surface and then dust it with semolina. Put a handful-size portion of the dough on the dusted surface, shaping it into a rough, thick log. Using your palms, roll the dough back and forth until you have a long rope about ¾ inch in diameter. Cut the rope on the diagonal into ¾- to 1-inch pieces. In batches, place the pieces in a wire sieve and shake gently to remove the excess semolina. Transfer to a lined sheet pan. Repeat with the remaining dough.

For gnocchi with pesto: Have one or two large bowls handy. In batches, add the gnocchi to the boiling water and cook until they all float to the surface, 3 to 4 minutes. To make sure they are done, bite into one; it should be tender yet still have some tooth. Using a wire skimmer or sieve, scoop the gnocchi out of the water into a large bowl and keep warm.

When all of the gnocchi is cooked, scoop out and reserve 1 to 2 cups of the cooking water.

Add the pesto to the gnocchi and toss gently, adding the cooking water as needed to loosen the pesto and coat the gnocchi with a light sauce. Pour onto one or more platters and serve immediately, with the grated Parmigiano on the side.

For panfried gnocchi with Parmigiano: Lightly oil one or two half sheet pans or roasting pans and set them near the stove. In batches, add the gnocchi to the boiling water and cook until they all float to the surface, 3 to 4 minutes. To make sure they are done, bite into one; it should be tender yet still have some tooth. Using a wire skimmer or sieve, scoop the gnocchi out of the water onto an oiled pan. Repeat until all of the gnocchi is cooked.

When all of the gnocchi is cooked, heat two large skillets over medium-high heat, then pour a thin film of olive oil on the bottom of each pan. Add the gnocchi in a single layer and cook, stirring gently, until they form a golden brown crust, about 4 minutes. Transfer to a platter, cover loosely to keep warm, and repeat with the remaining gnocchi. When all of the gnocchi are fried, top with shaved Parmigiano and serve immediately, with more Parmigiano on the side.

TOMATO-ALMOND PESTO

Makes about 1½ cups

This Sicilian-style pesto is best when tomatoes are at their peak, usually from July to mid-September, depending on where you live. Do not substitute canned tomatoes.

¾ cup almonds, lightly toasted
4 plum tomatoes, quartered
3 garlic cloves
2 bunches basil, leaves only (about 4 cups packed)
½ cup grated Parmigiano-Reggiano cheese
1 tsp kosher salt
½ cup extra-virgin olive oil, plus more for storage if needed

In a food processor, pulse the almonds until coarsely ground. Add the tomatoes, garlic, basil, cheese, and salt and process until a smooth paste forms. With the processor running, drizzle in the oil in a fine, steady stream. Use immediately, or transfer to an airtight container, top with a thin layer of oil, and refrigerate until needed.

ASHLEY CHRISTENSEN

poole's diner macaroni au gratin

Single Batch
Makes about 12 servings

Double Batch
Makes about 24 servings

MAKE AHEAD

One secret of Ashley's macaroni au gratin is its freshness—it doesn't hold well. The macaroni can be boiled several hours in advance, covered with plastic wrap, and stored at room temperature. The cheese can be shredded or grated, packed in ziplock plastic storage bags, and refrigerated for up to 3 days.

ASHLEY CHRISTENSEN IS known for her epic macaroni and cheese. Since opening her original restaurant, Poole's Downtown Diner in Raleigh, North Carolina, she estimates that she has served roughly fifteen thousand orders of the rich, gooey, cheese-capped dish every year.

Featured in her cookbook, *Poole's: Recipes and Stories from a Modern Diner,* Ashley's macaroni is simple yet lucious. With only a few ingredients it is truly a revelation, making it known far and wide.

Ashley now owns several restaurants in downtown Raleigh and giving back has become a big part of her business model, from supporting local farms to raising funds for important causes to figuring out how restaurants can play a bigger role in making a difference. Ashley does a lot of work for Share Our Strength and with a number of local organizations trying to be a positive voice in the community. "And when I say community," says Ashley, "I don't mean a specific zip code. It is everything that our work and our friendship touch." This is the way a community grows, around a shared table and one plate of mac and cheese at a time.

INGREDIENTS	SINGLE BATCH	DOUBLE BATCH
Elbow macaroni	1¼ lb	2½ lb
Vegetable oil	1 Tbsp	2 Tbsp
Grana padano cheese, grated	6 oz	12 oz
Jarlsberg cheese, shredded	6 oz	12 oz
White Cheddar cheese, shredded	1¼ lb	2½ lb
Heavy cream	6 cups	12 cups
Fine sea salt	1 Tbsp	2 Tbsp

Bring a large pot of salted water (about 8 quarts) to a boil over high heat. Add the macaroni and return to a boil. Once the water is boiling, cook the pasta until barely al dente, 5 to 7 minutes, then drain well and divide between two (or more if making a double batch) half sheet pans. Drizzle the macaroni evenly with the oil and mix well to keep the noodles from sticking together. Let cool completely.

Position a rack about 4 inches from the heat source and preheat the broiler. Combine the grana padano, Jarlsberg, and Cheddar cheeses in a large bowl and mix well. Set aside 60 percent of the cheese mixture for the topping. Reserve the remaining 40 percent for mixing with the macaroni.

In the same large pot used for boiling the pasta, combine the cream and salt and bring to a boil. Let simmer for 2 to 3 minutes; the cream will foam up and then subside into a simmer. Add the macaroni and cook, stirring occasionally, until the cream starts to thicken just slightly and coat the macaroni, 2 to 4 minutes. Start adding the reserved 40 percent of the cheese mixture in small handfuls, stirring and waiting for each addition to melt and incorporate into the sauce before adding more.

Divide the mixture between two large, shallow, broiler-safe baking dishes, each about 9 by 13 inches if making a single batch or among four dishes if making a double batch. Mound the reserved cheese over the top, dividing it evenly.

Place a filled baking dish on a half sheet pan to catch any drips, then place under the broiler and broil, rotating the dish as needed to brown evenly, until the cheese melts and caramelizes into a golden brown crust, 3 to 5 minutes. Watch the gratin carefully, as every broiler is different. Remove from the broiler and let rest for 5 minutes before serving. Repeat with the remaining filled dish(es). Serve immediately.

EQUIPMENT

Large stockpot for parboiling the pasta and then cooking it further in the cream; two or three half sheet pans for holding the boiled macaroni; at least two flameproof baking dishes, each measuring about 9 by 13 inches (be sure they are flameproof, as the gratins will be broiled).

BIG BATCH NOTES

You can make one giant pan of macaroni and cheese in a hotel pan, or divide the mixture among a few baking dishes and broil them one after the other. They will not fit in the broiler all at once, but they do cook quickly, especially if the macaroni mixture is freshly mixed and warm.

SERVING

Incredibly rich, creamy, and filling, this macaroni gratin needs little in the way of accompaniment, though a green salad or other green vegetable is always welcome.

BRETT AND ELAN EMERSON

big pan seafood paella

NO MATTER WHERE they are in the world, Spaniards agree that the best way to cook paella is outdoors over an open fire, surrounded by family and friends. Paella is a communal dish: brought to the table, it becomes both main course and centerpiece as guests dig in from all sides. This rice-based dish, which originated around the city of Valencia on the Mediterranean coast, gets its name from the wide, shallow double-handled metal pan, or *paellera*, used for cooking it.

While paella pans come in only one shape, they come in many different sizes, from petite rounds that can serve three or four to enormous party pans measured in feet rather than inches. The ingredients can range from simple preparations of chicken or rabbit and fava beans to elaborate mixtures of shrimp, mussels, and clams along with chicken, sausages, green peas, and artichoke hearts. The rice is typically a plump, short-grain variety (the most popular are Bomba and Calasparra) and threads of saffron turn it a lovely gold. The *salmorra*, a heady mix of tomato, garlic, and ñora chiles, adds flavor. Once the rice is tender and the main ingredients are cooked, a final blast of heat sizzles the bottom of the dish into *socarrat*, a thin, crunchy layer of delicious toasty, crunchy rice.

Brett and Elan Emerson shared a lifelong passion for Spanish food, traveling to Spain numerous times before opening Contigo, their restaurant in San Francisco's Noe Valley neighborhood. Guests regularly requested they put paella on the menu, but Brett was concerned that they couldn't successfully produce paella to order over live fire, the way he had learned years earlier at a restaurant near the rice fields of the Albufera, just outside of Valencia. But when Tilden, his daughter, was two, he was inspired to cook a version for her on their gas grill at home. The dish came out beautifully and, more important, his usually finicky daughter loved it. Cooking paella quickly became a weekly family tradition, and Brett realized how fun and convivial it was to share a large pan of rice with people you love. That prompted Brett and Elan to start featuring paella on Tuesdays at Contigo, a tradition that grew so popular that their second restaurant, Barceloneta in downtown Santa Cruz, California, is devoted to the dish.

Single Batch
Makes 10 to 12 servings

Double Batch
Makes 20 to 24 servings

MAKE AHEAD

The salmorra can be refrigerated for up to 3 days. The beans and peas can be prepared up to 6 hours ahead and kept at room temperature. If you have the time, scrub the shellfish an hour before cooking, then soak them in salted ice water to cover until cooking.

One 18-inch paella pan for a single batch; one 28- or 32-inch paella pan or two 18-inch pans for a double batch; large charcoal or gas grill for a single batch or two large grills or one oversized propane burner with reinforced tripod for a double batch; long-handled metal spatula, long-handled wooden spoon; few half sheet pans for holding the ingredients.

Paella pans are easily purchased at well-stocked cookware stores, at specialty stores carrying Spanish goods, or online. Carbon-steel paella pans need to be maintained like cast-iron skillets (seasoned before use and cleaned without soap to keep the seasoning patina) or they will rust. If you are buying a large pan for the first time, the slightly more expensive enameled paella pans are a good investment because they take less care.

An 18-inch paella pan is the largest size that will fit on most charcoal or gas grills and still allow proper air circulation. The standard charcoal grill is 22 inches in diameter, allowing about 2 inches on all sides. Measure your gas grill to be sure the pan will fit. For larger paellas, you will need the propane burner described above.

BIG BATCH NOTES

You are restricted to one paella pan per standard grill. But a standard charcoal grill is transportable: just pull the three legs out from the kettle and you are good to go. So borrow a second grill (or rent a propane burner) when a double batch is on the menu.

SERVING

Spanish rosé is a wonderful beverage with this dish, so you might ask your guests to bring a selection. To start, serve Marcona almonds, olives, and assorted Spanish cheeses. For dessert, offer fresh fruit.

INGREDIENTS	SINGLE BATCH	DOUBLE BATCH
Salmorra		
Tomatoes, such as Early Girl	2 lb	4 lb
Extra-virgin olive oil	2 Tbsp	¼ cup
Garlic cloves, thickly sliced	6 to 8	12 to 15
Dried ñora or ancho chiles, stemmed, seeded, and torn into large pieces (see *Ingredient Notes*)	4	7
Sweet smoked Spanish paprika (pimentón dulce)	½ tsp	1 tsp
Kosher salt	2 tsp	4 tsp
Paella		
Romano or green beans, trimmed and cut on the diagonal into 2-inch lengths	1 lb	2 lb
Shelled green peas	1 cup	2 cups
Saffron threads	1 to 1½ tsp	2 to 2½ tsp
Skinned halibut, cod, or other firm white fish fillets, cut into 2-inch pieces	2 lb	4 lb
Jumbo shrimp (21/25 count), preferably head on, peeled and deveined, with heads and tails left on	1 lb	2 lb
Squid, cleaned, bodies cut into ½-inch-wide rings, and tentacles left whole	1 lb	2 lb
Kosher salt		
Extra-virgin olive oil, or as needed	½ cup	1 cup
Manila clams, scrubbed	1 lb	2 lb
Mussels, scrubbed and beards removed if necessary	1 lb	2 lb
Bomba or Calasparra rice (see *Ingredient Notes*, page 124)	4 cups	8 cups
Fish stock	10 cups	20 cups
For Serving		
Cherry tomatoes, halved	1 cup	2 cups
Lemons, cut into wedges, for serving	2	4
Aioli (page 191), for serving	1 recipe	2 recipes

Make the salmorra: Cut the tomatoes in half crosswise. One at a time, grate the tomato halves on the large holes of a box grater set over a large bowl until you are left with nothing but the skin; discard the skin. Heat the oil in a large saucepan over medium heat. Add the garlic and cook until softened, about 2 minutes. Add the chiles and cook for 1 minute. Add the tomato pulp, paprika, and salt and cook, stirring occasionally, until most of the juices have evaporated, 10 to 15 minutes for a single batch and 20 to 30 minutes for a double batch.

Remove from the heat and let cool slightly. In batches, transfer to a blender and puree until smooth. Set aside.

Ñora chiles, which are widely cultivated around Valencia, are considered essential to the classic paella. They are round, small sweet chiles that are typically used dried. Look for them in shops selling Spanish foods or online. Ancho chiles are an acceptable substitute, but use 2 fewer anchos than ñoras in a single or double batch.

Make the effort to purchase a Spanish short-grain rice variety (sometimes marked medium grain), such as Bomba or Calasparra (Sollana), for the best result. The Spanish varieties are known for their ability to absorb a larger amount of liquid than is typically used for cooking rice without becoming soft and mushy.

If romano beans, peas, and cherry tomatoes aren't in season, feel free to substitute whatever looks good at the market. Shelled fava beans in the spring and early summer; green beans, leeks, green onions, and bell peppers year-round; and sunchokes in the winter are just a few ideas.

Make the paella: Bring a large saucepan of salted water to a boil over high heat. Fill a large bowl with ice water, line a large plate with paper towels, and set both near the stove. Add the beans to the boiling water and cook until crisp-tender, about 3 minutes. Using a wire skimmer, transfer the beans to the ice water until cool, then arrange on the towel-lined plate to drain. Add the peas to the same boiling water and boil until just tender, 3 to 5 minutes, depending on their freshness. Drain, immerse in the ice water to cool, then drain on the towel-lined plate with the beans. Transfer the beans and peas to separate bowls.

In a small, dry skillet, heat the saffron threads over medium heat, stirring and shaking the pan, until aromatic, about 2 minutes. Transfer to a mortar, let cool, then grind to a powder with a pestle.

Set up all of the paella ingredients near the grill: the fish, shrimp, and squid, with the salt and oil nearby; the clams and mussels; the salmorra and the saffron; and the beans and the peas. You'll also want a bowl to hold the cooked shellfish, some thick potholders for handling the pan, and a long-handled wooden spoon for stirring.

Prepare a charcoal or gas grill (or two grills if making a double batch) for direct cooking over high heat (500°F). For a charcoal grill, be sure the vents in the kettle are wide open. For a gas grill, set the burners to their highest setting.

Place the paella pan on the grill and let it heat. To precook the seafood, season the fish, shrimp, and squid with salt. When the paella pan is very hot, pour a thin film of oil (about 3 tablespoons) on the bottom of the pan. Add the fish pieces, skinned side up. When the underside is browned, using a long-handled spatula, flip the pieces and cook briefly on the second side, about 3 minutes total. The fish should not be fully cooked. Transfer the fish to a large platter. Add more oil to the pan as needed to maintain a thin film and repeat with the shrimp and then with the squid, again not cooking them fully. The shrimp should just firm up slightly (about 1 minute), and the squid should just turn opaque around the edge touching the pan (no longer than about 30 seconds). When the shrimp and squid are done, add them to the platter holding the fish.

If using a charcoal grill, add more fuel to your fire so it is extremely hot once again, then return the paella pan to the grill and let it heat. When the pan is hot, add about 3 tablespoons oil, then add the salmorra and saffron and cook briefly, being careful not to burn the saffron, and then pour in the stock. When the stock comes to a boil, season to taste with salt. Pour the rice into the pan, spreading it in an even layer over the bottom.

Once the rice is added, it takes 18 to 20 minutes to cook. Your aim is to cook the rice at a rolling boil for the first 10 to 12 minutes and then gradually let the heat decrease, adding fuel or spreading out the coals of a charcoal grill or adjusting the burners of a gas grill as needed. Do not stir the rice. Shake the pan occasionally and/or rotate it if needed to ensure the rice cooks evenly.

When the rice is about half-cooked, after about 10 minutes, start arranging all of the clams and mussels, followed by the partially cooked ingredients in the pan, starting with the fish and followed by the shrimp, squid, beans, and peas. When the rice is cooked, the seafood is hot, and, ideally, a crust—the soccarat—has formed on the bottom of the pan, transfer the pan to the table where you will be serving it. Discard any clams or mussels that failed to open.

Cover the paella with kitchen towels and let the rice rest and steam for 5 to 10 minutes. Just before inviting everyone to the table, garnish the paella with the cherry tomatoes and lemon wedges. Serve the aioli on the side.

HOW TO HOST A PASTA SUPPER

Nearly everybody likes pasta, which makes a pasta supper a great way to feed a crowd. Here is how to put together a menu that allows you to do most of the work in advance and offers enough variety to please everyone at the table.

o **Choose your pasta.** Three different shapes of pasta give guests enough variety without being overwhelming. Short shapes like radiatori, rotelle, ziti, or rigatoni are easier for guests to serve themselves and hold up better on a buffet than long, floppy spaghetti or linguine.

If you're preparing a pasta supper for a group larger than eight to ten people, it's best to cook the pasta ahead of time until almost al dente. (It is difficult to cook more than 2 pounds of pasta on the average home stove because the heat output from the burner is insufficient to return the water to a boil. That means, even if you have a huge stockpot, you must cook the pasta in batches.) Drain the pasta in a large colander and rinse under cold running water to stop the cooking. Toss the cold pasta with a bit of oil to prevent sticking, then cover and refrigerate for up to 1 day.

When you're ready to serve, dunk the precooked pasta in boiling water for a minute or two to heat it through and finish cooking. (A pasta pot with a perforated insert is the perfect cooking vessel for reheating the cooked pasta.) In terms of quantities, plan on 1 pound dried pasta for every four or five guests.

o **Offer a variety of sauces.** It's the mixing and matching that makes a pasta supper fun. Plan on about ⅔ cup sauce per guest (or about ⅓ cup for pesto), and serve three different varieties, like a classic marinara (page 154), a basil pesto (page 54), and a hearty, meaty Bolognese (page 96). The sauces can (and should!) be made ahead and reheated as necessary just before serving. You can also provide butter or garlicky olive oil for purists and pint-size guests.

o **Provide a few garnishes.** Set out bowls of grated Parmesan and pecorino cheeses; fresh herbs, such as finely shredded basil and finely chopped flat-leaf parsley and oregano; and red pepper flakes.

o **Make the sides simple.** A basic green salad and some crusty bread are all you need to serve alongside pasta, though you could also serve meatballs (page 93) or sausages, cut into rounds.

CAROLYN PHILLIPS

sesame noodles

Single batch **6 servings**

Double Batch **12 servings**

MAKE AHEAD

You can make the sauce up to 3 days ahead of time and keep refrigerated.

The full recipe can be made up to 2 days in advance and refrigerated. Bring to room temperature (and loosen with warm water, if needed) before serving.

EQUIPMENT

One or two large pots for cooking the noodles; one or two large woks or skillets for combining the noodles with the sauce.

BIG BATCH NOTES

If you are making a double batch, make the sauce in one wok or skillet and the divide it between two woks for combining with the noodles.

SERVING

To transform these noodles into a meal, top each serving with a fried egg with crispy edges or with leftover chopped or shredded pork, sausage, or other meat. You can also serve the noodle alongside or garnished with steamed greens such as bok choy, chard, or spinach. Use 1 pound greens for a single batch and 2 pounds for a double (weigh before cooking).

FOOD WRITER AND scholar Carolyn Phillips is the author of the widely praised *All Under Heaven: Recipes from the 35 Cuisines of China*. Her recipe for sesame noodles is an ideal dish for a crowd, served on its own or alongside stir-fried vegetables, tofu, or meat. It calls for only a handful of ingredients and comes together in a matter of minutes—the perfect formula for the busy host.

Carolyn discovered this no-frills street food—fresh noodles dressed with toasted sesame paste, plus a dash of black vinegar, soy, and sugar—at a little stand on Nanhai Road in Taipei. Over the years, she used that simple combination as a template to come up with her own version, introducing peanut butter for added creaminess and garlic for fragrance. She also sometimes uses her homemade citrus-infused chile oil (along with some of its "goop" of ground chiles, fermented black beans, garlic, and ginger) in place of the sesame oil, which results in a dish that tastes similar to Sichuan's popular *dan dan* noodles.

INGREDIENTS	SINGLE BATCH	DOUBLE BATCH
Asian sesame oil	¼ cup	½ cup
Chinese sesame paste (see *Ingredient Notes*)	¼ cup	½ cup
Crunchy or smooth peanut butter	¼ cup	½ cup
Cloves garlic, finely chopped	2 to 4	3 to 6
Green onions, white and green parts finely chopped and kept separate	2	4
Soy sauce	3 Tbsp	6 Tbsp
Black vinegar (see *Ingredient Notes*)	2 Tbsp	4 Tbsp
Sugar	2 tsp	4 tsp
Dried Chinese wheat noodles of any kind	1 lb	2 lb

In a wok or large, heavy-bottomed skillet, stir together the sesame oil, sesame paste, peanut butter, garlic, white parts of the green onions, soy sauce, vinegar, and sugar. Place over medium-low heat and heat slowly, stirring constantly, until the flavors have blended and the rawness of the garlic has mellowed, 8 to 11 minutes. Taste and adjust the seasoning.

Bring a large pot of water to a rolling boil over high heat (for a double batch, use two pots). Add the noodles and boil until barely done. Using a wire skimmer, scoop out the noodles and add them to the wok or skillet (or divide the sauce between two pans for a double batch; add half the noodles to each pan). Toss the noodles until they are well coated with the sauce, adding some of the hot noodle water as needed to keep them from clumping together. (This will take more water than you expect the first time around, usually at least 1 cup.)

Divide the noodles among individual bowls, sprinkle with the green onion tops, and serve hot or at room temperature. Carolyn likes to offer small bowls of the pasta cooking water on the side as a simple soup that can be used to thin down the sauce further as needed.

A QUICK GUIDE TO STIR-FRIED VEGETABLES

Carolyn uses this basic how-to for making stir-fried vegetables. For a garnish, she uses 1 bunch (about 12 ounces or so) spinach or other leafy vegetables, or 8 ounces bok choy or other similarly heftier vegetables, for every four to six people as a garnish, not a side dish. If you'd like to serves these as a side dish, double the quantity. More is always okay, if that's what you'd like.

1. All leafy vegetables should be soaked and swished around in a big bowl of warm water to loosen any sand or dirt. Getting rid of the grit is incredibly important, so don't rush this step. Rinse the vegetables until you no longer see sand in the bottom of the bowl. Drain the vegetables well and cut into more or less bite-size pieces.

2. Place your dry wok over high heat. When it is very hot, add a small bit of oil—no more than a tablespoon is needed—and a sprinkle of salt and swirl the oil to coat the bottom and sides of the pan. Next, add whatever aromatics you like, such as chopped garlic or ginger, and stir until fragrant, 15 to 20 seconds.

3. Now begin adding the vegetables by the handful to the hot wok. Let each handful wilt before you add the next handful, as this keeps your wok nice and hot. Push the wilted greens up the side of the pan and place the raw ones in the very bottom. Repeat until done.

4. Once all of the vegetables have been heated through this way, begin tossing them around to distribute the seasonings and cook them just until the rawness has disappeared.

5.
meat and poultry: braises, roasts, grills, and fries

WHETHER COOKED ON the grill, in the oven, or on the stove top, a big piece of meat is a traditional celebratory centerpiece. Browned and beautifully roasted porchetta, slow-cooked brisket, succulent carnitas tacos, spicy Korean pork belly wraps—these meaty dishes are easily shared with big groups of family and friends.

In summer, a smoky grilled tri-tip or slabs of sticky barbecued ribs might be on the menu, while in winter, fragrant braised lamb shanks or bubbling, cheese-topped chicken parm might anchor a holiday spread. Whatever the season or the occasion, coming together to eat is a big part of the fun, as is swapping stories while tending the grill or making condiments and sides to accompany the main course.

If you like to eat meat, we encourage you to be conscientious about where it comes from and how it was raised. To this end, make friends with your butcher who can help you source high-quality, sustainably raised meat, including unusual cuts for special dishes. A great butcher can be a font of information and advice on cooking techniques and tips.

ANYA FERNALD

wine-braised brisket

THIS BRISKET RECIPE from *Home Cooked*, Anya Fernald's celebrated cookbook, has become the centerpiece of my family's annual latkes-and-vodka party (page 47). Tender brisket is always a comforting dish, but it is at its best when it's cold outside. Made with wine and herbs, the fragrance of the long braise will welcome your guests to the party.

Throwing a big party comes easily to Anya. In addition to being the CEO of the Belcampo meat company, a farm-to-table business that raises and sells organic sustainable meat, she is also the founder of Eat Real, an annual Oakland, California, food festival that brings farmers, regional food producers, and eaters together. Says Anya, "I love to serve brisket because it's a relatively affordable cut that, when braised, turns out to be a delicious, inexpensive main dish. At a more casual gathering, I like how everyone ends up pulling at the brisket, sopping up the juices with bread, and getting their elbows deep in the dinner."

The beauty of brisket is that it is relatively easy to make ahead of time. Anya's three-step technique ensures a moist brisket that can be sliced without falling apart, which is essential for party serving. First, the brisket is seared on the stove top. Next, it's placed in a heavy pot and braised with wine for a few hours. Just before serving, the meat is transferred to a sheet pan and browned with a blast of heat in a hot oven. Once you get the technique down, you can vary the cooking liquid, herbs, and spices to suit your taste, swapping beer, beef stock, or hard cider for the wine, adding thyme in place of rosemary, or amping up the braise with citrus or whole garlic cloves.

The brisket is sliced and served on platters either family-style or on a buffet table along with the latkes and a green salad. Leftovers—if there are any—are delicious tucked into sandwiches or shredded and folded into a potato hash.

Single Batch **Makes 6 servings**
Double Batch **Makes 12 servings**

MAKE AHEAD

The brisket and its cooking liquid can be covered in the roasting pan with aluminum foil and refrigerated for up to 2 days. Reheat in a low oven (still in the braising liquid) until the brisket is warmed through, then transfer to a sheet pan, increase the oven temperature to 375°F, and give the brisket a final blast of dry heat to brown the exterior. The brisket can also be frozen: Let cool completely, then cut into large pieces (do not slice) and transfer to plastic freezer storage bags. Spoon in some of the braising liquid, seal closed, and freeze for up to 2 months. Let thaw for 2 days in the refrigerator, then transfer the brisket and liquid to a pan, cover, and reheat in a 300°F oven. Just before serving, slice the brisket and season the sauce with salt and a squeeze of lemon juice, if needed to brighten the flavor.

INGREDIENTS	SINGLE BATCH	DOUBLE BATCH
First-cut beef brisket (see *Ingredient Notes*, page 134)	5 lb	10 lb
Kosher salt and freshly ground black pepper		
Large red onion(s), cut into 8 wedges	1	2

continued on following page

133

Large skillet for browning the brisket; one or two large roasting pans; one or two half sheet pans.

BIG BATCH NOTES

Some cooks simmer brisket in a pot on the stove top, but oven braising is easier. If you're making brisket for a large crowd, brown the meat all at once, then transfer it to one or two roasting pans (if making a double batch, you may need only one pan if the briskets will fit without overlapping). If using two pans, they can go into the oven at the same time. Brisket shrinks a lot during cooking, so allow 12 to 14 ounces raw meat per person, depending on appetites.

SERVING

As noted, brisket is great paired with latkes (page 47) or it might follow a first course of matzo ball soup (page 61). A big salad of bitter greens would match either menu.

INGREDIENT NOTES

Whole beef briskets are divided into two cuts, the first (or flat) cut, which has an even thickness and a fat cap on only one side, and the second (point or deckle) cut, which is thicker, has more internal marbling, and is typically smaller. First cuts are more commonly available and are usually preferred because they are leaner and more uniform.

INGREDIENTS	SINGLE BATCH	DOUBLE BATCH
Fresh rosemary sprigs	2	4
Whole cloves	2	4
Juniper berries	4	8
Black peppercorns	1 tsp	2 tsp
750-ml bottle(s) hearty red wine	1	2

Preheat the oven to 300°F. For a double batch, position racks in the center and bottom third of the oven.

If necessary, trim the visible fat cap on the brisket to about ¼ inch thick. Generously season on both sides with salt and pepper.

Heat a large cast-iron skillet over high heat. When the pan is very hot, add the brisket, fat side down, and sear until deep golden brown, 5 to 6 minutes. Flip the brisket and sear on the second side until brown, 5 to 6 minutes. (If the brisket is too large for your largest skillet, brown the brisket in the roasting pan spanning two burners.)

Transfer the brisket to a large roasting pan. Add the onions, rosemary, cloves, juniper berries, and peppercorns. Pour in the wine, then add water as needed for the liquid to reach halfway up the side of the brisket. Tightly cover the pan with aluminum foil.

Braise until the brisket is fork-tender but not falling apart, 3 to 3½ hours. Remove from the oven.

Carefully transfer the brisket to a sheet pan. Increase the oven temperature to 375°F. When the oven has reached temperature, place the sheet pan in the oven and bake until a dark brown crust begins to form on the meat, about 20 minutes.

Meanwhile, pour the braising liquid through a fine-mesh sieve into a clear measuring pitcher and discard the solids. Using a large spoon, skim off and discard any fat from the surface. If the braising liquid is not as reduced as you would like, transfer it to a saucepan, bring to a boil over medium heat, and boil until reduced and thickened. If it is thick enough, simply heat it to serving temperature. Season with salt and pepper.

When the brisket is ready, transfer to a cutting board and cut against the grain into ½-inch-thick slices. Arrange the slices on a platter and spoon some of the braising liquid on top. Pour the remaining liquid into a pitcher or bowl. Serve the brisket and the braising liquid immediately.

GAYLE PIRIE AND ANDREW DOVEL

porchetta

A CLASSIC PORCHETTA is made using most of a pig, which is deboned, seasoned, rolled, tied, and roasted outdoors on a spit for hours. Numerous regions of Italy claim the porchetta as their own, and throughout the year, special festivals (*sagre*) are held in its honor that bring together locals and tourists alike to feast on the succulent pork and the local wine at long communal tables set up in the town square.

This recipe, which was created by chef Andrew Dovel with Gayle Pirie of Foreign Cinema restaurant in San Francisco, using farm-fresh meat from Llano Seco, respects the grand scale of Italian porchetta. It also mirrors the generosity of Gayle and her husband, John Clarke, who have been chefs and co-owners of Foreign Cinema for over twenty years.

The pork cut you will need for this recipe is known as the pork middle, or porchetta cut. It is a single piece of pork belly, with the ribs removed, attached to the loin, and must be special ordered from the butcher. If you cannot find this cut, you can use two separate cuts—a pork belly and a pork loin. Season the flesh side of the belly then wrap the belly around the loin for roasting as directed.

Although this recipe definitely takes time, the method skips the traditional spit in favor of a home oven. Andrew suggests roasting it in two stages: a long, slow roast at 250°F, then a fast blast at 450°F to crisp up the skin. Ideally, you need to let the seasoned pork rest overnight before you start cooking and then again overnight between cooking, so start this dish at least two days before you plan to serve it. However, to refrigerate a cut this big will require an entire refrigerator or a commercial refrigerator, so keep this in mind. If you don't have adequate refrigerator space, consider making this in one day or trying the recipe that follow this one.

INGREDIENTS

Whole skin-on, boneless pork loin with belly attached	1
Kosher salt	3 cups
Freshly ground black pepper	½ cup

continued on following page

Makes 30 to 40 servings

MAKE AHEAD

As noted, if you have the refrigerator space, it is best to season the pork and refrigerate it overnight before the initial roasting. The smear can be made and refrigerated at the same time. Once the pork has finished its initial roasting, you will need to let it cool and then return it to the refrigerator overnight before the final roasting.

Large roasting pan; half sheet pan, large sharp knife.

BIG BATCH NOTES

This is a huge piece of meat, which requires a big, flat work surface to prepare it and tie it off. Rolling and tying the meat is easier with two people.

If your oven is small you can cut the loin in half (see photos opposite). This is also helpful to fit in refrigerator space.

SERVING

Serve alongside Braised Tuscan Kale with White Beans.

BRAISED TUSCAN KALE WITH WHITE BEANS

Makes 12 servings

3 lb Tuscan kale
1 cup diced pancetta or prosciutto, in ¼-inch dice
2 Tbsp olive oil
4 garlic cloves, finely chopped
6 cups drained cooked cannellini beans (page 233)
Kosher salt and freshly ground black pepper

Strip the thick central stem from each kale leaf, then coarsely chop the leaves.

In a large saucepan, heat the pancetta and oil together over medium heat and cook, stirring occasionally, until the pancetta is lightly browned, about 5 minutes. Stir in the garlic and cook until fragrant, about 1 minute.

Working in batches, stir in the kale, letting each batch wilt slightly before adding more. Stir in the beans, reduce the heat to medium-low, and cover tightly. Cook, stirring occasionally, just until the kale is tender, about 8 minutes. Season with salt and pepper and serve.

INGREDIENTS

Smear

Garlic cloves, finely chopped	1 cup
Flat-leaf parsley, leaves only	3 bunches
Fresh thyme leaves	¼ cup
Chopped fresh rosemary	2 Tbsp
Fresh oregano leaves	¼ cup
Lemon zest, in long strips (from about 10 lemons)	1 cup
Olive oil–packed anchovy fillets (or 2 Tbsp anchovy paste)	8

Season the pork liberally and generously on both sides with the salt and pepper. Set in a roasting pan, cover loosely with plastic wrap, and, if possible, refrigerate overnight.

Make the smear: In a food processor, combine the garlic, parsley, thyme, rosemary, oregano, lemon zest, and anchovy fillets and process until a thick paste forms.

Roll, tie, and roast the porchetta: Cut ten pieces of butcher's twine, each 20 inches long. Put the pork, skin side down, on a clean work surface with a long side parallel to the counter edge. Rub the interior flesh side thoroughly with the smear. Roll the belly firmly around the pork loin into a fat cylinder. Tie the cylinder tightly using the lengths of butcher's twine, spacing them about 2 inches apart and tying each with a double knot. Wrap the pork cylinder with two layers of plastic wrap, then overwrap with two or three layers of heavy-duty aluminum foil, encasing the pork completely. Transfer to a half sheet pan and let stand at room temperature for 1 hour.

About 10 minutes before you are ready to roast the porchetta, preheat the oven to 250°F. When the oven is ready, roast the porchetta for 4 hours.

Remove from the oven but do not unwrap. Let cool to room temperature. At this point, the loin can be refrigerated overnight.

Remove all of the foil and plastic wrap over the sheet pan, being careful not to lose the juices that were created. Preheat the oven to 450°F.

Roast the porchetta until the skin is dark gold and has a crisp, crackling feel when touched, about 1 hour. Remove from the oven, tent with aluminum foil, and let rest for 15 minutes.

To serve, using a serrated knife, cut into ½-inch-thick slices and serve.

porchetta   137

SARA JENKINS

porchetta rustica

MAKE AHEAD

The porchetta can be rolled, tied, and refrigerated for up to 1 day. It is best served the same day it is roasted.

EQUIPMENT

One or two large roasting pans.

SERVING

Sara most often uses her porchetta for sandwiches made with crusty Italian rolls, but it can also be served with Polenta (see facing page).

INGREDIENT NOTES

Because the crispy skin is an important part of the final dish, you will want to purchase shoulder roasts with the fat and skin intact. That may mean you need to special order them from a butcher shop. If your butcher cannot supply them, purchase regular pork shoulder roasts and order a thin sheet of pork belly to wrap around each roast.

Fennel pollen has a fluffy texture that is much different from common fennel seeds. It is sold at Italian grocers and online. If you cannot find it, use half the amount of fennel seeds, ground in a spice grinder or with a mortar and pestle.

COOKS WHO LOVE a challenge will find a lot of pleasure in the traditional recipe for porchetta on page 135. But when you want to feed a smaller crowd, this recipe from *Olives and Oranges: Recipes and Flavor Secrets from Italy, Spain, Cyprus, and Beyond* by Sara Jenkins and Mindy Fox is the one to turn to. It is based on the version made famous by Sara at her first restaurant, Porchetta, and now occasionally served across the street at her new space, Porsena.

Sara spent much of her childhood in Italy, where she regularly ate porchetta from street-corner carts. She couldn't find an acceptable rendition in New York, so she created this receip to enjoy this herb-infused crispy-skin pork whenever she wanted.

Sara likes to experiment with different flavors to keep her porchetta relevant and interesting, like incorporating it into a cubano or bahn mi, but she always makes sure that her porchetta keeps its strong Italian roots.

INGREDIENTS

Skin-on boneless pork shoulder roasts, 4 lb each (see *Ingredient Notes*)	2
Fennel pollen (see *Ingredient Notes*)	½ cup
Finely grated lemon zest	½ cup
Fresh sage leaves, finely chopped	40
Leafy fresh thyme sprigs, leaves only, finely chopped	10
Leafy fresh rosemary sprigs, leaves only, finely chopped	10
Garlic cloves, coarsely chopped	10
Medium-coarse sea salt	1 Tbsp
Freshly cracked black pepper	1 Tbsp
Extra-virgin olive oil	¼ cup
Dry white wine	2 cups

Preheat the oven to 250°F.

Using a sharp knife, score the skin on each roast in a crosshatched pattern, making cuts ⅛ inch deep and about 1 inch apart. Then, using the tip of the knife, make ten incisions, each about ½ inch deep, all over each roast.

In a small bowl, combine the fennel pollen, lemon zest, sage, thyme, rosemary, garlic, salt, and pepper and mix well. (Alternatively, skip chopping the ingredients and instead combine them all in a mini food processor and pulse for about 30 seconds.)

Rub one-third of the herb mixture on the roasts, stuffing it into the incisions. Using butcher's twine, and shaping each roast into a round, tie each roast crosswise in three or four places to maintain its shape. Brush the oil over the pork skin, then rub the pork with the remaining herb mixture.

Place the roasts, skin side up and side by side, in a large roasting pan (or use two pans if needed) and roast for 2 hours. Remove from the oven, pour the wine over the pork, and then baste the pork with the wine and accumulated pork juices.

Return the roasts to the oven and continue roasting, basting every hour, until the skin is well browned, the meat is fork-tender, and an instant-read thermometer inserted into the center of each roast registers about 175°F, 2½ to 3 hours.

Remove the roasts from the oven. Position an oven rack near the heat source and pre-heat the broiler. Broil the pork, turning it to brown all sides, until the skin is sizzling and extra crisp, 1 to 2 minutes.

Remove from the oven and let rest for 15 minutes. Snip and discard the twine, then cut into ½-inch-thick slices to serve.

POLENTA AL FORNO

Born into an Italian family, cookbook author Domenica Marchetti included this polenta in her book *The Glorious Vegetables of Italy*. In parts of Italy polenta is poured out onto a board in the middle of the table, ragu is ladled on top, then everybody eats from the communal board. Topped with leftover Bolognese sauce (page 96) or ratatouille (page 205), it makes a hearty supper, but it is an excellent side for dishes like porchetta. It can be assembled up to a day in advance, covered, and refrigerated and then slipped into the oven just before the guests arrive.

Makes 6 servings

6 cups vegetable broth or
  chicken broth
1 ½ cups polenta
3 tbsp unsalted butter
¾ cup plus 2 tablespoons grated
  Parmigiano-Reggiano cheese
½ to 1 tsp fine sea salt
Extra-virgin olive oil for the
  baking dish
4 oz shredded Asiago fresco,
  percorino fresco or other good
  shredding and melting cheese

Heat the oven to 400°F. In a heavy-bottomed saucepan, bring the broth to a boil over medium-high heat. Sprinkle in the polenta, in a continuous stream, stirring with a wire whisk to prevent lumps. Reduce the heat to medium and continue to cook the polenta, stirring frequently with a wooden spoon, for 30 to 40 minutes, or until it is thick and pulls away from sides of the pan. Add in the butter, ¾ cup of the Parmigiano, and ½ teaspoon salt and stir until incorporated into the polenta. Taste and adjust the seasoning.

Lightly oil an ovenproof baking dish large enough to hold the polenta. Spread half the polenta onto the baking dish and sprinkle the Asiago over it. Spread the remaining polenta on top and smooth it out. Sprinkle the remaining 2 tablespoons parmigiano on top. Bake uncovered for 20 to 30 minutes, until firm and bubbly.

pomegranate-braised lamb shanks

Single Batch **Makes 12 servings**

Double Batch **Makes 24 servings**

MAKE AHEAD

Like nearly every braise, this one improves upon standing. Let the shanks cool in the liquid to room temperature. Cover the pans and refrigerate for up to 3 days. Skim off and discard any hardened fat on the surface. To reheat, place in a 325°F oven until the shanks are warmed through. Transfer the shanks to a deep serving platter, then strain, reduce, and season the braising liquid.

POMEGRANATE, LAMB, GARLIC, rosemary, and thyme are familiar favorite flavors to Sam Mogannam, a San Francisco native who grew up helping out at his parents' small grocery store in the city's Mission District. He and his family still run that store, and now Bi-Rite Market and its expanded family of businesses have become much more than just places to buy ice cream and apples, kale salads, and sandwiches. Part community gathering place, part kitchen away from home, the markets are always lively, always crowded, always offering something delicious you've never tasted before. And now, Sam and his wife, Anne Walker, are watching their two daughters grow up in the store. Their lives are not just about the food; they are about feeding a community, too.

Sam began cooking this recipe for Christmas ten years ago, and it quickly became a favorite of his extended family. The idea was to bring together all of his aunts, uncles, and cousins to give everyone the opportunity to engage with the entire family, thus ensuring members of the next generation a deeper connection to their roots. His extended family numbers around fifty people, so he made a big batch of these shanks the first year, and they were devoured. When he decided to change the menu the following year, the family (especially his aunts!) expressed deep disappointment (*Where are the shanks?*). The next Christmas he went back to the original recipe, and the shanks have been on the menu ever since. Now he makes extra so his aunts can take some home and eat them over the following days.

A signature of these slow-braised lamb shanks is the use of tangy, ruby-red pomegranate juice, which imparts a fruity brightness. Cooking the shanks for several hours in a low-temperature oven keeps them fork-tender and full of flavor.

BIG BATCH NOTES

Unless you have a large rondeau or other large-capacity pot, it is easiest to brown the shanks and vegetables in two Dutch ovens, side by side on the stove top, then transfer the contents of both vessels to a roasting pan (or pans, if you're making a double batch) for braising.

SERVING

Although a shank looks like a big piece of meat, the bone accounts for much of the weight, so plan on a shank per person. Accompany with Hummus (see facing page) or fava bean dip, olives, roasted eggplant, Maftoul couscous, and pita and/or sesame bread.

INGREDIENT NOTES

For the best price, buy the pome-granate juice in 1-quart bottles, which are typically available in Middle Eastern or Mediterranean groceries and occasionally in some supermarkets.

INGREDIENTS	SINGLE BATCH	DOUBLE BATCH
Lamb shanks, about 1 lb each	12	24
Kosher salt and freshly ground black pepper		
Olive oil, or as needed	¼ cup	½ cup
Large yellow onions, cut into large dice	2	4
Tomato paste	¼ cup	½ cup
Large carrots, peeled and cut into large dice	6	12
Celery ribs, cut into large dice	6	12
Pomegranate juice (see *Ingredient Notes*)	4 cups	8 cups
Chicken or beef stock, preferably homemade	4 cups	8 cups
Head(s) garlic, halved crosswise, outer skin removed	1	2
Fresh thyme sprigs	6	12
Fresh rosemary sprig(s)	1	2

Preheat the oven to 275°F. Generously season the lamb shanks all over with salt and pepper.

Have ready a large roasting pan (or two pans if making a double batch). Heat two large, heavy Dutch ovens over medium-high heat. Add half of the oil to each pot and heat until hot but not smoking. In batches, add the lamb shanks and cook, turning occasionally and adding more oil if needed, until deeply browned on all sides, about 10 minutes. Transfer to a roasting pan and repeat until all the shanks have been browned, adding more oil to the pots as necessary.

Divide the onions between the Dutch ovens and cook, stirring occasionally, until light golden, 5 to 8 minutes. Stir half of the tomato paste into each pot and cook, stirring, for about 2 minutes. Divide the carrots and celery between the pots and cook, stirring occasionally, until they begin to soften, about 5 minutes. Divide the pomegranate juice and stock between the pots and bring to a simmer, scraping up any browned bits on the bottom with a wooden spoon, then season lightly with salt (the liquid will reduce during cooking, so you don't want to over season). Pour the contents of the pots into the roasting pan(s) with the lamb shanks and add the garlic, thyme, and rosemary. Cover the roasting pan(s) tightly with aluminum foil.

Braise until the meat is tender and the sauce is reduced, 4 to 5 hours, checking every 30 minutes after the 3-hour mark (some shanks cook faster than others, so it is best to begin checking early for doneness).

Remove the shanks from the oven. Using a slotted spoon, carefully transfer the shanks to one or more deep platters and cover with aluminum foil to keep warm. Pour the braising liquid through a fine-mesh sieve into a large saucepan and let stand for 10 minutes. Using a ladle or large spoon, skim off and discard the fat from the surface of the liquid. Bring the liquid to a simmer over medium-high heat and simmer until the sauce has reduced and thickened slightly, about 10 minutes. Taste and adjust the seasoning with salt and pepper.

To serve, spoon some of the sauce over the lamb shanks and serve the remainder in a pitcher or bowl alongside.

HUMMUS

Makes about 1½ cups

Sam says that his mother's hummus is the benchmark for all other versions. She taught Eddy, the Bi-Rite chef, how to make it, and he in turn trained all of the kitchen crew.

2 large garlic cloves, smashed
1½ cups drained cooked chickpeas (page 233), or 1 (15-oz) can chickpeas (garbanzo beans), drained and rinsed
3½ Tbsp fresh lemon juice
3 Tbsp warm water
2 Tbsp extra-virgin olive oil
1½ Tbsp tahini
¾ tsp kosher salt, plus more if needed
⅛ tsp ground toasted coriander
⅛ tsp ground toasted cumin
Pinch of cayenne pepper

In a food processor, pulse the garlic a few times to chop. Add the chickpeas, lemon juice, water, oil, tahini, salt, coriander, cumin, and cayenne and process until smooth. Adjust the consistency with a little more water if needed (it will stiffen further when chilled), then taste and adjust the seasoning with lemon juice and salt if needed. It should taste brightly of lemon rather than heavy with beans and tahini. Store in an airtight container in the refrigerator for up to 4 days.

pomegranate-braised lamb shanks   143

GONZALO GUZMAN

carnitas

THE CARNITAS AT Nopalito is one of Gonzalo Guzman's signature dishes and for good reason: it's succulent and wonderfully delicious. To make it, he slowly cooks pork shoulder with lard, milk, and seasonings like oranges and cinnamon until it shreds easily. Here, it is used in a favorite guise, as a filling for soft tacos. Pickled vegetables, a salsa cruda, and cabbage salad help balance the richness of the pork.

Gonzalo came to the United States when he was just fifteen years old, ending up in San Francisco. He started as a dishwasher and gradually worked his way up, learning to cook through years of double shifts at Jardinière, Boulevard, and finally at Kokkari, where he met Laurence Jossel. He helped Laurence open Chez Nous (now closed), then Nopa, a beloved neighborhood restaurant. Nopalito, Nopa's little sister, was their shared dream. Nopalito serves regional Mexican food featuring dishes from Guzman's native Veracruz made with the best ingredients available. The idea for the restaurant grew out of the staff meals Guzman would prepare, including carnitas, now a customer favorite at Nopalito.

In Mexico, carnitas is often sold by the pound at big outdoor markets. At Nopalito, Gonzalo originally served it family-style as a takeaway item for people putting together picnics at nearby parks. But it is a wonderful food for gathering family and friends around the table for any occasion.

For Gonzalo, feeding people is a way to stay connected: "I'm trying to represent my people by cooking dishes with a tradition and a history."

INGREDIENTS	SINGLE BATCH	DOUBLE BATCH
Boneless pork shoulder (preferably butt), cut into 3-inch chunks	5 lb	10 lb
Kosher salt		
Navel orange, cut into wedges	1/4	1/2
White onion, cut into thick wedges	1/2	1
Garlic cloves, crushed	3	6
Bay leaves	1	2
Cinnamon stick, about 3 inches	1/2	1

continued on following page

Single Batch
Makes 10 to 12 servings

Double Batch
Makes 20 to 24 servings

MAKE AHEAD

The carnitas can be cooked, cooled in the lard, covered, and refrigerated for up to 1 day. Reheat over low heat until the lard is melted and the meat is warmed through. If you are making the carnitas the same day as serving, note that the pork should be salted at least 2 hours before cooking. The pickled vegetables can be made up to 1 month ahead. The salsa cruda can be covered and refrigerated for up to 3 days. The cabbage salad can be covered and refrigerated for up to 1 day.

EQUIPMENT

One or two 5-quart Dutch ovens (or one 8-quart or larger Dutch oven for a double batch); cheesecloth for the seasoning bundle.

A tortilla warmer, available in ceramic or insulated cloth models, is a great serving piece for this kind of party. The insulated type works especially well, as it can be heated in a microwave to maintain more efficiently the optimal temperature of the tortillas.

DENNIS LEE

korean crispy pork belly

bo ssäm

BO SSÄM IS Korean comfort food at its best: tender pork belly slices wrapped in lettuce and topped with spicy condiments. This recipe, the work of Dennis Lee, does not come together quickly, though the hands-on time is minimal. It can be done ahead, however, and it is a wonderful participatory group feast. This meal is best when served at a table with all of the components within easy reach of the diners, so if you make a big batch for sixteen, keep this advice in mind.

Dennis is the co-owner and head chef of Namu Gaji restaurant in San Francisco. He and his two brothers, Daniel and David, not only run the restaurant together but also operate a one-acre farm that employs traditional Korean natural farming techniques and uses no petroleum fuel. They grow most of the produce used in the restaurant on their own land.

Dennis's mother would make bo ssäm for special occasions and for Sunday family get-togethers. This recipe is inspired by that tradition, down to the ssämjang, a salty, spicy, thick condiment that traditionally accompanies not only bo ssäm but also any grilled meat that is wrapped. The pickled daikon needs to sit overnight, but it is made in minutes and is a refreshing counterpoint to the pork belly. Ice-cold oysters are a good addition to the bo ssäm table.

Every Korean meal is accompanied by bowls of *banchan*, small shared side dishes of various types—fermented, steamed, braised, stir-fried with sauce, marinated and stir-fried, panfried—that are typically replenished as diners finish them. In this feast, the banchan are represented by kimchi and pickled daikon, but you can add to them, of course, with the number limited only by the space on the table. If you don't have time to make banchan, they can often be purchased at Asian markets.

Single Batch **Makes 8 servings**

Double Batch **Makes 16 servings**

MAKE AHEAD

The daikon can be refrigerated for up to 1 month, and the Ssämjang Sauce can be refrigerated for up to 1 month. The simmered pork belly must be cooled and refrigerated for at least 3 hours but will keep overnight. (Indeed, the longer it has been chilled and weighted, the easier it is to slice.)

One or two large, oval Dutch ovens
or roasting pans (the latter placed
over two burners) for simmering
the pork belly; one or two large,
heavy, high-sided pots for frying
the pork belly in oil.

BIG BATCH NOTES

If you decide to serve the oysters,
be sure you have someone on hand
who is adept at opening them,
or ask the fishmonger to shuck
them and to reserve the liquor and
bottom shells.

SERVING

Divide each component of the
meal between two or more plates
or bowls to cut down on passing
them at the table. Because bo
ssäm is eaten as a lettuce wrap out
of hand, have extra napkins on the
table. For beverages, offer soju,
a clear, vodka-like Korean liquor
distilled from rice; and Korean
beer, such as OB or Hite; and visit
a Korean market to find additional
banchan to serve.

INGREDIENT NOTES

You can find the *dwenjang*
(soybean paste sold in a brown
container), *gochujang* (red pepper
paste sold in a green container),
and *kimchi* (spicy fermented
cabbage pickle) at Korean or other
Asian markets and in some regular
supermarkets. The color coding of
the plastic containers will help you
identify the pastes, which are often
sold with only Korean labeling.

INGREDIENTS	SINGLE BATCH	DOUBLE BATCH
Boneless, skin-on pork belly, in a single piece	4 lb	8 lb
Fresh ginger, peeled and thinly sliced	4 oz	8 oz
Head(s) garlic, cloves separated, peeled, and coarsely chopped	1	2
Fine sea salt	6 Tbsp	¾ cup
Fish sauce	3 Tbsp	6 Tbsp
Grapeseed, rice bran, or canola oil, for frying		
For Serving		
Fine sea salt		
Pickled Daikon (see facing page)	1 recipe	2 recipes
Ssämjang Sauce (see facing page)	1 recipe	2 recipes
Heads red leaf or bibb lettuce	2	4
Jalapeño chiles, cut into thin rounds	2	4
Store-bought kimchi	2 cups	4 cups
Dashi-Brined Oysters (page 152), optional	1 recipe	2 recipes

The day before serving (or at the latest, the morning of serving), prepare the pork belly (if making a double batch, treat both pieces of pork belly the same way). Cut the pork in half lengthwise to make two long rectangles. Arrange the rectangles skin side up and with a long side facing you. Using a sharp knife, score the skin side of each rectangle, spacing the slashes 1 inch apart and cutting no deeper than to the flesh.

Place the pork in a large, wide pot (or two pots if making a double batch). Add the ginger, garlic, salt, and fish sauce and then pour in water to cover the meat by about 1 inch. You will have to add water to the pot continually during the cooking, so the exact amount is not important as long as the pork is covered with water.

Bring to a rolling boil over high heat. Reduce the heat to a steady simmer, cover the pot, and cook, adding water as needed to keep the pork covered with water, until the pork is tender enough to tear with your fingers, but not so tender that it falls apart. The timing will depend on your stove and the size and shape of your pot, but it should take between 1¾ and 2½ hours.

Using tongs, and being careful they do not break apart, transfer the pork pieces to a half sheet pan (or two pans if making a double batch) and let cool to room temperature. Wrap each pork piece with a double layer of plastic wrap, pulling it tightly so the scored skin and fat are compressed together. Top with a second half sheet pan and weight down the top pan with a couple of bricks (a 5-pound hand weight or heavy food cans would also work). Refrigerate from 3 hours up to overnight.

PICKLED DAIKON

Makes about 2 cups

1 large (1.5 lb) daikon radish,
  peeled and thinly sliced
2 cups unseasoned rice vinegar
2 Tbsp sugar
½ tsp fine sea salt

Put the daikon into a widemouthed
jar. In a bowl, whisk together the
vinegar, sugar, and salt until the
sugar and salt have dissolved.
Pour the vinegar mixture over the
daikon and press down on the daikon slices so they are submerged.
Cover and refrigerate for at least
12 hours before serving.

SSÄMJANG SAUCE

Makes about 1½ cups

½ cup *dwenjang* (Korean soybean
  paste) (see *Ingredient Notes*)
½ cup *gochujang* (Korean red chile
  paste) (see *Ingredient Notes*)
¼ cup unseasoned rice vinegar
2 Tbsp water
1 garlic clove, minced
1 jalapeño chile, seeded and
  minced (optional)

In a bowl, whisk together the
dwenjang, gochujang, vinegar,
water, garlic, and chile (if using),
mixing well. Transfer to a glass
container (the gochujang can
stain porous materials red),
cover tightly, and refrigerate until
serving.

korean crispy pork belly   151

DASHI-BRINED OYSTERS

Makes 16 oysters

Bonito Brine
6 cups water
2-inch square kombu seaweed
½ cup bonito flakes
½ tsp soy sauce

16 oysters

To make the bonito brine, in a saucepan, bring the water to a boil over high heat. Remove from the heat, add the kombu and bonito flakes, and let steep for 15 minutes. Strain through a fine-mesh sieve into a bowl and stir in the soy sauce. Let cool to room temperature, then cover and refrigerate until cold.

Shuck the oysters over a fine-mesh sieve set over a bowl. Set aside the liquor captured in the bowl and the bottom shell of each oyster. Gently rinse the shucked oysters to rid them of any shell fragments and then place them in the cooled bonito brine. Rinse the reserved shells in cold water, set on a plate, and chill in the refrigerator. Cover and chill the reserved oyster liquor.

When ready to serve the bo ssäm, line a large platter with crushed ice and nestle the oyster shells, hollow side up, in the ice. Using a slotted spoon, place a brined oyster in each shell, then spoon a little of the reserved oyster liquor over each oyster.

After pressing, the bellies will be flat and it should be difficult to see the original score lines. Remove the pork from the refrigerator, unwrap, and discard the plastic wrap. With a sharp knife, lightly score the skin side of each pork piece again, this time in a crosshatch pattern and make the slashes only about ⅛ inch deep, spacing them about ½ inch apart.

Pour the oil to a depth of ½ inch into a large, heavy high-sided pot. Place the pork pieces, skin side down and side by side, into the cold oil and cover the pot with the lid slightly ajar so steam can escape but the oil won't splash out and burn you. Depending on the size of your pot, you may need to do each piece of belly separately, as each piece must lie flat in the pot. (If you are making a double batch, try to use two pots.) Place over high heat, then reduce the heat to medium when the fat starts popping and crackling. Continue frying until the edges of the skin look brown and the skin stops crackling, about 20–25 minutes. Adjust the heat as needed so the pork heats through and browns evenly but not too quickly. Remove from the heat and let cool for about 5 minutes.

Using tongs or a metal spatula, transfer the pork pieces, skin side up, to a cutting board. Using a sharp knife, and using the original deep score lines as a guide, cut the pork into strips 1 inch wide. Turn each strip skin side down and gently cut through the meat, creating ¼-inch-thick slices and being careful not to separate the skin from the meat. Shingle the slices on a large platter and sprinkle with salt.

Serve the pork belly warm or at room temperature, with the daikon, Ssämjang Sauce, lettuce, chiles, kimchi, and oysters (if serving) alongside. Invite guests to use the lettuce leaves as wrappers for the pork slices, garnishing with their choice of condiments.

LIZA SHAW

old-school chicken parm

DEEPLY INFLUENCED BY a Sicilian family friend who would cook for big family get-togethers in Maryland, Liza eventually moved to California to pursue a career in cooking Italian food. She began as an extern and line cook at Acquerello, leaving to open A16, where she became partner and Executive Chef.

One of the things she missed from Maryland was the classic East Coast chicken parm, so she opened the now-closed Merigan Sub Shop, a pint-size spot in San Francisco that specialized in high-quality sandwiches including chicken parm. In this case, the sub came before this dinner-party version.

Liza adds grated Parmigiano-Reggiano cheese, minced garlic, red pepper flakes, and dried oregano to the bread crumb mixture she uses to coat the chicken, and prefers chicken thighs (more robust flavor, resilient texture) over breasts.

Although chicken parm is not difficult to make, it does involve many components. Happily, much of the work can be done in advance, so Liza prepares it in stages. For example, she recommends pounding and seasoning the chicken a day or two before breading, panfrying, and baking it. "It is worth taking a step back and realizing the value of gathering people around the kitchen and preparing food together, putting in some time, maybe learning a new technique, and achieving greatness rather than quickness," says Liza. "After all, we are feeding ourselves—our friends and families."

Liza's chicken parm would make a popular meal on New Year's Day; it was dubbed by many of her customers as "the best hangover cure." Serve the dish, family-style alongside a few of these sides: tricolore salad, pasta dressed with some of the marinara sauce, garlic bread, and braised greens. Perhaps a new New Year's Day tradition is in order?

Single Batch
Makes 10 servings

Double Batch
Makes 20 servings

MAKE AHEAD

The marinara sauce can be refrigerated for up to 5 days or frozen for up to 2 months. The seasoned bread crumbs can be refrigerated for up to 2 days or frozen for up to 2 months. If frozen, thaw at room temperature before using. The pounded and seasoned chicken can be refrigerated for up to 2 days. The breaded chicken can be covered with plastic wrap and refrigerated for up to 1 day, or it can be transferred to plastic freezer bags, frozen for up to 1 month, and then allowed to thaw completely in the refrigerator before frying. The assembled dish can be refrigerated for up to 1 day. The chicken will absorb some of the sauce while refrigerated; add some sauce around the sides of the pans to moisten before baking, if desired, and increase the baking time by 10 to 12 minutes to heat through.

One large stockpot for making the sauce; two or four 10-by-15-inch baking dishes; three or four half sheet pans for holding the breaded and fried chicken. If making the double batch, you will need a double oven. The chicken can be slightly overlapped in the baking pans.

BIG BATCH NOTES

The marinara sauce purposely yields a large batch to serve on the side or to provide leftovers for another use.

Liza feels that freshly made bread crumbs make this dish special, but in a pinch, you can substitute store-bought panko (Japanese bread crumbs), using 8 cups (about 1¼ pounds) for a single batch or 16 cups (about 2½ pounds) for a double batch. Any leftover home-made bread crumbs can be stored in the freezer for up to 2 months and used for any other breading project (scaloppine, eggplant parm, meatballs, etc.).

To make the chicken-breading pro-cess easier, Liza suggests a "wet hand, dry hand" technique: keep one hand devoted to touching wet ingredients (chicken, egg) and the other reserved for dry ingredients (flour, bread crumbs).

INGREDIENTS	SINGLE BATCH	DOUBLE BATCH
Marinara Sauce		
Extra-virgin olive oil	¾ cup	1½ cups
Slivered garlic	2 Tbsp	¼ cup
Dry white wine	2 cups	4 cups
Large bunch of basil	1	2
28-oz cans crushed tomatoes, preferably Bianco DiNapoli brand	4	8
Kosher salt	1 Tbsp	2 Tbsp
Red pepper flakes	1 tsp	2 tsp
Dried oregano	¾ tsp	1½ tsp
Bread Crumbs		
Day-old bread, preferably rustic, crusts removed (see *Ingredient Notes*, page 156)	2 lb	4 lb
Grated Parmigiano-Reggiano or grana padano cheese	1 cup	2 cups
Large garlic cloves	10	20
Red pepper flakes	1½ tsp	1 Tbsp
Dried oregano	2 tsp	1 Tbsp
Chicken		
Boneless, skinless chicken thighs	5 lb	10 lb
Kosher salt		
Unbleached all-purpose flour	3 cups	6 cups
Large egg whites	6	15
Canola oil, for deep-frying		
Low-moisture mozzarella cheese, shredded or thinly sliced	1 lb	1½ lb
Grated Parmigiano-Reggiano or grana padano cheese	1 cup	2 cups
Fresh basil leaves, whole or julienned, for serving		

Make the marinara sauce: Combine the oil and garlic in a large stockpot over medium heat and cook, stirring often, until translucent, 3 to 5 minutes. Do not allow the garlic to brown. Add the wine, bring to a boil, and boil until reduced by half, 10 to 15 minutes.

While the wine reduces, pick the basil leaves from their stems and set the leaves aside. Tie the stems into a bundle with kitchen string. When the wine has reduced, add the tomatoes, salt, red pepper flakes, oregano, and basil stems to the pot and bring slowly to a simmer, stirring occasionally. Keep an eye on the tomatoes, as they will scorch

SERVING

Because this will be served straight from the oven, have trivets waiting on the table. Large, wide spoons will help serve the chicken with the cheese and sauce.

A very simple tricolore salad (green lettuce, red radicchio, and white Belgian endive) would be a good pairing. Pasta, dressed with some of the marinara sauce, and garlic bread are the classic side dishes. Liza is a big fan of braised bitter greens, like broccoli rabe, chard, or dandelion, to balance the richness of this dish.

INGREDIENT NOTES

If you wish, use one #10 can crushed tomatoes for the single batch or two #10 cans crushed tomatoes for the double batch in place of the smaller cans. Look for these large cans at restaurant supply shops or wholesale clubs.

If you don't have stale bread on hand and you are starting with fresh bread, the night before, trim off and discard the crust, then tear the bread into 2- to 3-inch chunks. Spread the chunks in a single layer on half sheet pans and let stand, uncovered, at room temperature for at least 12 hours or up to 24 hours before making the crumbs.

In a time crunch, you can use store-bought marinara. Substitute 6 cups for a single batch and 12 cups for a double batch.

if unattended. Simmer the sauce, stirring occasionally, for about 10 minutes to blend the flavors.

Remove from the heat and let cool until just warm. Remove and discard the basil stem bundle, then tear the basil leaves into pieces and stir into the sauce. Let cool to room temperature. You should have 3½ quarts if making a single batch or 7 quarts if making a double batch. Transfer to covered containers and refrigerate until needed.

Make the bread crumbs: Tear the bread into chunks and set aside. In a food processor, combine the cheese, garlic, red pepper flakes, and oregano and pulse to finely chop the garlic. Transfer to a bowl. Fill the processor about half full with bread and add about ½ cup of the cheese mixture. Process until the mixture is evenly blended and is the texture of sand. Transfer to a large bowl and repeat with the remaining bread and cheese mixture. You should have 8 cups (2 quarts) seasoned crumbs if making a single batch or 16 cups (4 quarts) if making a double batch. Transfer to large ziplock plastic bags or other airtight containers until needed.

Prepare the chicken: Use a paring knife to trim off any excess chicken fat. Slip five or six chicken thighs into a 1-gallon ziplock plastic bag, arranging them in a single layer. Lay the bag flat on a work surface and, using a meat pounder or heavy pan, pound the chicken thighs to a thickness of about ½ inch. The thighs might separate into smaller pieces during this process, but that doesn't matter in the end. Remove the chicken from the bag, arrange the pieces in a single layer on a half sheet pan, and repeat with the remaining chicken thighs. Season each piece well on both sides with salt.

Put the chicken at one end of your work surface. Line up three rimmed dishes or shallow bowls next to the chicken (large pie or cake pans work well) and put an empty half sheet pan beyond the third bowl (or two pans if making a double batch). Put the flour in the first dish, lightly beat the egg whites until foamy in the second dish, and put the seasoned bread crumbs in the third dish. (If you are making a double batch, you will want to start with just half of each ingredient and then replenish.) To streamline what can be a messy process, keep one hand devoted to touching wet ingredients (chicken, egg) and the other reserved for dry ingredients (flour, bread crumbs).

With the "wet" hand, put two or three pounded chicken thighs in the flour dish and use your "dry" hand to shake them around in the flour, flipping the pieces so they are evenly coated. Shake off any excess flour and put them into the egg whites, using the wet hand to turn the chicken pieces so they are coated on both sides. One at a time, using the wet hand, remove the thighs from the egg whites, letting the excess egg white drip off, and toss them into the bread crumbs. Using your dry hand, shake and flip the pieces to coat evenly on both sides with the crumbs. Transfer the coated pieces to the clean sheet pan, arranging them in a single layer. Repeat the breading process until all of the chicken has been breaded, stacking the chicken and separating the layers with parchment paper as needed.

Pour the oil to a depth of 1½ inches for a single batch and 3 inches for a double batch into a large Dutch oven and heat over medium-high heat to 350°F on a deep-frying thermometer. (Keep in mind that once the chicken hits the oil, the oil will bubble and its level will rise significantly, so always choose a pot that is larger than you think you need for frying.) Line two half sheet pans with paper towels and set nearby.

Working in small batches, carefully add the chicken to the oil and fry, turning once, until golden brown and just barely cooked through, 4 to 5 minutes. Because the chicken will be cooked a second time in the oven, you don't want to overcook it at this point. It is okay if it is pink inside. Using tongs, transfer the chicken to the prepared sheet pan to drain. Repeat until all of the chicken has been fried.

Assemble and bake the chicken: Position oven racks in the top third and center of the oven and preheat the oven to 425°F. Have ready two 10-by-15-inch baking pans.

Pour about 1 cup of the marinara sauce into each pan, spreading it so it covers the entire bottom. Shingle chicken pieces on top of the sauce, filling the entire pan. Top each pan with 2 cups of marinara, spooning it over in stripes so the chicken pieces aren't completely coated. (You'll use 6 cups sauce for a single batch and 12 cups for a double batch.) Arrange the mozzarella over the sauced parts, then top with the Parmigiano-Reggiano.

Transfer to the oven and bake until the cheese is golden and bubbling, 15 to 20 minutes. Remove from the oven and let stand for 4 to 5 minutes. Scatter the basil over the top and serve hot.

PIERRE THIAM

senegalese grilled chicken with lime-onion sauce

yassa ginaar

TERANGA, A WOLOF word that translates roughly to "hospitality," is a key component of life in Senegal, along Africa's west coast. As Senegalese-born chef Pierre Thiam describes it, families traditionally eat sitting on the floor on straw mats arranged around a communal bowl of food. An extra space is always left, so that anyone visiting, whether honored guest or unexpected stranger, can be invited to join the circle and enjoy the grilled meats, spicy stews, fresh seafood, vegetables, and rice that make up Senegal's varied cuisine. This generosity, he says, is the spirit of *teranga*.

Pierre, who grew up in the capital city of Dakar and now lives in Brooklyn, is the author of two cookbooks about Senegalese food, *Yolele! Recipes from the Heart of Senegal* and *Senegal: Modern Senegalese Recipes from the Source to the Bowl*. The flavors of Senegal, he says, are deep and rich, coaxed out of simple ingredients and shaped by many cultures, from the traditions of the local Wolof, Diola, and Foula peoples to the European influences of the French and Portuguese colonial eras and the more recent influx of Lebanese, Vietnamese, and Chinese immigrants. In this recipe, known as yassa ginaar, slowly caramelizing the onions gives a complexity and sweetness to the finished dish that is nicely balanced by the tanginess of fresh lime juice and zest, the heat of habanero chiles, and the smokiness of grilled chicken.

This recipe is ideal for the cook who likes tending food on the grill, as it goes together easily once the chicken is well browned. Pierre, who suggests serving the chicken over hot rice, has also shared a recipe for the black-eyed pea salad that is typically served alongside the chicken.

Single Batch **Makes 8 servings**

Double Batch **Makes 16 servings**

MAKE-AHEAD

The onions can be sliced a day ahead of time and stored in an airtight container in the refrigerator. If you are concerned the odor of the onions will permeate other foods in your fridge, store them in an ice chest. The chicken must be marinated at least 2 hours and up to overnight in the refrigerator before cooking. The black-eyed peas for the salad must be soaked overnight and can be cooked and refrigerated up to 2 days in advance. The salad can be refrigerated for up to 4 hours; bring to room temperature before serving.

Charcoal or gas grill for browning the chicken, one or two large pots for the onions and finishing the dish, one or two large bowls for marinating the chicken; half sheet pans for holding the chicken before and after grilling

BIG BATCH NOTES

If you do not have a big grill, you will need to grill the chicken in two batches.

SERVING

Keep it simple and easy, and serve with rice and Pierre's black-eyed pea salad.

INGREDIENTS	SINGLE BATCH	DOUBLE BATCH
Limes	10	20
Peanut oil	5 Tbsp	10 Tbsp
Cubes chicken bouillon, crumbled	2	4
Kosher salt and freshly ground black pepper		
Yellow onions, cut into thin half-moons	5	10
Chickens, each about 3–4 lbs and cut into 8 serving pieces	2	4
Water	1 cup	2 cups
Habanero chiles, seeded and minced	1	2
Classic Steamed Rice (page 76), made with basmati rice	6 cups	12 cups
Black-Eyed Pea Salad (see facing page)	1 recipe	2 recipes

Grate the zest from 3 limes if making a single batch and from 6 limes if making a double batch, working over a medium bowl. Juice all of the limes (you should have about 1¼ cups juice if making a single batch or 2½ cups juice if making a double batch) and add to the bowl. Add 2 tablespoons of the peanut oil for a single batch or 4 tablespoons for a double batch. Add the bouillon cubes, season with salt and pepper, and stir to mix. Place the onions and chicken in one large bowl if making a single batch or two large bowls if making a double batch. Pour the marinade over the onions and chicken and turn to coat on all sides. Cover and marinate in the refrigerator for at least 2 hours or up to 24 hours. Turn the chicken every 30 minutes or so for the first hour to make sure all the pieces are evenly marinated.

Prepare a charcoal or gas grill for direct cooking over medium-high heat. Transfer the chicken to half sheet pans (reserve the onion mixture) and allow to come to room temperature.

Pour the remaining 3 tablespoons oil into a very large Dutch oven if making a single batch or divide the 6 tablespoons between two Dutch ovens if making a double batch and heat over medium heat. Drain the onions well in a colander, reserving the marinade. Add the onions, cover, and cook, stirring occasionally to avoid scorching and gradually adding the water, ¼ cup at a time if making a single batch and ½ cup at a time if making a double batch, until the onions are nicely caramelized, 20 to 30 minutes.

Place the chicken, skin side down, on the grill. Grill, turning occasionally, until the chicken is well browned, about 15 minutes. If flare-ups occur, for a charcoal grill, move the chicken to the cooler, outer edges of the fire, not over the coals. For a gas grill, turn one side of the grill off and move the chicken to the cooler area. Transfer the chicken to clean half sheet pans.

Add the grilled chicken and any accumulated juices from the sheet pans to the Dutch oven(s), along with the reserved marinade and habanero(s). Stir gently, bring to a boil, lower the heat to medium-low, cover, and simmer until the chicken is cooked through, 15 to 20 minutes.

Transfer the chicken and the onion sauce to one or more big, deep platters. Serve with the rice and salad.

BLACK-EYED PEA SALAD

Makes 8 servings

Black-eyed peas are common in Africa, and in the American South where they are often served on New Year's Day to bring good luck. This simple salad is typically served alongside yassa ginaar, but it would also make a nice addition to other menus. If you are short of time, substitute 3 cups thawed frozen black-eyed peas for the freshly cooked ones.

1¼ cups dried black-eyed peas
Kosher salt and freshly ground
    black pepper
1 large tomato, peeled and diced
1 English cucumber, seeded
    and diced
1 red bell pepper, seeded and diced
6 green onions, chopped
1 cup coarsely chopped fresh flat-
    leaf parsley
Juice of 2 limes
1 Tbsp ground cumin
1 habanero chile, seeded
    and minced
½ cup extra-virgin olive oil

The night before cooking, sort through the black-eyed peas and remove any debris, then rinse them well. Put them in a large bowl and add water to cover by 1 inch. Let soak overnight.

The next day, drain the beans, transfer to a large saucepan, and add fresh water to cover by 1 inch. Bring to a boil over high heat, reduce the heat so the liquid is gently simmering, and cook, uncovered, until the beans are tender, about 1½ hours, adding 1 tablespoon salt near the end of cooking. Drain, rinse under cold running water, and let cool completely.

In a large bowl, combine the tomato, cucumber, bell pepper, green onions, and parsley and stir to mix. Add the drained black-eyed peas and stir again. In a small bowl, whisk together the lime juice, cumin, and habanero, then gradually whisk in the oil. Pour over the bean mixture and mix well. Season to taste with salt and pepper.

TANYA HOLLAND

fried chicken and cornmeal waffles

TANYA HOLLAND'S BROWN Sugar Kitchen, in Oakland, California, is bright and welcoming, busy with diners from all walks of life. Tanya takes her love of soul food and puts a spin on it, using all the skill and know-how she learned in culinary school in France. Her chicken and waffles recipe, by the far the most popular dish at her restaurant, perfectly showcases Tanya's ability to modernize classic soul food.

When Tanya was growing up, her parents often threw big dinner parties for their family and friends, so cooking for others has always been very personal for Tanya and central to her family's best times. She took that passion and love of food and directed it into Brown Sugar Kitchen and into her work with two important organizations that help others, Share Our Strength's "No Kid Hungry" campaign and Community Food Banks across the country.

Tanya's signature dish owes its fame to her careful preparation of every batch. She soaks the chicken overnight in an herb-seasoned buttermilk brine, a mixture that deeply infuses the poultry with flavor. Tanya's waffles are especially light, thanks to the yeast in the batter and an overnight rise in the refrigerator.

This irresistible combination of chicken and waffles was long ago popularized in jazz clubs as a late evening supper—or very early morning breakfast. Nowadays, it is a popular breakfast or brunch order, but don't dismiss it for lunch or dinner. Crunchy chicken and crisp waffles are delicious any time of day. Both the chicken in its brine and the waffle batter sit in the refrigerator overnight, so this is a perfect prep-ahead meal. When it's time to start cooking, a friend or two helping out in the kitchen— cooking chicken, making waffles—are welcome.

Single Batch **Makes 10 servings**

Double Batch **Makes 20 servings**

MAKE AHEAD

The chicken must be refrigerated in its brine overnight. The waffle batter must be refrigerated for at least 8 hours or up to 18 hours before using. The cooked waffles can be cooled, stacked, and frozen in ziplock plastic freezer bags for up to 1 month. To reheat, place the frozen waffles on the oven racks (don't use a sheet pan) of a pre-heated 350°F oven until warmed through and crisp, 5 to 7 minutes.

The chicken is best when served within 2 hours of cooking. Fry the chicken first and keep it warm on one rack of the oven, then make the waffles and keep them warm on the second rack. For a big batch, serve the chicken at room temperature and use the oven to hold the waffles. Of course, if you have a double oven, you are home free.

One to two large bowls for brining the chicken; two large Dutch ovens for frying the chicken; two waffle irons to cook the waffles; half sheet pans and large cooling racks for the chicken and the waffles.

BIG BATCH NOTES

The theme of this meal is "divide and conquer," which means everything will go much more easily with two Dutch ovens for frying the chicken and two waffle irons, so borrow the extra equipment if necessary.

You may even want to have a third Dutch oven and extra oil handy if the frying oil gets too dark, which sometimes happens when you are cooking a lot of chicken.

SERVING

Tanya serves mimosas, coffee, and orange juice with her chicken and waffles. This is a filling meal on its own and doesn't need side dishes. You can put out butter along with the maple syrup for the waffles, and a favorite hot-pepper sauce for the chicken. A salad of fresh fruit is the perfect finish.

INGREDIENTS	SINGLE BATCH	DOUBLE BATCH
Chicken and Brine		
Dried tarragon	2 Tbsp	¼ cup
Sweet paprika	2 Tbsp	¼ cup
Onion powder	2 Tbsp	¼ cup
Garlic powder	4 tsp	8 tsp
Kosher salt	4 tsp	8 tsp
Dried oregano	2 tsp	4 tsp
Dried thyme	2 tsp	4 tsp
Cayenne pepper	2 tsp	4 tsp
Freshly ground black pepper	1 tsp	2 tsp
Chickens, each 3½ lb and cut into 8 pieces	2	4
Finely chopped fresh flat-leaf parsley	¼ cup	½ cup
Buttermilk	2 cups	4 cups
Cornmeal Waffles		
Warm water (about 105°F)	¾ cup	1½ cups
¼-oz envelopes active dry yeast	1	2
Large eggs	3	6
Whole milk	3 cups	6 cups
All-purpose flour	2 cups	4 cups
Cornmeal (medium-grind)	1 cup	2 cups
Kosher salt	1½ tsp	1 Tbsp
Sugar	1½ tsp	1 Tbsp
Unsalted butter, melted and cooled slightly	¾ cup	1½ cups
Baking soda	½ tsp	1 tsp
For Frying		
All-purpose flour	3 cups	6 cups
Freshly ground black pepper	½ tsp	1 tsp
Kosher salt	2 tsp	1 Tbsp
Vegetable oil, for deep-frying		
For Serving		
Maple syrup, warmed	1½ cups	3 cups

Brine the chicken: In a small bowl, stir together the tarragon, paprika, onion powder, garlic powder, salt, oregano, thyme, cayenne pepper, and black pepper.

Place the chicken in a large bowl if making a single batch or divide between two large bowls if making a double batch. Sprinkle the spice mixture and parsley evenly over the chicken and toss to coat. Pour the buttermilk over the chicken, turn the chicken as needed to coat evenly, cover, and refrigerate overnight.

Make the waffle batter: Pour the water into a small bowl, sprinkle with the yeast, and stir to dissolve the yeast. Let stand until foamy, about 10 minutes.

Meanwhile, whisk together the eggs and milk in a large bowl. When the yeast mixture is ready, add to the egg mixture and stir to combine.

Sift together the flour, cornmeal, salt, and sugar into a bowl. Whisk the dry ingredients into the egg-milk mixture, followed by the butter. Cover the bowl with plastic wrap and refrigerate overnight.

Fry the chicken: In a large bowl, stir together the flour, black pepper, and salt. Remove the chicken pieces from the buttermilk mixture, letting the excess liquid drip off. Dredge the chicken pieces in the seasoned flour.

Set a wire cooling rack over a half sheet pan (or use two pans with racks if making a double batch). Position oven racks in the center and top third of the oven and preheat the oven to 250°F.

Pour the oil to a depth of 3 inches into two large, deep Dutch ovens and heat over medium-high heat to 350°F on a deep-frying thermometer. Carefully add as many chicken pieces as possible to the oil without crowding the pan. Cook the chicken, turning occasionally and adjusting the heat as needed to maintain the oil temperature, until the chicken is cooked through and an instant-read thermometer inserted near (but not touching) the bone registers 165°F, 14 to 18 minutes. Using tongs, transfer the chicken to the cooling rack to drain. Keep the chicken warm in the oven while you fry the remaining chicken.

Cook the waffles: Stir the baking soda into the waffle batter. Set a wire cooling rack over a half sheet pan (or use two pans with racks if making a double batch). Preheat the waffle iron according to the manufacturer's directions and brush lightly with vegetable oil. Following the manufacturer's directions for amount (usually a generous ¾ cup), pour the batter into the waffle iron, close the lid, and cook until golden and cooked through, 3 to 6 minutes, depending on the iron. As the waffles are ready, transfer them to the cooling rack (do not stack them or they will get soggy) and keep them warm in the oven while you cook the remaining waffles.

Serve the waffles and fried chicken, accompanied with warm maple syrup.

RICK RODGERS

root beer barbecued spareribs

COOKBOOK AUTHOR AND cooking teacher Rick Rodgers's immediate family isn't too large (he has two brothers, also excellent cooks), but his extended family is very big. His great-grandmother had nine children, and his maternal grandmother had seven, so, many relatives show up for the family reunions that occur on an irregular basis. "We often use my mom's birthday as a reason for us all to get together—last year it was thirty-five hungry people. Spareribs are the favorite main course. My method grew out of a necessity to serve everyone." Rick says that he prefers big, meaty spareribs to baby backs because he can get more servings from the spareribs. He also recommends having many filling side dishes as a way to keep everyone's plate filled and to cut down on the work required by the person attending the grill.

A Rodgers family backyard party is usually a potluck affair. "We don't stray too much from the standard fare because these recipes have become icons and represent our family history. My brother Doug makes Caesar salad, my brother Greg makes the beans, my sister-in-law Linda brings a Mexican dip, and one of my cousins can be relied on to provide our family's famous recipe for potato salad. Two things are always served: garlic bread and chips with back-of-the-box onion dip. Retro? Yep. But it isn't a party at Mom's house without them."

A great-quality artisanal root beer makes the best-tasting sauce, so don't settle for less.

Single Batch
Makes 6 to 8 servings

Double Batch
Makes 12 to 16 servings

MAKE AHEAD

The sauce can be refrigerated for up to 3 weeks. The rub can be stored at room temperature for up to 3 weeks. The ribs can be rubbed, wrapped, and refrigerated for up to 1 day. The ribs can be cooked, cooled, stacked, wrapped in fresh aluminum foil, and refrigerated for up to 8 hours before browning. Brown and sauce the ribs just before serving.

INGREDIENTS	SINGLE BATCH	DOUBLE BATCH
Barbecue Sauce		
Unsalted butter	2 Tbsp	4 Tbsp
Yellow onion(s), finely chopped	1	2
Peeled and finely chopped fresh ginger	1 Tbsp	2 Tbsp
Garlic clove(s), finely chopped	1	2
12-oz bottle(s) root beer (not diet)	1	2

continued on following page

One or two charcoal or gas grills; heavy-duty aluminum foil, preferably extra wide; extra-long kitchen tongs; ice chest for keeping the sauced ribs warm (optional).

BIG BATCH NOTES

An average (22-inch) charcoal grill will accommodate no more that 6 or 7 pounds of ribs. Keep the first batch of browned and glazed ribs hot in a cooler (without ice) while you finish the second batch.

SERVING

Follow the Rodgers family lead and offer the best picnic food, such as chips and dip and coleslaw, macaroni salad, potato salad, or maybe a broccoli salad. A recipe for the family's favorite baked beans is on the facing page. For dessert, you can't go wrong with the brownies on page 277, perhaps à la mode with a warm chocolate sauce (see page 277). Ribs are a sticky finger food, so pass around plenty of napkins—and maybe water bowls, too—before dessert so everyone can clean up.

INGREDIENTS	SINGLE BATCH	DOUBLE BATCH
Ketchup	1 cup	2 cups
Cider vinegar	⅓ cup	⅔ cup
Molasses (not blackstrap)	⅓ cup	⅔ cup
Worcestershire sauce	2 Tbsp	¼ cup
Sriracha or other hot sauce	1 tsp	2 tsp
Rub		
Smoked sweet paprika	1 Tbsp	2 Tbsp
Kosher salt	1 Tbsp	2 Tbsp
Garlic powder	1½ tsp	1 Tbsp
Onion powder	1½ tsp	1 Tbsp
Freshly ground black pepper	1½ tsp	1 Tbsp
Cayenne pepper	½ tsp	1 tsp
Pork spareribs (in 4 slabs for a single batch, 8 slabs for a double batch)	6 lb	12 lb
Pecan, apple, or cherry wood chips	1 cup	2 cups

Make the sauce: In a heavy saucepan, melt the butter over medium heat. Add the onion(s) and cook, stirring occasionally, until lightly browned, about 5 minutes. Add the ginger and garlic and cook until fragrant, about 1 minute. Stir in half of the root beer, increase the heat to high, bring to a boil, and boil until the root beer is reduced to a thick syrup, 10 to 15 minutes. Reduce the heat to medium-low and stir in the remaining root beer, the ketchup, vinegar, molasses, Worcestershire sauce, and Sriracha and bring to a simmer. Simmer, stirring often, until the sauce is thickened and slightly reduced, 20 to 30 minutes. Remove from the heat and let cool.

Make the rub: In a small bowl, whisk together the paprika, salt, garlic powder, onion powder, black pepper, and cayenne pepper, mixing well.

Prepare the ribs: Remove the membrane from the bony side of each rib slab. To do this, slip a small, sharp knife under the membrane at one corner on the bone side of the ribs to loosen an inch or so of the membrane. Using a paper towel for traction, pull the membrane away from the ribs. This may take a couple of tries to remove most of the membrane. Trim off any extraneous surface fat, as well.

Season the ribs all over with the rub. Wrap each slab in heavy-duty aluminum foil, creating a package. Wrap the package again, with a flat side of the foil covering the first folded seam, which will help keep the juices trapped in the foil as you cook and flip the ribs.

Grill the ribs: Prepare a charcoal or gas grill for direct cooking over medium-high heat. If using a charcoal grill, let a chimney filled with about 6 pounds charcoal briquettes burn until it is just covered with white ash. Pour the coals out onto the grate and spread them in an even layer. Let the coals burn down for 5 to 10 minutes. If using a gas grill, preheat the grill with all burners on. Turn half of the burners off and adjust the heat to medium-high (400°F to 450°F).

If making a double batch, cook the ribs in two batches. Place the rib packets, seam side up, on the grill. Cover the grill and cook until the meat has shrunk and exposed about ½ inch from the rib bone ends (open a packet to look), about 1¼ hours. (For a charcoal grill, after 45 minutes, add about twelve briquettes to the coals to help maintain the temperature.) During cooking, carefully turn the packets two or three times with long tongs, taking care not to pierce the foil and release the juices (which would cause flare-ups).

Remove the packets from the grill and let them cool for about 30 minutes. Unwrap the ribs, discarding the fat and juices. Let the ribs cool for another 30 minutes until tepid.

Prepare the grill again for direct cooking over medium-high heat to brown and sauce the ribs. For a charcoal grill, spread the ashed-over coals in an even layer and let them burn for about 20 minutes so they aren't too hot. Sprinkle the wood chips over the coals. (If making a double batch and grilling in two batches, you will need 1 cup chips for each batch.) For a gas grill, preheat the grill on high, then adjust the heat to medium-high (400°F to 450°F). Wrap the chips in an aluminum foil packet and tear open the top of the packet. (If making a double batch and grilling in two batches, you will need to wrap each cup of chips in a separate foil packet.) Place the packet directly on the ignited heat source and heat until the chips are smoking. (If you have a smoker box, omit the foil packet and put the chips in the box.)

Place the now-tepid unwrapped ribs on the grill. Cover the grill and cook, turning the ribs occasionally, until browned on both sides, about 10 minutes. Continue grilling, occasionally brushing with the sauce and keeping the lid closed, until the ribs are glazed, about 10 minutes more.

Transfer the ribs to a cutting board and let stand for 3 to 5 minutes. Cut between the bones and serve the ribs with any remaining sauce.

BACON AND BOURBON BEANS

Makes 8 to 12 servings

You can make the beans a day in advance, then cool, cover, and refrigerate them. To reheat, stir in 1 cup hot water, cover, and place in a preheated 350°F oven. Bake, stirring occasionally, for about 30 minutes, then uncover and bake for 10 to 15 minutes to glaze the top.

6 bacon slices, cut into 1-inch pieces
1 large sweet onion, such as Vidalia or Maui, chopped
1 jalapeño chile, seeded and finely chopped
2 garlic cloves, chopped
1 (15-oz) can pinto beans, drained and rinsed
1 (15-oz) can small white beans, drained and rinsed
1 (15-oz) can black beans, drained and rinsed,
1 (15-oz) can kidney beans, drained and rinsed
1 cup barbecue sauce, homemade (page 169) or store-bought
½ cup ketchup
½ cup bourbon

Preheat the oven to 350°F.

In a Dutch oven or flameproof casserole, cook the bacon over medium-high heat, turning occasionally, until crisp, about 5 minutes. Transfer the bacon to paper towels to drain and cool, leaving the fat in the pot. Crumble the bacon.

Add the onion, jalapeño, and garlic to the pot and cook over medium heat, stirring occasionally, until the onion is golden, about 5 minutes. Stir in the pinto, white, black, and kidney beans, followed by the barbecue sauce, ketchup, bourbon, and crumbled bacon. Bring to a boil.

Cover and bake for 30 minutes. Uncover, stir, and continue baking until the cooking liquid has thickened, about 15 minutes. Serve the beans directly from the pot.

JOE CARROLL

santa maria-style tri-tip

MAKE AHEAD

This dish is very simple, so the only thing you might do ahead of time is make the salt, pepper, and garlic rub and soak the wood chips.

EQUIPMENT

Charcoal or gas grill.

BIG BATCH NOTES

You should be able to fit three roasts on the average (22-inch) charcoal grill or four roasts on a standard gas grill. When serving, if possible, have a couple of cutting boards (the ones with wells are best to catch the juices) and sharp carving knives and enlist someone in the group to second you as a carver.

SERVING

Salsa (page 147) and tortilla chips are an easy appetizer, and Central Coast red wine goes well with the tri-tip and beans (see facing page).

TRI-TIP IS THE star of Santa Maria barbecue, a tradition of wood-fired grilling that got its start at the big cattle ranches of the Central Coast of California, between San Luis Obispo and Santa Barbara. To feed the hungry, hardworking *vaqueros* (cowboys) after a successful roundup, slabs of beef were grilled over aromatic hardwood fires of the native coast live oak and served alongside pots of *pinquitos* (the local pink beans), tortillas, and fresh salsa.

Today, restaurants specializing in hefty portions of dry-rubbed beef grilled over crackling wood fires line the streets of Santa Maria, a lively agricultural town. The local Elks Lodge hosts hundreds of people for its frequent community dinners, where the head grillers, some well into their seventies and eighties, wear shirts emblazoned with "Santa Maria Elks Bar-B-Que Team."

Joe Carroll, author of *Feeding the Fire*, a primer on barbecue, and the owner of restaurants Spuyten Duyvil, Fette Sau, and St Anselm in Brooklyn, fell in love with Santa Maria–style barbecue during a cross-country deep dive into lesser-known regional barbecue styles.

True to its name, the tri-tip is a triangular cut located between the flank and the round. Your butcher may know it as bottom sirloin tip, bottom sirloin butt, or Newport steak. Because it is a lean cut, it is best cooked on the rare side.

INGREDIENTS	SINGLE BATCH	DOUBLE BATCH
Kosher salt	2 Tbsp	¼ cup
Freshly ground black pepper	1 tsp	2 tsp
Garlic powder	1 tsp	2 tsp
Tri-tip roasts, each about 2 lb	2	4
Oak chips	1 cup	2 cups

In a small bowl, combine the salt, pepper, and garlic powder and mix well. Generously season the beef all over with the salt mixture and let stand at room temperature for 1 hour. Soak the oak chips in water for at least 30 minutes.

Prepare a charcoal or gas grill for direct cooking over high heat. If using a charcoal grill, let the coals burn in 1 chimney for a single batch and 3 chimneys for a double batch until covered with white ash, dump them onto the grate, and then rake two-thirds of them to one side and leave the remainder on the other side, to create one hot zone and one cooler zone. If using a gas grill, turn one of the burners to medium-low to create two heat zones, one hot and one cooler. Drain the chips, wrap in an aluminum foil packet, and tear the top open.

Brush clean and lightly oil the grill grate. Place the beef over the hotter side of the grill and sear, turning once, until well charred on all sides, about 3 minutes per side.

If using a charcoal grill, put the wood chip packet on the coals on the cooler side of grill. If using a gas grill, place the packet under the grate on the medium-low burner. Continue grilling the meat over a low flame/low heat, turning it every 10 minutes or so, until it reaches the desired doneness. The timing will be 30 to 35 minutes for medium-rare; an instant-read thermometer inserted into the center of the roast should register 125°F. Listen to the meat to know if your grill is at the right temperature: you should be able to hear the meat gently sizzle. If cooking over gas, simply adjust the temperature as needed. If cooking over charcoal, adjust the temperature by moving the meat to different parts of the grill, or move some of the coals from the hot side of the grill to maintain an even, steady heat source beneath the meat.

When the meat is done, transfer it to a cutting board, tent loosely with aluminum foil, and let rest for 10 minutes. Cut the meat against the grain into ¼-inch-thick slices and transfer the slices to a platter. Pour any accumulated juices over the top and serve.

SANTA MARIA-STYLE BEANS

Makes 12 servings

This bean recipe from Rick Rodgers can be cooked up to 1 day in advance, cooled, covered, and refrigerated. To reheat, stir in ½ cup water and place over low heat, stirring gently, until heated through, about 10 minutes.

2 Tbsp olive oil
½ cup diced cured smoked linguica or Spanish chorizo, in ¼-inch pieces
1 yellow onion, chopped
2 garlic cloves, minced
2 Tbsp unbleached all-purpose flour
1 Tbsp chili powder
½ tsp ground cumin
1¼ cups chicken stock or water
1 (8-oz) can tomato sauce
4 (15-oz) cans pink beans, drained and rinsed
Kosher salt

In a large saucepan or a Dutch oven, heat together the oil and linguica over medium heat and cook, stirring occasionally, until the linguica is lightly browned, about 3 minutes. Add the onion and cook, stirring occasionally, until softened, about 3 minutes. Stir in the garlic and cook until fragrant, about 1 minute. Sprinkle with the flour, chili powder, and cumin and stir well. Stir in the stock and tomato sauce, increase the heat to high, and bring to a boil. Reduce the heat to medium-low and simmer, stirring often, until no raw flour taste remains, about 5 minutes.

Stir in the beans and season to taste with salt. Return to a simmer and cook, stirring often, until the sauce has thickened and reduced by about one-fourth, 15 to 20 minutes. Taste and adjust the seasoning with salt, then serve.

JAMES SYHABOUT

thai curry chicken wings

phat garlee peek gai

Single Batch
Makes 8 to 10 servings

Double Batch
Makes 16 to 20 servings

MAKE AHEAD

The curry can be made up to
2 days in advance and refrigerated.
Reheat gently over medium-low
heat until hot.

WHEN JAMES SYHABOUT was two years old, his family left their native northeast Thailand and settled in Oakland, California. From the time he was ten, James helped out in the kitchen of his mother's Thai restaurant. He went to the California Culinary Academy straight out of high school, then worked at Michelin-starred Manresa restaurant in Los Gatos, California, before opening his first restaurant, Commis, a destination spot in Oakland. But when his mother, Udon, wanted to retire, James took over the lease on her Thai restaurant. Returning to his roots with the opening of Hawker Fare, he began serving the Isan Thai and Laotian food he had grown up eating, which also became the subject of his first cookbook.

At home, James likes to pound his lemongrass and shallots the way his mother taught him, in a jumbo-size mortar. However, a food processor does the job just as well. A few pantry staples—oyster sauce, fish sauce, and yellow curry powder—add big flavor to Syhabout's version of this easy home-style curry, known as *phat garlee peek gai*. Made with chicken wings and served over fragrant jasmine rice, it's an easy, inexpensive meal to share with friends.

INGREDIENTS	SINGLE BATCH	DOUBLE BATCH
Curry Paste		
Lemongrass	1 stalk	2 stalks
Chopped shallots	1 cup	2 cups
Garlic cloves	6	12
Yellow curry powder (see *Ingredient Notes*)	3 Tbsp	6 Tbsp
Kosher salt	1 Tbsp	2 Tbsp

INGREDIENTS	SINGLE BATCH	DOUBLE BATCH
Curry		
Canola oil	1 cup	2 cups
Dried árbol chiles	½ cup	1 cup
Chicken wings, tips chopped off at the joint (see *Ingredient Notes*)	5 lb	10 lb
Oyster sauce	½ cup	1 cup
Asian fish sauce	¼ cup	½ cup
Water	1 cup	2 cups
Kosher salt		
Green onions, cut into 2-inch lengths	8	16
Cilantro, roughly chopped, including stems	1 bunch	2 bunches
Classic Steamed Rice (page 76), made with jasmine rice	10 cups	20 cups

Make the curry paste: Trim off and discard the grassy top from each lemongrass stalk, leaving the pale, plump bottom part, then trim off the root end. Peel off and discard the woody outer layers and slice the remainder crosswise into thin rounds. Transfer to a food processor, add the shallots, garlic, curry powder, and salt, and pulse until a coarse paste forms.

Make the curry: Pour the oil into a large Dutch oven and add the curry paste and chiles. (If using two pots for a double batch, divide the oil, curry paste, chiles, and the remaining ingredients between them.) Turn the heat to medium and fry, stirring often, until the mixture is very fragrant, about 5 minutes. (Starting with a cold pan and cold oil helps keep the garlic in the paste from burning.)

Add the chicken wings, oyster sauce, and fish sauce and mix to coat the wings. Add the water and increase the heat to high, stirring constantly. Cook until the oil starts to separate from the rest of the sauce and the wings are tender, about 15 minutes.

Remove from the heat and season to taste with salt. Transfer to one or more serving platters and top with the green onions and cilantro. Serve serve hot with the rice.

EQUIPMENT

One or two large Dutch ovens.

BIG BATCH NOTES

Save yourself some time and ask your butcher to trim the wing tips from the chicken wings.

SERVING

Serve the curry and rice with a simple salad of sliced cucumbers and red onion tossed with a dressing of lime juice, fish sauce, oil, garlic, and a little sugar. Don't forget to put out bowls for the bones and plenty of napkins.

INGREDIENT NOTES

Look for yellow curry powder at specialty Asian food markets.

Be sure to use fresh, not frozen, chicken wings for this dish for the best flavor. Each wing is made up of three parts (in order from the body): the drumette, the flat, and finally the tip, which is mostly cartilage and skin. Arm yourself with a heavy knife or cleaver to chop off the boney wing tip from each wing.

6.
seafood boils, bakes, and roasts

THE MOST MEMORABLE seafood meals are often the least fussy: platters of cracked crab served with melted butter, a seafood boil on newspaper-covered picnic tables, whole roasted salmon, or ladles of grilled clams alongside country-style bread.

Fresh fish feasts are most often linked to place and local catch. Along the West Coast, the opening of Dungeness crab season in the fall launches weeks of community crab boils. On the sandy shores of New England, summertime means clambakes, as families and friends get together year after year for beachside feasts of clams, lobsters, corn, and potatoes. In New Orleans, Gulf shrimp are simmered with blue crabs and smoky andouille sausage in liquid spiked with plenty of cayenne and hot sauce. There are fish fries in the Midwest, lobster festivals in Maine, and blue crab days in Maryland. Typically hosted outdoors, these big-batch traditions readily lend themselves to all-day feeds, fund-raisers, and family reunions.

TROY MACLARTY

bollywood theater spicy shrimp curry

Single Batch
Makes 8 to 10 servings

Double Batch
Makes 16 to 20 servings

MAKE AHEAD

The sauce, without the shrimp, can be refrigerated for up to 2 days or frozen for up to 2 months; if frozen, thaw in the refrigerator for about 24 hours. Reheat the sauce in a large skillet or Dutch oven over medium heat, stirring often, until simmering. Add the shrimp and proceed as directed. The parboiled rice can be kept at room temperature, in its baking dish and tightly covered with aluminum foil, for up to 1 hour.

EQUIPMENT

Large (12- to 14-inch) skillet for making the sauce; a large Dutch oven if making a double batch.

BIG BATCH NOTES

When making a double batch, it is essential that you stir the shrimp slowly over medium heat to ensure all of them cook through. For ease of preparation the day of serving, prepare the curry sauce in advance.

TROY MACLARTY DIDN'T always want to be a chef. With a degree in biology, he initially became intrigued with the science of food, but soon began experimenting with cooking. Although he got his kitchen training at Chez Panisse, in Berkeley, California, he fell in love with the heady spices and complex cuisines of India while traveling there. Returning to Portland, Oregon, he opened Bollywood Theater, a colorful, lively restaurant whose décor is an homage to Indian cinema and whose menu features Troy's own contemporary West Coast interpretation of Indian street foods.

Coconut milk adds a creamy, tropical note to this well-balanced, fragrant, tangy shrimp curry, a favorite among Bollywood Theater customers. You can prepare much of it up to a couple of days in advance, and then finish it with a few quick steps before serving. Troy serves the curry with Saffron Rice (see facing page), though plain steamed basmati rice (page 76) is fine, too.

INGREDIENTS	SINGLE BATCH	DOUBLE BATCH
Vegetable oil	½ cup	¾ cup
Thinly sliced large yellow onions	4 cups	8 cups
Packed fresh curry leaves (see *Ingredient Notes*)	½ cup	1 cup
Black mustard seeds (see *Ingredient Notes*)	1 Tbsp	2 Tbsp
Thinly sliced serrano chiles	¼ cup	½ cup
Finely chopped garlic	2 Tbsp	¼ cup
Peeled and finely chopped fresh ginger	2 Tbsp	4 Tbsp
Green cardamom pods, cracked to expose seeds (see *Ingredient Notes*)	6	12
Cinnamon sticks, about 2 inches	2	4
Whole cloves	4	8
Ground turmeric	2 tsp	4 tsp
Canned crushed tomatoes	1⅓ cups	2⅔ cups
Peeled, seeded, and pureed fresh plum tomatoes	2 cups	4 cups

INGREDIENTS	SINGLE BATCH	DOUBLE BATCH
Water	3 cups	6 cups
Coconut milk	1⅓ cups	2⅔ cups
Kosher salt		
Fresh lime juice, or to taste	2 Tbsp	¼ cup
Extra jumbo shrimp (16/20 count), peeled and deveined	2½ lb	5 lb
Saffron Rice (see right)	1 recipe	2 recipes

In a large skillet, heat the oil over medium heat. Add the onions and cook, stirring often, until they turn a nutty brown, about 15 minutes. Remove the onions from the pan with a slotted spoon and set aside. (If making a double batch, switch to a large Dutch oven at this point, adding any oil remaining in the skillet to the pot.) Reduce the heat to low, add the curry leaves and black mustard seeds, and heat, stirring frequently, until the seeds pop and the leaves are crunchy, about 2 minutes. Add the serranos and cook, stirring occasionally, until they start to soften, about 2 minutes. Add the garlic, ginger, cardamom pods, cinnamon sticks, and cloves and cook, stirring and taking care the spices do not burn, until aromatic, about 1 minute. Add the turmeric and cook, stirring, for about 1 minute.

Return the onions to the skillet and stir in the canned and pureed fresh tomatoes. Cook at a brisk simmer over medium heat until the tomatoes have thickened and reduced and the oil starts to separate, 25 to 30 minutes. Add the water and coconut milk, stir well, and season to taste with salt and lime juice.

Lightly season the shrimp with salt. Add the shrimp to the sauce, return to a simmer, and cook over medium heat, stirring occasionally, until just cooked through, about 5 minutes. Serve immediately with rice.

SERVING

Serve the shrimp with Saffron Rice (below) and something fresh and green to balance the richness of the dish. Sliced cucumbers, tomatoes, or any green salad will go well. Troy likes to serve a salad with watercress and shallots lightly dressed with salt and lime juice.

INGREDIENT NOTES

Curry leaves, black mustard seeds, and green cardamom pods can all be found at Indian markets. Look for the leaves in the refrigerated produce section or the frozen food section.

SAFFRON RICE

Makes 8 to 10 servings

This delicately flavored, golden rice dish scales easily for a crowd and pairs well with many dishes, such as the lamb shanks on page 140.

¼ cup whole milk
2 tsp unsalted butter
1 tsp saffron threads
2 cups basmati rice

Preheat the oven to 350°F. Butter a 9-by-13-inch or 6 cup–capacity ovenproof baking dish.

In a small saucepan, combine the milk, butter, and saffron and bring to a simmer over medium heat. Remove from the heat and let stand while you parboil and bake the rice.

Bring a large pot of generously salted water to a boil over high heat. Keep in mind that the rice will almost triple in volume, so be sure to have a large enough pot. Add the rice and boil until the rice is 80 percent cooked, about 6½ minutes; the rice should still be a bit crunchy in the center. Do not overcook. Drain the rice, transfer to the prepared dish, and cover tightly with aluminum foil.

Bake until the rice is tender, about 20 minutes. Remove from the oven, uncover, and drizzle evenly with the milk mixture. Re-cover with the foil and let stand for 10 minutes. Fluff with a fork and serve immediately.

MARIA FINN AND JOHN INGLE

dolphin club dungeness crab feed

Single Batch **Makes 10 servings**

Double Batch **Makes 20 servings**

MAKE AHEAD

The butters can be made up to 2 days in advance and refrigerated; melt over low heat just before serving. The crabs can be cooked the morning of the party and served chilled instead of warm. For this option, let the crab cool completely and then clean them. Put the crab into 2-gallon (jumbo) ziplock plastic bags and refrigerate or keep cold on ice in ice chests. (If you use the ice chests, be sure the bags are tightly closed so no water seeps in.) The lemons can be cut early in the day and refrigerated, too.

EQUIPMENT

One or more large stockpot(s) for cooking the crabs; long tongs for getting the crabs into and out of the pot(s); huge bowls to hold the cooked crabs; large knife or cleaver for chopping the crabs; large platters for serving; crab cracker sets.

THE WATERS OF the San Francisco Bay are notoriously rough and cold, but inside the Aquatic Park headquarters of the Dolphin Club, the mood is warm, friendly, and welcoming. Founded in 1877, this urban swimming and rowing club now has over a thousand members, brought together by their dedication to life on—and in—these unique waters at the edge of the Pacific Ocean.

Every Tuesday night, members gather to maintain, restore, and even build the club's collection of traditional Whitehall rowing boats. No members are allowed to take out a boat until they've done their fix-it time in the repair shop. It's a rite of passage that teaches each new member to respect the special vessels. As they sand, paint, and varnish, new members meet old ones and friendships are formed.

Dinner is served only after the work is done, so no slacking is allowed. Starting in late autumn, the savory steam of locally caught Dungeness crabs boiling in big pots fills the air as everyone gets together for a family-style crab feed in the boathouse.

Crab feeds are a mainstay of the West Coast, where the season for Dungeness crabs happily coincides with the start of the winter holidays. Communities come together to catch up, digging into heaps of steamed crabs. Three butter sauces are offered here and John also recommends serving the crab with aioli (see page 191). Crusty sourdough bread is a must at every crab feed.

INGREDIENTS	SINGLE BATCH	DOUBLE BATCH
One or more butters (see facing page) or aioli (see page 191)		
Bay leaves	4	8
Live Dungeness crabs, about 2 lb each	10	20
Lemons, cut into wedges, for serving	5	10
Unsalted butter	1 cup	2 cups

Make one, two, or all three butters. The recipes are easily doubled or even tripled, so make enough to feed your crowd.

Cook the crabs: Bring one or more large stockpots filled with salted water to a rolling boil over high heat and add the bay leaves. Then, using tongs, add as many crabs as will fit in the pot(s) without crowding. Cover, return to a boil, and cook until the shells are bright red, 12 to 16 minutes (about 7 minutes per pound). Using the tongs, carefully transfer the crabs to one or more very large bowl(s). (If serving warm, tent with aluminum foil while you cook the remaining crabs.) Let the crabs cool until easy to handle.

To clean the crabs, work on a cutting board with a well, preferably near a sink so you can discard the juices easily. Turn each crab so its belly is facing up. Grab the pointed end of the apron (the triangular-shaped shell on the belly), lift up, and pull off the apron. Then, starting at the small hole visible between the body and the top shell (or *carapace*), hold the body with one hand and pull off the entire top shell with the other. (If you like, scrape off the yellow crab "butter" from the top shell and stir into the drawn butter to flavor it.) Pull off and discard the spongy, finger-like gills, snap off the mandibles (near the front of the crab), and remove any other inedible parts from the body. Rinse away any innard remnants under cool running water.

Using a heavy knife, split each crab body in half lengthwise, then pile the halves onto a platter. Serve with butters.

To make drawn butter: In a small saucepan, melt 1 cup unsalted butter over medium heat, then allow to come to a boil. Let the butter boil without browning for about 1 minute. Remove from the heat and let stand for 5 minutes. Skim off the foam from the top of the butter, then carefully pour the clear yellow liquid into a small bowl, leaving the milky white solids behind in the saucepan. (Alternatively, skim off the foam as directed, then pour the butter into a small bowl, let cool, cover, and refrigerate until solid, at least 8 hours. Lift off the disk of hardened butter, discard the milky solids in the bowl, and wipe away any solids on the butter with a paper towel.) Serve warm with the crab.

To make Sriracha-Garlic-Lime Butter: Make the drawn butter, rewarm, then remove from the heat. Stir in 2 tablespoons fresh lime juice, 2 tablespoons finely chopped fresh cilantro, 2 teaspoons Sriracha sauce, 2 teaspoons minced garlic, and ½ teaspoon kosher salt. Serve warm.

To make Miso-Shallot Butter: Make the drawn butter and rewarm over low heat. Add ½ cup minced shallots and cook, stirring occasionally, until softened, about 3 minutes. Stir in ¼ teaspoon red pepper flakes and cook for 30 seconds, then whisk in 2 tablespoons white (shiro) miso and 2 tablespoons mirin until smooth. Remove from the heat and serve warm.

Live crabs take up a lot of space in the refrigerator, so don't even try to store them unless you have access to a walk-in refrigerator. The best plan is to order the crabs in advance and pick them up from the fishmonger a few hours before serving. Transport them on ice in ice chests, but be sure to leave the lid ajar or they will suffocate. Live crabs are feisty, so watch your fingers! Long tongs help when handling the crustaceans.

Your stove may have only one burner big enough to heat a stockpot in a reasonable amount of time and keep it boiling after the crabs are added. That's fine, but you can also use a high-powered electric hot plate. If the weather cooperates, you can cook the crabs outside on a propane stove (the kind used for frying turkey or for community fish fries). If you have only one big stockpot, you can boil the crabs in batches.

Recruit extra helpers for cleaning the crabs. It is a messy job (the crab juices squirt and run all over), so provide the team with aprons.

SERVING

Along with crusty bread and a big green salad, John will use the hot crab water to boil up a big batch of spaghetti served with a sauce of sautéed shallots, butter, wine, and the crab mustard. You might also serve steamed asparagus or artichokes, which pair well with any extra drawn butter. Be sure to line your table with big bowls for the spent shells and to outfit your guests with crab crackers and picks (nutcrackers will work too) and plenty of napkins.

RYAN PREWITT

louisiana shrimp and crab boil

SEAFOOD BOILS ARE a much-loved staple of community life in the South. Poured onto long tables covered with newspapers, a seafood boil is a wonderfully casual (often raucous) celebratory gathering. Boils are found throughout the coastal South, with regional variations depending on local ingredients and traditions. In Louisiana, blue crabs, Gulf shrimp, corn, potatoes, and links of andouille sausage are boiled in liquid generously spiked with cayenne and Louisiana hot sauce. Churches and community organizations often sponsor seafood boils for fund-raisers, and they are great for weekend get-togethers and summer holidays.

Ryan Prewitt, chef and partner of Pêche Seafood Grill in New Orleans, grew up in Memphis, where seafood boils are a rare event. It took moving to the Big Easy and working for chef Donald Link to gain a true appreciation for boiled seafood. "The quality of the food is a big part of it," explains Ryan, "but the conviviality of a group of people standing around a table getting dirty with their food is just as important. My wife and I do small boils in our backyard, and it makes me happy to think that my children are going to grow up with this tradition."

A seafood boil requires serious heat—more BTUs than most home stoves can muster—to keep the cooking liquid at a boil, so it is best if you buy, borrow, or rent a propane burner (the kind used for deep-fried turkey and fish fries).

When Ryan hosts a seafood boil, he looks for the best domestically caught wild seafood he can find. Take his lead and look for fresh white, pink, or brown Gulf or Florida shrimp, rather than cheaper farmed imports. The pickled peppers on page 187 are optional, but Ryan highly recommends them, along with plenty of ice-cold beer.

Single Batch **Makes 8 to 10**

Double Batch **Makes 16 to 20**

MAKE AHEAD

The spice mix can be made up to 2 weeks in advance and stored in an airtight container at room temperature. The garlic-lemon butter can be refrigerated for up to 2 days or frozen for up to 2 weeks; soften at room temperature before using. The stock is best when freshly made, but it can be refrigerated for up to 1 day.

For a single batch, you will need: at least a 16-qt stockpot for cooking the stock and a second large stockpot or other large container for holding the strained stock; for a double batch, you will need four large stockpots. You'll also need a large wire skimmer, an ice chest, a stack of newspapers or roll of butcher paper for covering the table, and tools for cracking and eating the crabs (small wooden mallets, seafood forks, and shell crackers).

BIG BATCH NOTES

Although it is possible to cook this boil in a pot on the stove top, it is much easier to set up a high-power propane burner outdoors. If you are making a double batch, divide it between two large pots and cook over two burners. If the stock in the stockpot seems too heavy to handle safely, put a second stockpot near the stove, fit a large colander into the top, and use a large ladle to transfer the stock to the colander.

SERVING

This boil is a complete meal. Ryan advises serving it with lots of cold beer and plenty of napkins. Be sure to set out big bowls for all of the debris, from shells to corncobs.

INGREDIENT NOTES

To save money, buy the hot sauce by the quart at a wholesale club.

Because the spices in this recipe are used in such large quantities, the price will quickly soar unless you purchase in bulk at a spice store, Indian grocer, or wholesale club.

INGREDIENTS	SINGLE BATCH	DOUBLE BATCH
Spice Mix		
Chili powder	3 Tbsp	6 Tbsp
Cayenne pepper	2 Tbsp	¼ cup
Sweet paprika	2 Tbsp	¼ cup
Kosher salt	2 Tbsp	¼ cup
Freshly ground black pepper	1 Tbsp	2 Tbsp
Garlic powder	1 Tbsp	2 Tbsp
Garlic-Lemon Butter		
Unsalted butter, at room temperature	1 cup	2 cups
Garlic cloves, minced	3	6
Lemon(s), zest only, finely grated	1	1½
Freshly ground black pepper	½ tsp	1 tsp
Stock		
Water	12 qt	24 qt
Dry white wine	2 qt	4 qt
Louisiana Hot Sauce (or Crystal hot sauce or Tabasco)	2 qt	4 qt
Heads of celery, roughly cut into ½-inch-thick slices	1	2
Yellow onions, coarsely chopped	3	6
Carrots, peeled and roughly cut into ¼-inch-thick slices	4	8
Cups unpeeled garlic cloves (about 3 heads and 6 heads, respectively)	2	4
Lemons, halved	8	16
Kosher salt	1 cup	2 cups
Black peppercorns	½	1 cup
Cayenne pepper	½ cup	1 cup
Bay leaves	8	16
Boil		
Ears corn, husked and halved	6	12
Small Yukon Gold or red potatoes (1½ to 2 inches in diameter)	3 lb	6 lb
Andouille or other smoked sausage, cut into 2-inch lengths	2 lb	4 lb
Heads garlic, unpeeled, tops trimmed	6	12
Live blue crabs	16	32
Jumbo shrimp (21/25 count), preferably heads on, unpeeled	5 lb	10 lb
Lemons, quartered	8	16
For serving		
Pickled Banana Peppers (see facing page), optional	1 recipe	1 recipe

Make the spice mix: In a bowl, whisk together the chili powder, cayenne pepper, paprika, salt, black pepper, and garlic powder. You should have about ¾ cup if making a single batch or 1½ cups if making a double batch.

Make the garlic-lemon butter: In a large bowl, combine the butter, garlic, lemon zest, and pepper and stir with a wooden spoon or rubber spatula until thoroughly mixed. (If you like, use a handheld mixer.) Cover and refrigerate, then bring to room temperature before using.

Make the stock: In a large stockpot, combine the water, wine, hot sauce, celery, onions, carrots, garlic, lemons, salt, peppercorns, cayenne pepper, and bay leaves. Cover, bring to a boil over high heat, then remove the cover, and let boil for 20 minutes to bring the flavors together.

Strain the stock through a large-mesh sieve placed over a second large pot or other large container. Discard the solids, then rinse the pot and return the stock to the pot.

Make the boil: Return the stock to a rolling boil over high heat. Add the corn, potatoes, sausage, and garlic, return to a boil, and boil for 4 minutes. Add the crabs and cook for 4 minutes more. (The water should come back to a strong simmer during this time.) Add the shrimp and cook until they just start to turn pink, about 2 minutes. Turn off the heat and let the whole mixture stand for 10 minutes. Meanwhile, cover your dining table with newspapers or butcher paper.

Using a handheld sieve, scoop the ingredients out of the cooking liquid into a large container, such as a cooler without ice or several large bowls. As you place each batch of ingredients in the container, sprinkle on some of the spice mix. Once all of the ingredients have been removed from the pot and sprinkled with spice mix, add the lemon quarters, dot the surface with the garlic butter, and mix gently so the butter melts.

Pour the boil out onto the paper-covered table and let everyone dig in. Serve immediately with the pickled peppers (if using).

PICKLED BANANA PEPPERS

Makes about 2 quarts

This is a great side dish to the Louisiana boil, but the tangy-sweet rings are also good on sandwiches and for nibbling.

1 lb hot banana peppers, cut into
   ¼-inch-wide rings
1 yellow onion, thinly sliced
2 cups cider vinegar
2 cups distilled white vinegar
¾ cup sugar
1 Tbsp kosher salt

In a heatproof, nonreactive bowl, combine the peppers and onion and toss to mix. In a nonreactive saucepan, combine the cider and white vinegars, sugar, and salt and bring to a rolling boil over high heat, stirring until the sugar dissolves. Immediately pour the hot liquid over the peppers and onion and let sit for at least a few hours or up to overnight before serving. The peppers will keep in an airtight container in the refrigerator for up to 1 month.

IHSAN AND VALERIE GURDAL
WITH STEVEN JOHNSON

grilled clambake

ONE OF THE best ways to gather around food is to forage together. Ihsan and Valerie Gurdal, owners of the Formaggio Kitchen, a wonderful gourmet shop with branches in Boston and Cambridge, Massachusetts, and New York City, host a big clamming event every year with friends and chefs Steve Johnson and Chris Schlesinger. With rakes and buckets in tow, the crew heads out to the beaches of Westport, Massachusetts, where they dig for dinner. Once their buckets are full with briny bivalves, they fire up a backyard grill and roast the clams over the fire until the shells pop open, then nestle the open clams in a savory sauce of tomatoes, onions, garlic, parsley, butter, wine, and, in a nod to Ihsan's Turkish heritage, Maras pepper flakes. The tradition started with just a few friends and has since grown into a yearly ritual.

When people talk about a traditional New England clambake, they usually mean an all-day affair next to a beachside fire pit. But this version can be made easily at home with much less work. Use whatever clams are best in your area. Cherrystones are much larger than littlenecks, for example, so you will want to use less of the former. If you don't have a grill, you can place the clams on sheet pans and bake them in the oven. As soon as the clams pop, use the tongs to pull them off the heat, taking care to reserve the juices, then toss the clams into the sauce. Ihsan and Steve often serve the clams with lightly grilled country bread for sopping up the sauce, or over pasta.

Single Batch
Makes 8 to 10 servings

Double Batch
Makes 16 to 20 servings

MAKE AHEAD

The tomato base can be made up to 3 days ahead and refrigerated. It can also be frozen in plastic bags and kept in the freezer for up to 2 months. Bring to a simmer before adding the clams.

INGREDIENTS	SINGLE BATCH	DOUBLE BATCH
Tomato Base		
Tomatoes, coarsely chopped	4 lb	8 lb
White onions, coarsely chopped	2	4
Large heads of garlic, clove separated, peeled, and thinly sliced	1	2
Dry white wine or beer (such as an IPA)	1 cup	2 cups

continued on following page

Charcoal or gas grill (or half sheet pans if using the oven). Two big pots for a double batch.

BIG BATCH NOTES

Depending on the size of your grill, you may want to prepare the tomato mixture on the stove top instead of cooking it on the grill. If you have a very large grill, you may be able to simmer the sauce and open the clams at the same time. For a double batch, consider borrowing a second grill, an additional pot, and some helping hands so you can have two grills going. If a bigger crowd is expected, it is easy to up the quantity of clams as they can be cooked in batches, but you may need to add more sauce. If you don't have a grill, you can arrange the clams in a single layer on half sheet pans and place them in a preheated 400°F oven until they open.

SERVING

Seafood forks are a nice touch for eating the clams, but any dinner forks will do. If you prefer to serve the clams and their sauce on pasta, the smaller batch is enough for 1½ pounds dried spaghetti or other thin pasta. Use a large stockpot to cook the pasta in salted water according to the package directions, then drain, reserving 1 cup of the cooking water. In a large bowl, toss together the pasta and clam and tomato mixture, adding the reserved pasta water as needed to thin to a good sauce consistency. Accompany the grilled bread or pasta version with a green salad.

INGREDIENT NOTES

Native to Turkey, Maras peppers are mild, fruity chiles typically sold in the form of dried flakes. They are a key flavor in Turkish cuisine (you'll find bowls of the flakes on restaurant tables in Istanbul) and are easy to find in well-stocked spice stores, specialty food markets, and online. Aleppo pepper flakes are a good substitute.

INGREDIENTS	SINGLE BATCH	DOUBLE BATCH
Flat-leaf parsley, leaves only, coarsely chopped	1 bunch	2 bunches
Unsalted butter, cut up	4 Tbsp	½ cup
Maras or Aleppo pepper flakes (see *Ingredient Notes*)	2 Tbsp	¼ cup
Kosher salt	1 Tbsp	2 Tbsp
Freshly ground black pepper	1 Tbsp	2 Tbsp
Clams in the shell, well scrubbed	60 to 80	120 to 160
Slices country-style bread, ½ inch thick	10	20
Extra-virgin olive oil, for drizzling		

Prepare a charcoal or gas grill for direct cooking over medium-high heat (450°F).

Make the tomato base: Combine the tomatoes, onions, garlic, wine, parsley, butter, Maras pepper, salt, and black pepper in a large pot, sauté pan, or flameproof roasting pan that can sit on the grill. Place the pan on the grill and cook, stirring occasionally, until the tomatoes begin to break down, about 10 minutes. For a charcoal grill, the coals will burn down naturally, or use long tongs to spread them out to disperse the heat. For a gas grill, reduce the heat to medium-low (about 350°F). Continue cooking until the sauce thickens, 10 to 15 minutes more. Taste and adjust the seasoning. Remove from the heat and cover with aluminum foil to keep warm.

Cook the clams and grill the bread: For a charcoal grill, add about two dozen more briquettes or the equivalent of charcoal chunks to the coals. Let them burn until covered with white ash (about 15 minutes), then use long tongs to spread them out. For a gas grill, return the heat to medium-high (450°F).

Working in batches, place the clams directly on the grill grate and let them cook until the shells pop open, about 5 minutes. With tongs, carefully transfer the clams to the pan with the tomatoes, taking care not to spill the clam juice. If desired, remove the top shell of each clam. Give the mixture a stir to coat the clams with the sauce.

Drizzle both sides of the bread slices with olive oil. Place directly on the grill grate and cook, turning once, until toasted on both sides and charred in spots, about 2 minutes total. Return the clam pan to the grill and cook, uncovered, just until the sauce begins to simmer. Do not overcook or the clams will toughen.

Serve the clams and sauce immediately with the grilled bread for sopping up the sauce.

GEORGEANNE BRENNAN

grand aioli with roasted salmon

GEORGEANNE BRENNAN, AUTHOR of *My Culinary Journey: The Food and Fêtes of Provence, La Vie Rustic, A Pig in Provence*, and many other books, has owned a house in rural Provence for many years. Every summer on August 15, the whole town hosts a *grand aioli*, a village fête that lasts for days and culminates with a feast and a *pétanque* (a form of French boules, similar to Italian bocce) tournament. This big meal centers around aioli, the famous garlic mayonnaise of Provence, which is both the name of the sauce and the party. Hundreds of people gather to share a meal of steamed potatoes, green beans, beets, hard-cooked eggs, and salt cod, cooked by the people of the town and served family-style with great bowls of aioli and plenty of local rosé.

Held in late summer when the weather is warm and the produce is at its peak, this communal feast is fun to make for a crowd because you can serve as many as your table is long, making a beautiful celebration of the pleasures of the outdoors.

Georgeanne brought this tradition with her to her home in California, where she often makes it with her daughter, Ethel, for family get-togethers. Although salt cod is traditional, this version features roasted whole sides of salmon, a nod to the nearby Pacific waters. The specific vegetables can be varied depending on what is in season. You might add cherry tomatoes, radishes, sugar snap peas, sliced raw fennel, or blanched cauliflower—all of them good with the garlicky mayonnaise.

Aioli calls for only a few ingredients and can "break" (the emulsion separates) if it isn't whipped properly. The key to getting it to set up is patience, and good arm strength. If your mayonnaise breaks, you may be adding the oil too quickly. Make sure to drip it into the egg yolks slowly in a thread-like stream—like a steady series of drips, and the slower the better. This might be a two-person job, with one whipping and one dripping.

Makes 8 to 10 servings; about 3 cups aioli

MAKE AHEAD

Georgeanne makes this simple meal the day of serving so everything retains its freshness. But the vegetables can be prepped a day in advance and then cooked the day of the party. The vegetables and salmon should be cooked no more than 1 hour in advance of serving. Cover them to keep them moist and bright looking. The aioli can be refrigerated for up to 4 hours.

BIG BATCH NOTES

Because of the water on the bottom shelf of the oven, you are restricted to baking one whole salmon fillet at a time. If you want to double your guest list, you will need a double oven or you will need to borrow a neighbor's oven. You cannot double the aioli recipe either, as it can be tricky to make and may not whip properly. If you decide you need twice as much, you will need to make two separate batches.

For a larger gathering, engage your guests to make multiple batches of aioli.

SERVING

A grand aioli is best when served on a long table with the food down the middle in multiple mismatched bowls and platters. Allow one bowl of aioli and a platter of vegetables for every four or five guests. French bread and glasses of rosé round out the meal.

INGREDIENTS

Aioli

Garlic cloves	6 to 8
Coarse sea salt	1 tsp
Extra-virgin olive oil or grapeseed oil, or a mixture (see *Ingredient Notes*)	3 cups
Large egg yolks, at room temperature	6
Freshly ground black pepper	½ tsp

Salmon

Extra-virgin olive oil, for brushing	
Skin-on whole salmon fillet, 3½ to 4 lb, pin bones removed	1
Kosher salt and freshly ground black pepper	

Vegetables

Small beets, red, gold, or a mixture	1½ to 2 lb (16 to 24 beets)
Small boiling potatoes, such as Yellow Finn, White Rose, or Yukon Gold	1½ to 2 lb (12 to 15 potatoes)
Small carrots, scrubbed or peeled (or use larger carrots, cut into 2-inch lengths), tops trimmed to ½ inch	1½ to 2 lb (16 to 24 carrots)
Green beans, trimmed	1½ lb
Hard-cooked large eggs, halved	8 to 10

Make the aioli: Using a mortar and pestle, pound the garlic and salt together to form a paste. (Alternatively, using a knife, chop the garlic, then finely mince the garlic together with the salt to a paste.)

Have the oil ready in a liquid measuring cup. In a large bowl, lightly beat the egg yolks. Set the bowl on a moistened dish towel to provide traction and to hold the bowl in place. Whisking constantly, begin drizzling in the oil, drop by drop at first, until the mixture begins to thicken and emulsify. Once the emulsion is stable, continuing to whisk constantly, increase the speed slightly, pouring the oil in a slow, steady, fine stream. When all of the oil has been added, gently stir in the garlic mixture. If the aioli is too thick, whisk in a tablespoon or two of warm water. Season with the pepper, then cover and refrigerate until serving, whisking again vigorously just before serving.

Cook the salmon: Position racks in the bottom third and center of the oven and pre-heat the oven to 200°F. Put a baking pan of warm water on the bottom rack. Brush a half sheet pan with oil.

Place the salmon, skin side down, on the pan. Brush the flesh with oil and season with salt and pepper. Bake until the fish feels slightly firm to the touch and the tip of a small, sharp knife easily flakes the flesh, 1 to 1½ hours, depending on the thickness of the fillet.

Remove the salmon from the oven and let cool slightly, then transfer to a platter.

Cook the vegetables while the salmon bakes: Cut off any leafy tops from the beets, leaving ½ inch of the stem intact.

Put the beets in a large saucepan, add salted water to cover by 2 inches, and bring to a boil over high heat. Reduce the heat to medium and simmer until tender when pierced a knife tip, about 50 minutes. Drain the beets, set aside to cool until they can be handled, then slip off the skins. (Remember that red beets will stain any food and some work surfaces they touch.) Cut the beets into wedges or halves and set aside.

Put the potatoes in a large saucepan, add salted water to cover generously, and bring to a boil over high heat. Reduce the heat to medium and simmer until the potatoes are tender when pierced with the tip of a knife, 15 to 20 minutes. Using a slotted spoon, transfer the potatoes to a colander and rinse under cold running water to stop the cooking. Cut the larger potatoes into halves or quarters.

Line a large plate or half sheet pan with paper towels. Add the carrots to the potato cooking water and bring to a boil over high heat. Reduce the heat to medium and simmer until the carrots are tender when pierced with a knife tip, 8 to 10 minutes. Using the slotted spoon, transfer the carrots to the towel-lined plate.

Fill a large bowl with ice and water and set near the stove and line a second large plate or sheet pan with paper towels. If the water level in the saucepan has dropped, add more water, then return the water to a boil over high heat. Add the green beans and cook until tender, about 5 minutes. Drain the green beans in the colander, then transfer to the ice bath and let stand until cold. Drain the beans and transfer to the towel-lined plate.

Arrange the beets, potatoes, carrots, green beans, and eggs on platters. Serve the salmon and vegetables with the aioli alongside.

baked whole rockfish

Single Batch **Makes 8 servings**

Double Batch **Makes 16 servings**

MAKE AHEAD

The fish can be salted and refrigerated for up to 8 hours before baking.

EQUIPMENT

One or two large, round ceramic or glass baking dishes or ovenproof skillets.

BIG BATCH NOTES

The rule of thumb for a whole fish is 1 pound per person. The larger the fish, the larger the baking vessels will need to be. You will be able to fit two fish in most vessels, arranging them in a yin-yang pattern as described.

SERVING

This fish is best served simply with some grilled bread rubbed with the flat side of a raw garlic clove, and a hearty vegetable side, such as roasted peppers with capers and balsamic, or a shredded carrot salad with a minty vinaigrette.

A BAKED WHOLE fish is a dramatic and easy way to feed a group, especially after a successful fishing expedition. Rockfish is a relatively inexpensive choice for fish lovers, though you can use any mild-flavored whole fish with medium to firm texture, such as sea bass or steelhead trout.

According to Russell Moore, chef-owner of Camino restaurant in Oakland, California, cooking fish on the bone is a great way to give yourself a little safety net if you happen to overcook the fish. The skin and bones keep the fish juicy, and there's more wiggle room for timing than with fillets. The long communal tables at Camino make it an ideal place for hosting big feasts. Over the years Russ and his wife, Allison Hopelain, the restaurant's general manager, have hosted many special dinners, especially on Monday nights when they have often featured kebabs and other fire-roasted dishes. Camino has also been the site of many cookbook celebration dinners, bringing together authors and chefs warmed by the huge wood-fired hearth and grill at the heart of the restaurant.

Although Russ typically cooks rockfish in the wood-fired grill at Camino, he's adjusted this recipe for the oven, an easier method for the home cook.

INGREDIENTS	SINGLE BATCH	DOUBLE BATCH
Whole rockfish, sea bass, or other mild, medium- to firm-textured white fish, 4 to 5 lb each, cleaned	2	4
Sea salt	6 Tbsp	¾ cup
Loosely packed soft fresh herb leaves, such as flat-leaf parsley, chervil, cilantro, tarragon, mint, or garlic chives, or a mixture, stems reserved	3 cups	4 to 5 cups
Extra-virgin olive oil, plus more for serving	½ to ⅔ cup	⅔ to ¾ cup
Lemons and/or limes, cut into wedges	3	6

Preheat the oven to 400°F. Rinse each fish inside and out and pat dry.

Using a very sharp knife, make four or five vertical slashes on both sides of each fish, spacing them about 1½ inches apart, and cutting almost to the bone. Season each fish

196

liberally inside and out with the salt, picking up the fish as needed to coat it evenly and making sure the salt gets into the cuts you have made. Refrigerate the fish while you complete the next step.

Place the herb stems in a saucepan and add water to cover barely. Bring to a simmer over high heat, then immediately remove from the heat and strain the liquid through a fine-mesh sieve into a bowl. Discard the stems. Roughly chop the herb leaves.

Rub the oil all over the salted fish, inside and out, reserving some for drizzling on the fish just before it goes into the oven. Sprinkle two-thirds of the herbs all over the fish, inside and out, again picking up the fish as needed to coat evenly and making sure the herbs get into the cuts you have made.

Place the fish in one or two ovenproof glass or ceramic dishes, preferably round. If you don't have baking dishes, one or two trusty ovenproof skillets (which have slightly sloped sides, rather than the straight sides of a sauté pan) will work great, too. You want to rest each fish on its belly, spreading the belly apart to keep the fish upright. Two fish will usually fit in a single vessel if arranged in a yin-yang pattern, though it is fine to put only one fish in each vessel.

Pour enough of the "herb tea" around the fish to come ¼ inch up the sides of the pan. Drizzle a bit more oil over the fish, then transfer to the oven.

The tricky part is to know when the fish are done. It depends on your oven, the density of the fish, and the temperature of the fish before they went into the oven. Peek at the fish after 8 to 10 minutes to see what's happening. You should also baste the fish at this time with the herby juices in the pan. Then continue to check the fish every 5 minutes until the flesh is just opaque. To test, use a small knife to pry away the flesh to see if it is cooked at the bone. It should pull away easily and flake readily.

If you think the fish are done, pull them from the oven and let stand for 4 to 5 minutes, then check the flesh at the bone again to see how it looks. If it is not opaque and flaky, return the fish to the oven for a few minutes and then check again.

You can serve the fish directly from the dish or pan or take them out and put them on platters. Sprinkle the remaining herbs over the fish and drizzle with more olive oil, if you like, then let your guests dig in. Spoon some of the delicious herby juices over each person's portion or serve them on the side. Accompany with the lemon wedges.

MARGO TRUE

herbed baked fish with pearl couscous

Single Batch
Makes 10 to 12 servings

Double Batch
Makes 12 to 24 servings

MAKE AHEAD

The tomato sauce can be made up to 2 days in advance and refrigerated until ready to use. The dish itself can also be made and refrigerated up to 2 days in advance.

EQUIPMENT

One or two roasting pans

SERVING

This is a satisfying one-pan meal on its own, but is also great with a loaf of crusty bread and a plate of seasoned vegetables or a green salad.

MARGO TRUE, WRITER and longtime food editor at *Sunset* magazine recommends this quick and simple dish to feed a crowd without fuss. It is ideally prepared in summer when ripe, juicy tomatoes are plentiful. You can use any small or short pasta you like, but pearl couscous (aka Israeli couscous) is Margo's favorite because "it looks like caviar and the slippery little beads are fun to eat." You can choose your favorite white fish too, but a flatter fillet, like Pacific flounder or rockfish (aka Pacific snapper), will cover the pasta more impressively than chunky blocks of halibut or lingcod, both of which are also pricier. This dish also tastes good served cold, making it ideal for preparing a day ahead. Serve on a warm summer evening.

INGREDIENTS	SINGLE BATCH	DOUBLE BATCH
White fish fillets, such as flounder, rockfish, Pacific cod, halibut, lingcod, or tilapia, each ½ to 1 inch thick, skinned	About 2 lb	About 4 lb
Fine sea salt or kosher salt		
Tomato-Basil Sauce		
Fresh tomatoes, preferably in different colors and sizes, large ones cut into wedges and cherry tomatoes halved	4½ lb	9 lb
Extra-virgin olive oil	⅓ cup	⅔ cup
Garlic cloves, thinly sliced	6	12
Loosely packed chopped fresh basil	¾ cup	1½ cup
Fresh thyme, minced	1½ tsp	1 Tbsp
Sea or kosher salt	1½ tsp	1 Tbsp
Red pepper flakes	¾ tsp	1½ Tbsp
Freshly ground black pepper	¾ tsp	1½ Tbsp
Bay leaves	2	4
White wine or unseasoned rice vinegar	⅔ cup or 1½ Tbsp	1⅓ cup or 3 Tbsp

Pearl couscous	3 cups	6 cups
Grated lemon zest (from 1 to 2 lemons, preferably Meyer)	1½ Tbsp	3 Tbsp
Extra-virgin olive oil, for drizzling		
Sea or kosher salt		
Fresh small thyme sprigs and small basil leaves, for garnish		

Lightly season the fish on both sides with salt, then cover and chill for 30 minutes to 1 hour. Meanwhile, preheat the oven to 350°F and oil the bottom of a roasting pan large enough to accommodate the fillets in a single layer. (You will need two pans for a double batch.) Bring a large pot of generously salted water to a boil.

Make the Tomato-Basil Sauce: In a 4- to 6-quart saucepan (or one 8- to 10-quart sauce pot for a double batch), combine the tomatoes, oil, garlic, basil, thyme, salt, red pepper flakes, black pepper, and bay leaves, cover, and bring to a simmer over medium heat. Add the wine and cook, uncovered, until the sauce loses the sharpness of the alcohol and tastes mellow, about 5 minutes for a single batch or 10 minutes for a double batch (tomatoes should retain their shape). Re-cover and remove from the heat.

When the water is boiling, add the couscous and boil until barely tender, about 8 minutes (it will finish cooking in the oven). Drain well, then pour the couscous into the prepared pan.

Pour the sauce, then distribute the sauce evenly over the couscous. Stir gently to mix the sauce evenly with the couscous. Nestle the fish fillets in a single layer in the couscous, overlapping them slightly if necessary. Sprinkle the fillets with the lemon zest.

Cover the pan tightly with aluminum foil and bake until the fish is opaque throughout when tested with the tip of a sharp knife, 15 to 25 minutes; the timing will depend on the thickness of the fillets.

This dish can be served hot, warm, or chilled. Drizzle with a little additional oil, sprinkle with salt, and top with the thyme sprigs and basil leaves before serving.

THE PEARL PASTA FAMILY

The pearl pasta most common in the U.S., called *ptitim* in Israel, is factory-made by extruding durum wheat dough into small balls that are then toasted. It's a riff on the many older, bead-like pastas that extend from the Mediterranean to the Middle East. If you like the tender-chewy texture of Israeli couscous, try Palestinian maftoul, still made by hand from cracked wheat and durum flour, and steamed rather than toasted; chickpea-size Lebanese mograbieh and Algerian berkoukes; and deeply toasted Sardinian fregola. Any can be used in this recipe; just cook until almost tender before adding to the fish. Find them in Middle Eastern markets.

7.
from the garden: vegetables and salads

VEGETABLES AT THEIR peak are featured in dishes that would be right at home at a harvest celebration, a farm supper, or a simple meal put together with the bounty of a backyard vegetable plot. A trip to the market or a stop at a roadside stand in summer might lead to ratatouille, roasted eggplant, or a tomato-topped tart, while a hearty potato gratin is a welcome choice for a cold winter day.

The emphasis here is on substantial vegetable dishes that can be the centerpiece of a meal. If offered as a side dish, each recipe will yield about twice the number of servings. However, any of these dishes would also be good with poultry, seafood, or meat on the side and can be adapted to what you find at your farmers' market or in your garden.

Many of the recipes in this book call for a simple green salad to round out the meal. It can be as simple as arugula tossed in olive oil and a squeeze of lemon juice, or mixed chicories with a creamy vinaigrette. Because it is meant as as a complement, a great green salad doesn't need many ingredients. Just count on 1 to 1½ ounces (a big handful) of lettuce and/or greens per person. Include contrasting textures, and flavors, keep it seasonal and simple, stopping at not more than four or five of the best ingredients you can find. Of course, you can always adorn your salad with nuts, cheese, fruits, or vegetables, as long as it goes along with the main dish.

ANNA WATSON CARL

potato gratin with bacon-thyme bread crumbs

Single Batch **Makes 10 servings**

Double Batch **Make 20 servings**

MAKE AHEAD

The unbaked assembled gratin, without the bread crumb topping, can be refrigerated for up to 1 day. Because the gratin will be chilled, increase the baking time by 10 to 15 minutes. The bread crumb topping can be made up to 2 hours in advance and stored at room temperature.

AS AUTHOR ANNA Watson Carl writes in her cookbook, *The Yellow Table*, "Something magical happens when you gather people about a table to share a meal. They can be old friends or they can be strangers, but a transformation always occurs."

When Anna's mother gifted her their family's yellow dinner table—known as "the center of the home" growing up—Anna made sure it continued to be well loved. "Over the past twelve years," she writes, "I've thrown hundreds of gatherings, small and large, around the yellow table." In Nashville, she became known for hosting a weekly Tuesday-night dinner party. The yellow table seats twelve, "but if more people came, we'd add a card table and folding chairs, and eat off paper plates if we ran out of real ones. After dinner, we'd play music and sing 'til after midnight."

This hearty, creamy potato gratin, studded with bacon and topped with bubbling melted cheese, is perfect for sharing with family and friends around your own favorite table, especially on a chilly winter night. It makes a great side dish to round out a holiday meal or potluck, but it's also rich and satisfying enough to serve as a main course.

INGREDIENTS	SINGLE BATCH	DOUBLE BATCH
Extra-virgin olive oil	3 Tbsp	6 Tbsp
Garlic cloves	2	4
Yukon Gold Potatoes, peeled	4 lb	8 lb
Heavy cream	2 cups	4 cups
Whole milk	1½ cups	3 cups
Freshly grated nutmeg	¼ tsp	½ tsp
Fresh thyme sprigs	8	16
Kosher salt and freshly ground black pepper		
Grated Gruyère cheese (about 6 oz and 12 oz, respectively)	1½ cups	3 cups

INGREDIENTS	SINGLE BATCH	DOUBLE BATCH
Bacon slices, cooked until crisp (optional)	6	12
Panko (Japanese bread crumbs)	¾ cup	1½ cups
Grated Parmesan cheese	½ cup	1 cup

EQUIPMENT

A mandoline or plastic slicer is the best way to get uniform potato slices. A heavy knife and a steady hand works, too.

BIG BATCH NOTES

If making a double batch, bake the gratin in two pans or in one 12-by-20-by-4-inch hotel pan. If baking in a hotel pan, add 10 to 15 minutes to the baking time.

SERVING

Set out a green salad alongside the gratin. It is also a good side dish to roasted meats.

Preheat the oven to 375°F. For a double batch, position racks in the center and bottom third of the oven.

If making a single batch, lightly oil a 9-by-13-inch flameproof baking dish with 1 tablespoon oil. If making a double batch, lightly oil two 9-by-13-inch flameproof baking dishes, using 1 tablespoon oil for each dish. Smash the garlic cloves and remove the skins. Rub a garlic clove over each oiled dish. Set all of the garlic cloves aside.

Fill a large bowl with water. Using a mandoline or other slicer or a knife, cut the potatoes into uniform ⅛-inch-thick rounds. As you slice, add them to the water.

In a large, heavy saucepan, combine the cream, milk, nutmeg, 3 thyme sprigs (or 5 sprigs if making a double batch), and all of the garlic cloves and bring to a simmer over medium heat. Drain the potatoes, add them to the cream mixture, and season with salt and pepper. Return the mixture to a simmer and cook until the potatoes are just barely tender, about 5 minutes.

Using a slotted spoon, spread half of the potatoes in the prepared dish. Using a ladle, add about 1 cup of the cream mixture on top of the potatoes. Sprinkle with half of the Gruyère cheese. Again using the slotted spoon, spread the remaining potatoes over the cheese layer, add about 1 cup of the cream mixture, then top with the remaining Gruyère.

Coarsely chop the bacon (if using). Remove the leaves from the remaining thyme sprigs. In a bowl, combine the bacon, thyme, panko, and Parmesan and mix well. Sprinkle the bacon mixture evenly over the gratin(s) and then drizzle the top evenly with the remaining oil.

Bake until the top is golden and the cheese is bubbling, 25 to 30 minutes. Remove the gratin(s) from the oven and preheat the broiler. Position an oven rack about 6 inches from the heat source.

Place the gratin under the broiler and broil until the top is browned and crisp, about 1 minute, watching it carefully to be sure it doesn't burn. (If you have made two gratins, broil them one at a time.) Let stand for 10 minutes before serving.

ratatouille

WHEN 18 REASONS was screening *Ratatouille*, an animated Pixar film starring a gastronomically gifted rodent who dreams of becoming a famous French chef, San Francisco chef Melissa Perello, owner of Frances and Octavia restaurants, prepared a big batch of the film's namesake dish to feed the crowd. Ratatouille is a Provençal dish born of the abundance of the summer, when tomatoes and eggplants fill farmers' markets and every garden has an overzealous zucchini vine that seems to produce a dozen squashes overnight.

Single Batch **Makes 10 servings**

Double Batch **Makes 20 servings**

MAKE AHEAD

The ratatouille can be refrigerated for up to 2 days. Bring to room temperature before serving or gently reheat in a large Dutch oven over low heat, stirring occasionally, until warm.

The ratatouille is best made at least a few hours before serving to allow the flavors to meld.

INGREDIENTS	SINGLE BATCH	DOUBLE BATCH
Olive oil	1½ cups	3 cups
Very thinly sliced garlic (about 22 and 44 cloves, respectively)	1 cup	2 cups
Dry white wine	½ cup	1 cup
28-oz cans whole San Marzano tomatoes	4	8
Thinly sliced fennel (about 2 large and 4 large bulbs, respectively)	4 cups	8 cups
Yellow onions, cut into ½-inch dice	4	8
Basil, stems tied with kitchen string	½ bunch	1 bunch
Ground fennel or fennel pollen	1 Tbsp	2 Tbsp
Fine sea salt, plus more for the eggplant and seasoning	1 Tbsp	2 Tbsp
Freshly ground black pepper	1 tsp	2 tsp
Red pepper flakes	1 tsp	2 tsp
Globe eggplants, cut into 1½-inch cubes	4	8
Canola oil, for deep-frying		
Zucchini, trimmed and halved lengthwise	6	12

Preheat the oven to 325°F.

In a large Dutch oven, combine the olive oil and garlic over medium heat and cook, stirring often, until the garlic begins to turn a toasty blond and is fragrant, about 3 minutes. Once the garlic begins to take on color, watch it carefully so it doesn't burn. Add the wine to stop the browning.

If making a double batch, use a large Dutch oven with a capacity of at least 8 quarts.

SERVING

This salad makes a wonderful addition to a vegetarian meal that includes other grain or bean salads and roasted, spiced vegetables, such as cauliflower or sweet potato. Michelle also likes to serve it alongside roasted chicken or fish.

INGREDIENT NOTES

Farro is an ancient wheat variety popular in Italy. Read the label to determine how much of the germ and bran have been removed, as this will affect how the farro is cooked. Whole-grain farro retains these outer layers as well as the endosperm and is the most nutritious of the three available forms. It should be soaked overnight to speed the cooking. Pearled, or refined, farro has had these outer layers removed, and semi-pearled farro has had them partially removed. These two types do not need soaking.

Look for purslane, Armenian cucumbers, and sorrel in season at farmers' markets and well-stocked produce stores and supermarkets. Purlsane, which has smooth, succulent leaves and a tart flavor, grows as a weed, so you might even find it (unasked) in your garden. Spinach or other mild greens are good substitutes in this salad. (If substituting the purslane and sorrel, double the amount of lemon juice.) Armenian cucumbers are long, slender, curved, and firm. An English cucumber can be substituted. Sorrel, which is easy to grow in a home garden, is a leafy plant appreciated for its sour taste.

Freekeh, young green wheat kernels that have been toasted, have a wonderful smoky, grassy, sweet flavor. The kernels cook up fluffy, making it a perfect grain for salads like this one. To use it in this tabbouleh recipe, omit the soaking step and proceed as directed for the farro.

INGREDIENTS	SINGLE BATCH	DOUBLE BATCH
Dried árbol chile(s)	1	2
Fine sea salt		
Hot water	2½ cups	5 cups
Fresh lemon juice (see note)	1-2 Tbsp	2-4 Tbsp
Red wine vinegar, preferably Banyuls	2 Tbsp	¼ cup
Finely diced firm, crisp lettuce, such as romaine or Little Gem	4 cups	8 cups
Snipped purslane, in 1-inch pieces (see *Ingredient Notes*)	4 cups	8 cups
Armenian cucumber(s), cut into ¼-inch dice (see *Ingredients Notes*)	1 large	2 large
Coarsely chopped fresh flat-leaf parsley	2 cups	4 cups
Coarsely chopped sorrel (see *Ingredient Notes*)	1 cup	2 cups
Coarsely chopped fresh tarragon	1 cup	2 cups
Thinly sliced fresh chives	½ cup	1 cup
Pistachios, toasted and coarsely chopped	1 cup	2 cups
Pistachio or extra-virgin olive oil	1 Tbsp	2 Tbsp

If using whole-grain farro, put it in a large bowl, add water to cover, and let stand overnight in a cool place or in the refrigerator. Drain and rinse well under running cold water.

In a large pot, heat the butter, 3 tablespoons of the olive oil if making a single batch or 6 tablespoons if making a double batch, the garlic clove(s), and the chile(s) over medium heat. Add the farro, 2 pinches of salt, and the hot water, raise the heat to high, and bring to a boil. Reduce the heat to low, cover, and cook until all of the water is absorbed and the farro is tender, 15 to 20 minutes. Remove from the heat, cover tightly, and let stand for 10 minutes.

Add the lemon juice, vinegar, and the remaining olive oil to the farro and stir and fluff with a fork to mix well. Let the farro cool to room temperature. Remove and discard the garlic and chile(s), then taste and adjust the seasoning with salt and add additional lemon juice if needed.

Transfer the farro mixture to a large bowl, add the lettuce, purslane, cucumber(s), parsley, sorrel, tarragon, chives, pistachios, and pistachio oil and stir and toss gently. Taste and adjust the seasoning with salt, lemon juice, and oil if needed, then serve.

MAKE AHEAD

Although the curry powder can be made up to 3 months in advance, it is best if used within a week of grinding for the freshest flavor. You must toast the millet and then soak it overnight before making the salad. The roasted cauliflower can be covered and kept at room temperature for up to 4 hours. The salad can be made up to 2 days in advance and refrigerated. Bring to room temperature before adding the cilantro, tasting and adjusting the seasoning, and serving.

EQUIPMENT

A large saucepan for cooking the millet; at least two half sheet pans for roasting the cauliflower.

BIG BATCH NOTES

If making a double batch, you will probably have to roast the cauliflower in batches, as most ovens will accommodate only two half sheet pans at a time.

To save time, roast the cauliflower while the millet is cooking.

SERVING

See suggestions for Green Tabbouleh with Farro and Herbs (page 208).

TOASTED MILLET WITH CRISPY CURRIED CAULIFLOWER

Michelle uses her homemade curry powder here, which adds a unique burst of flavor. She makes extra curry powder to have on hand for seasoning everything from popcorn and soups to grilled meats and hummus. If you choose to use a store-bought powder, be sure to purchase a high-quality one.

INGREDIENTS	SINGLE BATCH	DOUBLE BATCH
Millet		
Millet	2 cups	4 cups
Boiling water	4 cups	8 cups
Stalks green garlic, thinly sliced	2	4
Dried árbol chile(s)	1	2
Fine sea salt		
Coconut oil or ghee, melted	¼ cup	½ cup
Fresh lime juice	1 to 3 Tbsp	3 to 6 Tbsp
Cauliflower		
Heads cauliflower	2	4
Coconut oil or ghee, melted	3 Tbsp	6 Tbsp
Dried árbol chiles	1	2
Fine sea salt		
Toasted Curry Powder (page 212)	2 Tbsp	4 Tbsp
Lime wedges	2 to 4	4 to 8
To Finish		
Green onions, thinly sliced	4	8
Serrano chiles, thinly sliced	3	6
Drained cooked chickpeas (see *Ingredient Notes*, page 212)	2 cups	4 cups
Cilantro, leaves only	1 bunch	2 bunches
Full-fat plain yogurt, preferably sheep's milk, or labne	2 cups	4 cups
Fine sea salt		
Limes, cut into quarters	2 to 3	4 to 5

Prepare the millet: The night before making the salad, toast and soak the millet. Heat a large Dutch oven or other deep pot over medium-high heat. Add the millet and toast, stirring occasionally with a wooden spoon, until it darkens slightly and a nutty aroma fills the room, 6 to 8 minutes. Remove from the heat and immediately pour cold water over the millet to cover by 1 inch. Cover and let soak overnight.

TOASTED CURRY POWDER

Makes about 1 cup

3 dried árbol chiles
¼ cup brown mustard seeds
¼ cup sesame seeds
¼ cup coriander seeds
2 Tbsp cumin seeds
1 Tbsp fenugreek seeds
1 tsp black peppercorns
1 Tbsp ground turmeric

In a dry skillet, combine the chiles, mustard seeds, sesame seeds, coriander, cumin, fenugreek, and peppercorns over medium-high heat and toast, shaking the pan often, until very aromatic, 4 to 5 minutes. Take care not to burn the spices. Pour onto a plate and let cool to room temperature. Working in batches, transfer to a spice grinder, grind to a fine powder, and then pour into a bowl. When all of the spices are ground, add the turmeric and whisk to combine. Transfer to an airtight container and store in a cool, dark place until needed.

INGREDIENT NOTES

While this salad is delicious made with chickpeas, Michelle often makes it with sprouted dried green peas, which are sold at natural food stores and can be cooked according to the package directions.

If green garlic is not in season, substitute with half the quantity of thinly sliced garlic cloves.

The next day, drain the millet and return it to the pot. Bring 2–4 cups of water to a boil. Place the pot with the millet over medium heat, and then slowly pour in the boiling water. Add the green garlic, chile(s), and 2 generous pinches of salt for a single batch or 4 pinches for a double batch. Bring to a boil over high heat, then reduce the heat to medium-low and simmer until the water is absorbed, 17 to 20 minutes. Remove from the heat, remove and discard the chile(s), and fluff the millet with a fork. Season to taste with salt, coconut oil (start with ¼ cup for a single batch and ½ cup for a double batch), and lime juice (start with 1 tablespoon for a single batch and 2 tablespoons for a double batch).

Roast the cauliflower: Position racks in the top third and center of the oven and preheat the oven to 450°F. Line two half sheet pans with parchment paper.

Trim off the base of each cauliflower, then cut each head into 2-inch florets and the core into 2-inch pieces. Transfer the florets, core pieces, and leaves to one or more large bowls and toss with the coconut oil to coat evenly. Add the chile(s) and 2 pinches of salt if making a single batch or 4 pinches if making a double batch. Divide the cauliflower between the two prepared pans (if making a double batch, you will be working with only half of the cauliflower at this point), spacing the pieces ½ inch apart.

Roast the cauliflower, switching the pans between the racks and rotating them back to front about halfway through roasting, until the cauliflower is lightly caramelized, about 35 minutes. Remove from the oven, sprinkle each pan with 1 tablespoon of the curry powder, and stir and toss until the cauliflower is evenly coated. Return the pans to the oven and continue to roast until the cauliflower is a deep golden brown and slightly crispy at the edges, 5 to 7 minutes longer. Remove from the oven again and squeeze a lime wedge or two over each pan. Remove and discard the chile(s).

Finish the salad: Gently toss together the millet, cauliflower, green onions, serrano chiles, chickpeas, and three-fourths of the cilantro. Taste and adjust the seasoning with salt. Transfer to one or more platters and sprinkle with the remaining cilantro. Serve at room temperature with the yogurt and the lime quarters passed on the side.

roasted eggplant with smoky yogurt and spicy almonds

EGGPLANT PLAYS MANY roles in the cooking of the London-based, Israeli-born chef and dazzlingly successful cookbook author Yotam Ottolenghi. Fried, roasted, grilled, or steamed, it becomes the star of dips, salads, main courses, and side dishes. Like so many of his creations, this vegetable-based dish, featuring oven-roasted eggplant slices topped with a smoky, roasted pepper yogurt and buttery spiced almonds, is delicious enough to stand on its own, though it can also be part of a buffet alongside grilled meat or an array of vegetarian dishes.

Yotam, who loves to entertain at home, is used to putting many hands to work in the kitchen. A family feast becomes a many-headed collaboration, with all ages pitching in on tasks delegated by inclination and ability. With an artist's eye for color and pattern, Yotam likes to begin the preparation for a meal by laying out the serving platters and bowls, so he can envision the beauty of the final spread before he even picks up a knife. It's a smart trick that prevents last-minute rummaging for the right-size dishes, and lets you feel one step closer to getting a gorgeous meal on the table.

This dish has three distinct parts—eggplant, yogurt sauce, and spiced almonds—most of which can be prepared in stages a day in advance. For the best results, however, do the final assembly just before serving.

Single Batch **Makes 8 servings**

Double Batch **Makes 16 servings**

MAKE AHEAD

The yogurt sauce can be made up to 1 day ahead and refrigerated. The eggplant can be roasted several hours in advance (or even the day before if needed) and refrigerated. Bring the sauce and the eggplant to room temperature before combining them. The almonds can be toasted up to a few hours in advance and stored in an airtight container at room temperature. Assemble the dish just before serving.

INGREDIENTS	SINGLE BATCH	DOUBLE BATCH
Smoky Yogurt		
Red bell peppers	2	4
Ancho chiles, soaked in boiling water for 30 minutes	2	4

continued on following page

213

BIG BATCH NOTES

Most ovens will be able to handle only two sheet pans at a time for roasting. If you have a convection oven that handles three pans, use it (set to 450°F) for this recipe; you will not have to switch the positions of the pans in a convection oven as the circulating air will help to brown the eggplant evenly.

SERVING

Accompany with a chicory salad for a vegetarian menu or grilled lamb or other meat for a nonvegetarian menu.

INGREDIENTS	SINGLE BATCH	DOUBLE BATCH
Olive oil–packed anchovy fillets, rinsed and patted dry	2	4
Fresh lime juice	2 Tbsp	¼ cup
Small garlic cloves, crushed	2	4
Kosher salt	½ tsp	1 tsp
Smoked sweet paprika (pimentón de la Vera)	½ tsp	1 tsp
Crème fraîche	1 cup	2 cups
Plain full-fat Greek yogurt	½ cup	1 cup
Eggplant		
Large eggplants (about 2¼ lb each)	6	12
Extra-virgin olive oil	½ cup	1 cup
Ground turmeric	1 tsp	2 tsp
Kosher salt	¾ tsp	1½ tsp
Freshly ground black pepper		
Almonds		
Unsalted butter	3 Tbsp	5 Tbsp
Sliced almonds	1 cup	2 cups
Coriander seeds	1 Tbsp	2 Tbsp
Sesame seeds	3 Tbsp	6 Tbsp
Kosher salt	1 pinch	2 pinches
Red pepper flakes	¼ tsp	½ tsp
Coarsely chopped fresh cilantro leaves, for serving	½ cup	1 cup

Make the smoky yogurt: Preheat the oven to 475°F. Line a quarter or half sheet pan with parchment paper.

Place the bell peppers on the prepared sheet pan and roast, turning occasionally, until the skin has started to blacken, about 20 minutes. Remove from the oven and let the peppers cool until they are easy to handle. Remove and discard the stems, skin, and seeds. Place the flesh in a food processor, add the ancho chiles and 1 tablespoon of their soaking water if making a single batch (and 2 tablespoons if making a double batch), the anchovies, lime juice, garlic, salt, and paprika, and process until smooth. Add the crème fraîche and yogurt and pulse to combine. Transfer to an airtight container and refrigerate for at least 1 hour before serving.

Roast the eggplant: Position oven racks in the top third and center of the oven and leave the oven set at 475°F. Line two half sheet pans with parchment paper. Halve each eggplant crosswise, then cut each half lengthwise into 1-inch-wide wedges. In one or more large bowls, toss together the eggplant wedges, oil, turmeric, salt, and a generous amount of pepper. Spread the eggplant wedges in a single layer on the prepared pans. (If making a double batch, you will need to do this in two or three batches.)

Roast the eggplant wedges, switching the pans between the racks and rotating them back to front about halfway through roasting, until the eggplant is crispy and cooked through, about 30 minutes. Remove from the oven and let cool to room temperature.

Toast the almonds: In a skillet, melt the butter over medium-high heat. When the butter begins to foam, add the almonds, coriander seeds, sesame seeds, and salt and cook, stirring, until the almonds are golden brown, 1 to 2 minutes. Remove from the heat, stir in the pepper flakes, and then spoon into a shallow bowl so the nuts do not continue to cook.

Just before serving, arrange the eggplant on one or more large platters. Spoon the smoky yogurt over the top, sprinkle with the almonds, and top with the cilantro.

CATHY BARROW

call-it-what-you-will cobb salad

FOOD WRITER AND cookbook author Cathy Barrow is known for her big batch cooking. In addition to contributing to many publications, she also authors the "Bring It" column for the *Washington Post*, which includes wonderful recipes for shared meals.

This recipe has been a centerpiece of one of those shared meals. "When I gather a gang of friends," says Cathy, "food is always foremost in our minds. Because there's never a shortage of rich, delicious dishes, I contribute a bright, flavorful salad with flexible topping opportunities. This salad is a mash-up of my favorite parts of three classic salads: Cobb, fattoush, and Niçoise."

The salad starts with beautiful greens like butter lettuce or Little Gem leaves, deconstructed into easy-to-serve salad cups, or with a tangle of oak leaf, romaine, and arugula. In winter, choose mâche, radicchio, endive, sturdy escarole, or feathery frisée.

From there, it's a panoply of possibilities, depending on the season. Rather than tossing everything together, Cathy offers the components on beautifully arranged platters, so guests can mix and match as they like. Shallot vinaigrette goes on the side for drizzling, while a bowl of homemade mayonnaise stands ready to be slathered on the boiled eggs and potatoes. And no salad is complete without crunchy, garlicky croutons.

Single Batch
Makes 8 to 10 servings

Double Batch
Makes 16 to 20 servings

MAKE AHEAD

The vinaigrette can be made up to 3 days in advance and refrigerated. The day before serving, the potatoes can be boiled, the haricots verts can be blanched, the radishes can be sliced, the eggs can be boiled and peeled, and the beets can be roasted. Store them in separate airtight containers in the refrigerator. Although the croutons are best served warm, they can be made up to 2 hours in advance and stored in an airtight container at room temperature.

INGREDIENTS	SINGLE BATCH	DOUBLE BATCH
Shallot Vinaigrette		
Shallot(s), minced	1	2
Sherry vinegar	¼ cup	½ cup
Kosher salt	¼ tsp	½ tsp
Dijon mustard	1 tsp	2 tsp
Freshly ground black pepper	½ tsp	1 tsp

continued on following page

BIG BATCH NOTES

This salad is infinitely expandable because you are using store-bought chicken or tuna. If you opt to serve beef, you can purchase roast beef from a good delicatessen to use in place of the home-cooked flank steak.

INGREDIENT NOTES

Purchase rotisserie chickens for the salad (2 chickens for a single batch or 4 chickens for a double batch). Bone and skin the birds and cut or shred the meat. For the tuna, use three 5-ounce cans olive oil–packed tuna, drained and flaked into large chunks, for a single batch or six 5-ounce cans for a double batch.

For the flank steak, use 2 pounds for a single batch or 4 pounds for a double batch. Season on both sides with salt and pepper, and broil or grill for 3 to 4 minutes on each side for medium-rare. Rest the meat for a few minutes before cutting across the grain into ¼-inch-thick slices and cover and set aside for up to 1 hour before serving.

INGREDIENTS	SINGLE BATCH	DOUBLE BATCH
Extra-virgin olive oil	¾ cup	1½ cups
Vegetables and Eggs		
Small beets, about 5 oz each, scrubbed but unpeeled	4	8
Small Yukon Gold potatoes, scrubbed but unpeeled	1½ lb	3 lb
Kosher salt		
Haricots verts or slender green beans, trimmed	1 lb	2 lb
Eggs	8	16
Garlic Croutons		
Extra-virgin olive oil	½ cup	¾ cup
Garlic cloves	3	6
Thick slices sourdough or ciabatta bread, torn into large pieces	8	16
Flaky sea salt, such as Maldon		
Assembly		
Little Gem or butter lettuce, separated into leaves	4 heads	8 heads
Cooked chicken, tuna in olive oil, or cooked flank steak (see *Ingredient Notes*)	3 to 4 cups	6 to 7 cups
Crumbled blue, feta, or goat's milk cheese	1½ cups	3 cups
Radishes, sliced	12	24
Kalamata olives, pitted	½ cup	1 cup
Avocados, halved, pitted, peeled, and each cut into 6 wedges	4	8
Mayonnaise, preferably homemade	1 cup	2 cups

Make the vinaigrette: In a bowl, stir together the shallot(s), vinegar, and salt and let stand for 10 minutes. Whisk in the mustard and pepper, then slowly whisk in the oil until the dressing is emulsified. Set aside until serving.

Roast the beets: Preheat the oven to 400°F. Cut off any leafy tops from the beets, leaving ½ inch of the stem intact. Wrap each beet in aluminum foil and place on a sheet pan. Bake until the beets are tender, about 1¼ hours, depending on their size. Let cool until easy to handle, then slip off the skins. Let cool to room temperature, then cut into wedges.

Cook the potatoes: In a large saucepan, combine the potatoes with water to cover by 1 inch, add a big pinch of salt, and bring to a boil over high heat. Meanwhile, ready a large bowl of ice water. When the potatoes are boiling, reduce the heat to medium-low and cook until the potatoes are just tender when pierced with the tip of a knife, about 20 minutes. Using a wire skimmer or slotted spoon, transfer the potatoes to the ice water. Keep the water boiling to cook the beans. Let the potatoes stand for 5 minutes, then drain well, let cool completely, and pat dry with paper towels. Cut the potatoes into halves or quarters, depending on their size.

Cook the haricots verts: Add the haricots verts to the boiling water and cook just until they turn bright green, about 2 minutes. (If using green beans, cook until crisp-tender, 3 to 4 minutes.) Drain into a colander, rinse under cold running water, and let cool, then pat dry with paper towels.

Boil the eggs: Arrange the eggs in a single layer in a large saucepan. Add cold water to cover by 1 inch and bring just to a boil over high heat. Remove from the heat, cover tightly, and let stand for 13 minutes. Meanwhile, ready a large bowl filled with ice water. After 15 minutes, carefully transfer the eggs to the ice water and let stand until thoroughly chilled, 10 to 15 minutes. Peel the eggs and cut in half lengthwise.

Make the croutons: Line a half sheet pan with paper towels. Heat the oil in a large skillet over medium heat until shimmering. Stir in the garlic cloves and cook, stirring often, until fragrant and golden, about 1 minute. Using a slotted spoon, remove and discard the garlic. Working in batches, add the bread and fry, turning as needed, until well browned on all sides, about 1 minute. Using the slotted spoon, transfer the bread to the towel-lined sheet pan and scatter the flaky salt over the top. Repeat with the remaining bread, adding more oil to the skillet as needed. Keep the croutons in a warm oven until you are ready to serve the salad.

On one or two large platters or boards, arrange some of the lettuce leaves as a foundation. Top with the cooked vegetables; eggs; chicken, tuna, or flank steak; cheese; radishes; olives; and avocados, arranging them in distinct quadrants. Serve the remaining lettuce and the croutons, vinaigrette, and mayonnaise on the side.

BRYANT TERRY

grits with grilled vegetables

GRITS ARE A staple on the menus of Oakland-based chef Bryant Terry, who pairs them with different ingredients year-round. Bryant is a James Beard award–winning chef, television host, social justice activist, educator, and the author of several cookbooks, including *Afro-Vegan, The Inspired Vegan,* and *Vegan Soul Kitchen.* He is the inaugural chef-in-residence at the Museum of the African Diaspora (MoAD) in San Francisco, creating programming that celebrates the intersection of food, farming, health, activism, art, culture, and the African diaspora. He's also a master at cooking for—and inspiring—large groups of people.

Bryant first served a version of this dish at the inaugural session of a series of breakfast gatherings called Grits and Greens, put together by his friend urban strategist Ashara Ekundayo to explore the intersection of food, art, and technology. Each gathering featured stone-ground grits along with savory finishes. For this version, he tops the grits with grilled vegetables for a simple summer meal. You can vary the vegetables with the season, featuring whatever you find at your local market. Instead of the typical cheese, this inspired recipe takes a modern vegan approach, using creamed cashews to enrich the grits. Both the grits and the cashews need to be soaked overnight, so plan accordingly.

Single Batch
Makes 6 to 8 servings

Double Batch
Makes 12 to 15 servings

MAKE AHEAD

The grits and the cashews must be soaked 1 day in advance. The cashew cream can be made up to 4 days in advance and refrigerated. The vegetables can be marinated for up to overnight in the refrigerator. The grits and vegetables are best served soon after cooking, but if you have all of the components ready, they come together quickly.

INGREDIENTS	SINGLE BATCH	DOUBLE BATCH
Grits		
Yellow corn grits (see *Ingredient Notes*)	1½ cups	3 cups
Vegetable stock or water	8 cups	16 cups
Kosher salt	2 tsp	4 tsp
Finely chopped fresh flat-leaf parsley	¼ cup	½ cup
Cashew Cream		
Raw cashews	1 cup	2 cups
Water	½ cup	1 cup

continued on following page

Grill to cook the vegetables (or two or even three grills to make the job go more quickly if feeding a large group); one or two large bowls for marinating the vegetables; one or two large, heavy saucepans for the grits (keep in mind, they increase dramatically in volume when cooked). If you want to cook the grits indoors, a propane burner is useful.

BIG BATCH NOTES

If making a double batch, you will need to cook the grits in two large saucepans, rather than a single large one, as it can be difficult to cook a big batch successfully on most home stoves.

Although you will likely be grilling the vegetables in batches, they can sit for up to an hour before serving. If you want warm vegetables, it is best to have one person cook the grits (or one or two people if making a double batch) and another person grill the vegetables so everything is done about the same time. To keep the vegetables warm as they come off the grill, you can tent them with aluminum foil. It is easy to feed more people by simply adjusting the amount of vegetables. Plan on ½ to 1 pound vegetables per person. The cashew cream can be scaled up as well, using 2 parts nuts to 1 part water.

INGREDIENT NOTES

Be sure to use yellow corn grits, which are made from dent corn and are ground more coarsely than coarse yellow cornmeal. Do not substitute cornmeal, polenta, or the highly refined white hominy grits sold in the cereal aisle of supermarkets. Soaking the grits in water overnight will help shorten the cooking time. Do not drain the grits.

INGREDIENTS	SINGLE BATCH	DOUBLE BATCH
Vegetables		
Seasonal vegetables such zucchini or summer squashes, onions, leeks, green onions, bell peppers, tomatoes, mushrooms, fennel, broccoli, asparagus, eggplants, and/or corn, in any combination	4 to 5 lb	8 to 10 lb
Marinade		
Extra-virgin olive oil	¾ cup	1½ cups
Fresh lemon juice or vinegar	4 to 6 Tbsp	½ to ¾ cup
Loosely packed fresh herb leaves, such as basil, rosemary, oregano, thyme, parsley, cilantro, chives, summer savory	1 cup	2 cups
Coarse sea salt	2 tsp	4 tsp
Freshly ground black pepper	1 tsp	2 tsp
Fine sea salt		
Freshly ground black pepper	1 tsp	2 tsp
Red pepper flakes	½ to 1 tsp	1 to 1½ tsp

Soak the grits and cashews: The night before you make the dish, in a large bowl, soak the grits in 6 cups of the water. If making a double batch, use two large bowls, soaking 1 ½ cups of the grits in 6 cups of the water in each bowl. In a medium bowl, combine the cashews with water to cover and refrigerate.

Make the cashew cream: The next day, drain the cashews and transfer to a blender. Add the water and process until smooth and creamy. You should have about 1½ cups if making a single batch or about 3 cups if making a double batch. Cover and refrigerate until needed.

Prepare the vegetables: Remove seeds, husks, and/or peels if any vegetables you are using require it. Slice vegetables such as zucchini, summer squashes, eggplants, yellow or red onions, and fennel into ½-inch-thick slices. Cut tomatoes in half crosswise. Seed bell peppers and cut lengthwise into 2- to 3-inch-wide strips. Snap off the tough ends from asparagus. Separate broccoli into large florets. Trim the stem end of mushrooms and leave the caps whole. Green onions can also be left whole, as can small leeks. Cut larger leeks in half lengthwise.

Make the marinade and marinate the vegetables: In a large bowl, whisk together the oil and lemon juice. Finely chop the herbs, add to the bowl with the salt and pepper, and whisk until combined. Divide the marinade between two large bowls to accommodate the vegetables if making a big batch. Add the prepared vegetables to the marinade and toss to coat evenly. Cover the bowl and let stand at room temperature for 1 to 2 hours or refrigerate for up to overnight.

Prepare a charcoal or gas grill for direct cooking over medium heat (400°F). For a charcoal grill, let the coals burn until covered with white ash, then spread them out.

Cook the grits: While the grill is heating, put the grits on to cook. Skim off any hulls or chaff that has risen to the top of the soaking liquid, then pour the grits and the liquid into a large, heavy saucepan and add the salt. If making a double batch, pour each bowl of grits and liquid into its own large, heavy saucepan and add 2 teaspoons salt to each pan. Bring to a boil over high heat, whisking vigorously so no lumps form. Immediately reduce the heat to low and simmer uncovered, whisking occasionally to prevent sticking, until the grits have absorbed most of the liquid and are beginning to thicken, 2 to 5 minutes. Add the remaining 2 cups stock if making a single batch, or divide the remaining 4 cups stock evenly between the two pans if making a double batch, and simmer, stirring often, for 10 to 15 minutes. Stir in 1 cup cashew cream if making a single batch, or divide 2 cups cashew cream evenly between the two pans if making a double batch (save the remaining cashew cream for another use), and continue to simmer, whisking frequently, until the grits are soft and fluffy, about 30 minutes longer. Just before serving, whisk in the parsley, dividing it evenly between the two pans if making a double batch. The grits should be firm and creamy; if they look too thick, thin with a bit more stock or water.

Grill the vegetables: As noted in the *Big Batch Notes*, it is ideal if you can assign someone to keep an eye on the grits, whisking them often, while you tend to the grilling, or you can mind the grits while someone else grills. Remove the vegetables from the marinade, reserving the marinade, and place them on the grill. Grill for 2 to 3 minutes, then flip the vegetables and grill for 2 to 3 minutes on the second side. Continue cooking, flipping as needed, until the vegetables are tender and charred in spots. The different vegetables will take different amounts of time to grill. As they are ready, transfer them to one or more large platters and finish with some fine sea salt.

To serve: Divide the grits among individual bowls or spoon onto one or more large platters. Top with the grilled vegetables, drizzle with the reserved marinade, and season with the red pepper flakes and black pepper.

frittata with charred leeks, roasted grapes, and camembert

CHARLOTTE DRUCKMAN, AUTHOR of *Stir, Sizzle, Bake: Recipes for Your Cast-Iron Skillet,* created the pan-luck, a casual get-together to which guests bring a skillet-made item in its eye-catching cooking vessel. One of her favorite dishes to make for these get-togethers is a frittata. Versatile and popular with omnivores and vegetarians alike, these traditional Italian egg-based dishes can be served warm or at room temperature. They are also a time-honored way to transform a refrigerator full of odds and ends (especially vegetables) into a dish that is delicious for brunch, lunch, or dinner.

Charlotte learned how to make frittatas from her dad when she was a little girl. On Sunday nights when her mother didn't feel like cooking, her dad would whip up a frittata with whatever he found in the fridge. Now when Charlotte makes a frittata, she follows his lead and lets the ingredients guide her: day-old bread, a dab of pesto, a bowl of ratatouille, a lone zucchini or leek, a bell pepper or two, or bunches of leftover herbs are incorporated into beaten eggs with ingenuity and a generous spirit. Frittatas are an extremely economical menu choice, but they can go high-end, too—think dollops of crème fraîche and caviar. One of her favorite combinations for any occasion is this mix of charred leeks, roasted grapes, Camembert, and fresh tarragon.

Makes 8 to 10 servings
(one 12-inch frittata)

MAKE AHEAD

The leeks and grapes can be cooked up to 4 hours in advance and stored at room temperature. If you are having a gathering you can make a flight of frittatas up to 2 hours in advance and store at room temperature; serve at room temperature or rewarm gently in a preheated 300°F oven for about 10 minutes.

INGREDIENTS

Large leeks	2
Extra-virgin olive oil, plus more for serving	2½ Tbsp
Seedless red grapes	2¼ cups
Fine sea salt and freshly ground black pepper	
Fresh thyme sprigs, leaves only	4

continued on following page

225

BIG BATCH NOTES

This recipe assumes you have one 12-inch skillet, so ingredients for only a single batch are given. If you have two 12-inch skillets, cook double batches of the leeks and grapes, double the remaining ingredients, divide them between the pans, and bake the frittatas at the same time on the top third and center oven racks. If you have only a single skillet, bake the frittatas one after the other, transferring the first one to a platter to free up the skillet for cooking the second one.

SERVING

Frittata is one of the all-time great brunch dishes. Serve with a grain salad (page 207) or cinnamon rolls (page 238) and/or a huge platter of fresh fruit.

INGREDIENTS

Large eggs	12
Dijon mustard	2 Tbsp
Chopped fresh tarragon	2 Tbsp
Camembert, cut into small bite-size chunks	6 oz

Preheat the oven to 425°F. Preheat a 12-inch cast-iron skillet on the stove top, gradually raising the heat from low to medium.

While the skillet is heating, cut off and discard the dark green tops of the leeks, leaving the white and pale green parts and the root end intact. Split each leek in half lengthwise, then rinse well under cold running water. Pat the leeks dry and place in a shallow dish.

Drizzle the leeks with 1½ teaspoons of the oil, then use your hands to make sure they are lightly and evenly coated. When the skillet is hot, place the leek halves in it and cook, flipping them occasionally, until both sides are noticeably charred but not burned, about 12 minutes. Transfer them to a cutting board and let cool until they can be handled. Reserve the skillet for roasting the grapes (no need to clean it).

In a bowl, immediately toss the grapes with 1½ teaspoons of the oil, a generous pinch of salt, a couple grinds of pepper, and half of the thyme leaves. While the skillet is still hot, add the grapes to it and put it in the oven. Roast the grapes until they begin to fall in on themselves, their exteriors blister, and their interiors get jammy, 20 to 25 minutes. (If a few of them do collapse and you get a little grapey goo in there, don't worry.) Remove from the oven and let cool slightly. Reduce the oven temperature to 300°F.

While the grapes are roasting, the leeks should have cooled enough to handle. Slice them into thin ribbons, trimming off and discarding the roots. Transfer them to a bowl large enough to accommodate the grapes and season with a pinch of salt and a couple of grinds of pepper. Transfer the grapes to the bowl with the leeks and let them stand for 5 minutes to cool slightly. While the grapes are cooling, rinse and dry the skillet.

Preheat the cleaned skillet on the stove top, gradually raising the heat from low to medium.

Meanwhile, in a large bowl, whisk together the eggs, mustard, ¼ teaspoon salt, and ½ teaspoon pepper just until combined. Add the leek and grape mixture, the tarragon, and the remaining thyme and stir to incorporate.

When the skillet is hot, add the remaining 1½ tablespoons oil. It should sizzle. Pour the egg mixture into the skillet, gently jiggling the pan to distribute the leeks, grapes, and herbs evenly. Increase the heat to high and cook for 1 minute so the very bottom of the frittata begins to set. Evenly dot the frittata with the Camembert pieces and transfer to the oven. Bake until the frittata is just set, about 30 minutes.

Garnish the frittata with a generous drizzle of oil and as much pepper as you like, then serve warm or at room temperature directly from the skillet.

If you want to turn the frittata out of the skillet onto a large plate for serving (either because you want to reuse the skillet or you prefer a less rustic presentation), first loosen the sides of the frittata from the edge of the skillet with a spatula. Then, gently lifting up an edge of the frittata, ease the spatula under it and carefully free the entire frittata from the bottom of the pan. At this point, you may be able to slide it, using the spatula and your hand, straight out of the pan onto a plate. If not, invert a large plate over the top of the skillet and flip the pan and plate over together, so the frittata plops onto the plate. Flip the frittata over again (if you have to use a second large plate, do so) and then garnish with a generous drizzle of oil and season with the pepper.

Because frittatas are so easy to make and can be cooked in advance and served at room temperature, you can prepare two or three different kinds for the same get-together. Start cooking a few hours before the party begins and create a flight of frittatas for your guests, or invite your guests to bring their favorite versions.

Use Charlotte's Charred Leek, Roasted Grapes, and Camembert Frittata for the basic instructions. The base for a 12-inch frittata is 12 large eggs whisked with about ½ teaspoon each fine sea salt and freshly ground black pepper (depending on how the filling is seasoned), to which you usually add about 3 cups filling, depending on the ingredients. Here are some fillings from Charlotte to get you started.

Asparagus, Fava Beans, and Peas: Mix 1 cup each chopped, cooked asparagus, cooked fava beans, and cooked peas into the eggs. Top the cooked frittata with 2 tablespoons grated Parmesan cheese.

Ham and Gruyère: Mix about 2 cups diced, smoked, or boiled ham, in ½-inch dice, and about 1 cup shredded Gruyère cheese into the eggs.

Herb: Mix about ⅓ cup finely chopped fresh leafy herbs like basil or dill into the eggs. If using more sturdy herbs, such as thyme or rosemary, use only 2 teaspoons.

Prosciutto and Peas: In a small skillet, sauté 4 ounces prosciutto or pancetta, cut into ¼-inch dice, until browned, about 5 minutes. Transfer to paper towels to drain and cool slightly, then add to the eggs along with 1 cup cooked peas.

Ratatouille: Mix 3 cups chopped Ratatouille (page 205) into the eggs.

Roasted Red Pepper and Goat Cheese: Mix 1 cup diced roasted red pepper, in ½-inch dice, and 1 cup crumbled fresh goat cheese into the eggs.

PHYLLIS GRANT

cherry tomato tart with anchovies and garlic confit

SAVORY TARTS ARE an easy and delicious way to feature seasonal produce and feed a crowd. Phyllis Grant, author of the blog *Dash and Bella*, makes this flatbread with cherry tomatoes and garlic confit for her family. She usually has homemade pastry dough in the freezer, so she is ready to bake at all times. But if you don't feel like making dough or don't have any on hand, this tart can be made with store-bought puff pastry or pizza dough.

You can play with the ingredients. Garlic confit is a wonderful addition, as are the anchovies, but you can substitute other ingredients, such as roasted corn, pancetta, prosciutto, or an egg or two cracked on top. Once you have the dough ready, this recipe goes together quickly, so make a few of these tarts and vary the toppings according to the season and your crowd.

Single Batch
Makes 8 to 10 servings

Double Batch
Makes 16 to 20 servings

MAKE AHEAD

The garlic confit can be made up to 2 weeks ahead and refrigerated. The pastry dough can be refrigerated for up to 2 days or frozen for up to 2 months; thaw in the refrigerator overnight before using, then let sit at room temperature for a few minutes before rolling. The baked tart can be kept at room temperature for up to 2 hours before serving.

INGREDIENTS	SINGLE BATCH	DOUBLE BATCH
Garlic Confit		
Large heads of garlic	1	2
Extra-virgin olive oil, to cover		
Fresh rosemary or thyme sprigs	1 or 2	2 to 4
Kosher salt		
Pastry Dough		
All-purpose flour	1¼ cups	2½ cups
Kosher salt	½ tsp	1 tsp
Unsalted butter, well-chilled	½ cup	1 cup
Ice water, as needed	¼ cup	½ cup

continued on following page

229

BIG BATCH NOTES

Bake the tarts at the same time on the top third and center racks of the preheated oven, switching their positions halfway during baking to ensure even browning.

SERVING

Accompany with a lightly dressed arugula salad, served on the side or on top of the tart.

INGREDIENT NOTES

If you decide to purchase commercial puff pastry dough (look for an all-butter brand) or pizza dough, you will need 1 pound puff pastry dough for each recipe. (Puff pastry dough is usually sold in 1 pound increments divided into 2 portions; each portion serves 6.)

INGREDIENTS	SINGLE BATCH	DOUBLE BATCH
Tart		
Oil from garlic confit, plus more for brushing	2 Tbsp	4 Tbsp
Cherry or grape tomatoes, any color	2 pints	4 pints
Fresh lemon thyme or classic thyme sprigs	4	8
Kosher salt		
Sugar		
Dijon mustard	2 Tbsp	4 Tbsp
Olive oil–packed anchovy fillets, drained	10	20
Grated Parmesan or pecorino cheese		

Make the confit: Discard the papery outer skins from the garlic head(s) and break apart into cloves. Using the tip of a small, sharp knife, poke a tiny hole in each clove to prevent the cloves from bursting, but do not peel. Put the garlic into a small, deep saucepan and pour in oil to cover. Add the rosemary and a pinch or two of salt if making a single batch or double the amount if making a double batch. Heat over medium-high heat until the oil bubbles, then reduce the heat to low and cook until the garlic is cooked through, soft, and creamy, 20 to 30 minutes. Remove from the heat and let cool to room temperature. Discard the herb sprigs. Transfer the garlic and its oil to a small covered container.

Make the dough: In a bowl, mix together the flour and the salt. Cut the butter into ½ inch square chunks and toss into dry ingredients. With your hands or a pastry cutter, incorporate the butter until the butter chunks are the size of peas. Gradually add in half of the cold water and mix it in with a fork until it just begins to clump together—just moist enough to form a dough when pressed into a mass. Add more water as needed. Pour the dough into a piece of plastic wrap and use the sides of the wrap to press the dough into a disc. If making a double batch, divide the dough in half and wrap and shape each half in plastic wrap. Refrigerate for at least 1 hour.

Make the tart: In a saucepan, heat the garlic oil over medium heat. Add the tomatoes and thyme and season with a big pinch each of salt and sugar if making a single batch or twice the amount if making a double batch. Cook, stirring occasionally, until the tomatoes just start to soften, about 3 minutes. A few tomatoes will probably burst. Remove from the heat and let cool to room temperature.

Preheat the oven to 350°F. For a double batch, position racks in the center and bottom third of the oven. Line a half sheet pan with parchment paper if making a single batch or two pans if making a double batch.

On a lightly floured work surface, roll out a dough portion into a rectangle to fit the bottom of the prepared pan. It should be about ¼-inch thick. Transfer the dough sheet to the prepared pan. If making two tarts, roll out the second dough portion the same way, transfer to the prepared pan, and refrigerate until ready to top.

Spread the mustard over the cold dough, leaving a roughly ½-inch border around the edges. (If making two tarts, divide the mustard and the remaining toppings evenly between two pastry sheets.) Drain the tomato mixture in a fine-mesh sieve set over a bowl. This step is important or the tart will be soggy. (The liquid can be reserved for another use, such as soup, if you like.) Scatter the tomatoes evenly over the dough. Drape the anchovies over the tomatoes. Remove the garlic confit cloves from their oil and squeeze them from their skins onto the tart. (Phyllis likes to place a clove next to each anchovy fillet.) If you like, place a few cloves at the center of the tart. Grate the cheese evenly over the tart. Paint the exposed tart dough edges with garlic oil.

Bake until nice and brown and beautiful. (If baking two tarts, switch the pans between the racks and rotate them from back to front halfway through baking to ensure even browning.) This should take between 30 and 40 minutes. A good test is to lift a corner of the tart to see if it's floppy or firm. Remove it from the oven when it doesn't bow at all. Or if you prefer the tart a bit gooey, take it out of the oven when it's not quite firm. Serve warm or at room temperature.

cherry tomato tart with anchovies and garlic confit   231

STEVE SANDO

italian white bean salad with tuna

A POT OF beans is one of the easiest, least expensive, and most delicious ways to feed a big group. It can be transformed into a soup, a stew, a chili, a salad, and more, and there are literally dozens of bean varieties to choose from. Here, Steve Sando, owner of Rancho Gordo, shares his classic recipe for a main-dish white bean salad that is both quick and easy once the beans are cooked.

Steve started Rancho Gordo with the intention of fostering the growth and popularity of heirloom beans, gathering bean seeds from Seed Savers Exchange and new varieties from Mexico. Since then, the company has grown to include hot sauce, dried pozole, and chiles, and Steve has authored *Heirloom Beans* (cowritten with Vanessa Barrington), *The Rancho Gordo Heirloom Bean Growers Guide*, *Supper at Rancho Gordo*, and *The Rancho Gordo Vegetarian Kitchen*.

Made with canned tuna, a typical pantry staple, this hearty and delicious main-course salad is a great dish anytime of the year. It can be served slightly warm in the winter or at room temperature as the centerpiece of a summer dinner. Make sure to use the highest-quality olive oil–packed tuna you can find, preferably an Italian or Spanish brand.

Single Batch **Makes 8 servings**

Double Batch **Makes 16 servings**

MAKE AHEAD

The beans can be cooked up to 2 days in advance. Let them cool in their cooking liquid, then refrigerate until ready to use. The salad can be prepared without fresh herbs and refrigerated for up to 1 day in advance. The finished salad can be refrigerated for up to 4 hours. Re-season with vinegar, oil, salt, and pepper before serving.

INGREDIENTS	SINGLE BATCH	DOUBLE BATCH
5-oz cans olive oil–packed tuna, drained slightly	2	4
Sweet onion(s), such as Vidalia, Walla Walla, or red, very thinly sliced	1	2
Celery ribs, halved lengthwise and cut on the diagonal into ¼-inch-thick slices	2	4
Finely chopped fresh flat-leaf parsley	⅔ cup	1⅓ cups
Drained, cooked white kidney, flageolet, cannellini, or other white beans (from about 1 lb/2 lb dried beans, respectively; page 235)	6 cups	12 cups
Extra-virgin olive oil	6 Tbsp	¾ cup

continued on following page

233

This is a hearty, satisfying salad
to serve as a main dish for a lunch
gathering; just add some lightly
dressed greens.

Red wine vinegar	1½ Tbsp	3 Tbsp
Finely grated lemon zest (optional)	2 tsp	4 tsp
Kosher salt and freshly ground black pepper		

Put the tuna in a large bowl and break it up slightly with a fork. Add the onion(s), celery, parsley, and beans. Drizzle with the oil and vinegar, add the lemon zest (if using), and season with salt and pepper, then toss gently to combine. Taste and adjust the seasoning. Serve at room temperature within 2 hours.

COOKING A BIG BATCH OF BEANS

ACCORDING TO STEVE SANDO, there is no single method for cooking beans. When you are in a hurry, you can use a pressure cooker, and when you have more time, a pot of beans can simmer slowly on the stove top.

Soaking the beans overnight in water to cover can speed up the process, though the main determinate of cooking time is the freshness of your dried beans; older beans take longer to cook. Steve normally soaks his beans in the morning in cold water. If you want to soak your beans, first rinse them and check for small bits of debris or pebbles. Then add cold water to cover by 1 inch and let sit for 2 to 6 hours.

To cook the beans, pour the beans and their soaking water into a large pot and add water as needed to cover the beans by 1½ inches. Cover the pot, place over medium-high heat, and bring to a hard boil.

Keep the beans at a boil for 5 minutes and then reduce the heat to a very gentle simmer. (If you have not soaked the beans, keep them at a boil for about 15 minutes.) If the simmer turns to a boil, remove the lid or set it ajar. Now allow the beans to cook. This can take 1 hour or it can take 3 to 4 hours, depending on the age of your beans. They are ready when they are cooked through—they should have no crunch—but still hold their shape.

When the beans are almost ready, add salt. Go easy, as it takes some time for the beans to absorb the salt. A scant 2 teaspoons salt per pot of 1 pound dried beans is usually ideal, though your palate may differ. Add any acidic ingredients, like tomatoes or vinegar, only after the beans are cooked through.

While fresh dried beans don't need a lot of fussing, you can flavor them as they cook with a ham bone, chicken broth, or a classic *mirepoix* (finely chopped carrot, celery, and onion sautéed in a little oil or other fat), if you like, though Steve prefers just sautéed onion and garlic.

In general, 1 pound (about 2 cups) will yield 6 cups of cooked beans.

8.
sweet gatherings

WHETHER IT'S A community ice cream social, a holiday cookie swap, or a fund-raising bake sale, dessert parties make sweet gatherings.

Maybe it's because they remind us of simple joys—making a wish on the candles of a birthday cake, sneaking spoonfuls of cookie dough, or licking the drips off summer ice cream cones—making dessert taps into our deepest sense of nostalgia. It's also a great place to start cooking with novices of any age. Any kitchen newcomer will be encouraged by the ease of mixing up a batch of brownie batter or the camaraderie of icing cupcakes.

Many of these recipes can be used as a base for others. With that in mind, you'll find a butter layer cake that becomes a Bundt cake and cupcakes, a berry trifle that has two great variations, a juicy crisp that can be made with different kinds of fruit, and a classic challah loaf for Shabbat that can be easily transformed into sweet cinnamon rolls ideal for a late morning get together.

Whatever the event, dessert is always welcome.

GABI MOSKOWITZ

challah cinnamon rolls with cream cheese icing

Single Batch **Makes 12 rolls**

Double Batch **Makes 24 rolls**

MAKE AHEAD

To serve cinnamon rolls in time for breakfast, make the dough the day before, through the first rise. Roll out and fill the dough, shape and cut the rolls, and transfer the rolls to the prepared baking dish. Cover tightly with plastic wrap and refrigerate overnight or up to 18 hours. The next day, remove the rolls from the refrigerator and let rise for 1 hour or so (until the rolls look puffy) before baking, then bake as directed.

NEARLY EVERY FRIDAY, Gabi Moskowitz, author of *The Brokeass Gourmet* and *Hot Mess Kitchen* and producer of the television show *Young and Hungry*, hosts a Shabbat dinner for family and friends. It's the perfect end to a hectic week. Follow her lead and turn off your cell phone, roast a chicken or cook a brisket (page 133), and fill your home with warm, savory smells. Then all you need is some wine and as many people as you can crowd around your table (or, if you're like Gabi, into your tiny apartment living room).

Whether Gabi is cooking for a few people or a large group, she always makes a double batch of challah dough. She braids half into a loaf for Friday dinner, then forms the remaining dough into cinnamon rolls that she pops into the refrigerator for a slow overnight rise. The next morning, she bakes them off, resets the table, and invites more friends over for brunch.

Because this is the sweets chapter, Gabi's classic challah dough, rich in eggs and oil and lightly sweetened with sugar, is used here to make her signature weekend cinnamon rolls. The dough can be made and the rolls baked the same day, but she advises a long, slow rise in the refrigerator (see *Make Ahead*), which is good for both the dough (allowing the various ingredients to mingle leisurely) and the baker (who doesn't have to get up early to make the dough). In case you want to do as Gabi does and bake a loaf or two of challah, directions for making the traditional braided bread are on page 243.

INGREDIENTS	SINGLE BATCH	DOUBLE BATCH
Dough		
Warm water (105° to 115°F)	⅔ cup	1⅓ cups
Sugar	¼ cup plus ¼ tsp	½ cup plus ½ tsp
Active dry yeast (1 and 2 envelopes, respectively)	2¼ tsp	4½ tsp

continued on following page

INGREDIENTS	SINGLE BATCH	DOUBLE BATCH
Olive or vegetable oil, plus more for the bowl	⅓ cup	⅔ cup
Large eggs	2	4
Kosher salt	1½ tsp	1 Tbsp
All-purpose flour, or as needed	3½ cups	7 cups
Filling		
Unsalted butter, at room temperature, plus more for the pan(s)	5 Tbsp	10 Tbsp
Granulated sugar	⅔ cup	1⅓ cups
Ground cinnamon	1½ Tbsp	3 Tbsp
Icing		
Cream cheese, at room temperature	3 oz	6 oz
Unsalted butter, at room temperature	3 Tbsp	6 Tbsp
Confectioners' sugar	⅔ cup	1⅓ cups
Vanilla extract	¼ tsp	½ tsp
Whole milk, if needed to thin	1 Tbsp	2 Tbsp

EQUIPMENT

One or two large bowls for mixing and proofing the dough: the dough is mixed and kneaded by hand, but you can use a stand mixer—the paddle attachment for mixing the dough, and the dough hook on medium speed for kneading—for both steps, if you prefer; one or two 9-by-13-inch baking dishes.

BIG BATCH NOTES

You will need a very large bowl for mixing and proofing the dough. If you decide to use a stand mixer for the double batch and you find it is straining during kneading, remove the dough from the bowl and continue kneading by hand on a work surface. If baking a double batch, rotate the dishes from back to front about halfway through baking.

Preheat the oven to 350°F and then turn it off. When it is time for the dough to rise, the oven will be warm but not hot.

Make the dough: In a large, heat-resistant bowl, whisk together the warm water, ¼ teaspoon sugar if making a single batch or ½ teaspoon sugar if making a double batch, and the yeast and let sit for 3 to 4 minutes to activate (it will become foamy). Whisk in the remaining ¼ cup sugar if making a single batch or ½ cup sugar if making a double batch, the oil, eggs, and salt, continuing to whisk until all of the ingredients are fully incorporated. Switch to a wooden spoon and slowly stir in enough of the flour until the dough is too stiff to stir.

Lightly flour a work surface and turn the dough out onto it. Knead the dough, adding more flour as necessary, until smooth, elastic, and slightly sticky, 8 to 10 minutes. Shape the dough into a ball.

Rinse the bowl you used for mixing the dough, dry well, and then coat with oil. Place the dough in the bowl and turn to coat it evenly with oil. Cover the bowl with a kitchen towel and place in the warm (not hot) oven. Let rise until roughly doubled in size, about 1 hour.

Make the filling: In a bowl, combine the butter, granulated sugar, and cinnamon and, using a rubber spatula, work together to make a smooth paste.

Shape and bake the rolls: Butter a 9-by-13-inch baking dish (or two baking dishes if making a double batch). Transfer the dough to a very lightly floured work surface and knead briefly to release excess air bubbles. (If making a double batch, divide the dough in half and work with half at a time to make each batch of rolls.)

On the lightly floured work surface, roll out the dough into a 13-by-10-inch rectangle, with a long side facing you. Use the rubber spatula to spread the filling evenly over the dough. Starting with the long edge farthest from you, roll the dough tightly toward you into a tight cylinder. Pinch the seam closed to seal the cylinder. Using a sharp knife, cut crosswise into 12 slices each about 1 inch thick. Arrange the slices, with a cut side up, in the prepared dish. (If making a double batch, repeat with the second half of the dough.) Cover tightly with plastic wrap and let the dough rise in a warm spot until the rolls look puffy, about 1 hour.

Preheat the oven to 350°F. Uncover the baking dish(es) and bake the rolls, rotating the dishes from back to front about halfway through baking if making a double batch, until nicely browned, 14 to 16 minutes. Let cool in the baking dish(es) on a wire rack for 15 to 30 minutes.

Make the icing: In a bowl with a handheld mixer, or in a stand mixer fitted with the paddle attachment, beat together the cream cheese, butter, confectioners' sugar, and vanilla on low speed until combined, then increase the speed to high and beat until smooth, thick, and spoonable. If the icing seems too thick, beat in milk to thin as needed.

Spread the icing over the warm rolls and serve.

CHALLAH

THE PERFECT CHALLAH is a gorgeous golden brown without any pale spots, so Gabi gives her loaf a double application of egg wash to ensure even coloring: as the bread rises, she brushes the new areas that appear with beaten egg.

Make the dough for the cinnamon rolls (page 240) and let rise as directed. Line a half sheet pan with parchment paper. Transfer the dough to a very lightly floured work surface and knead briefly to release excess air bubbles. (If making a double batch, line two half sheet pans with parchment paper, divide the dough in half, and work with half at a time to shape each loaf.) Divide the dough into three equal pieces. Using your palms, roll and stretch each piece into a rope 18 inches long, slightly tapering both ends of each rope. Lay the ropes side by side vertically, spacing them 1 inch apart.

Gently pinch the three strands together at the top and tuck the pinched end under. Lift the rope on the right and bring it over the center rope so it is now becomes the center rope and the original center rope is now the rope on the right. Next, lift the rope on the left and bring it over the center rope so it is now the center rope. Continuing braiding the ropes in this manner, alternately passing the right rope over the center rope and then the left rope over the center and keeping the loops fairly snug as you work. When you have reached the ends of the strands, pinch them together as you did the top and tuck the pinched end under. The loaf should be about 12 inches long. Transfer the loaf to the prepared pan. (If making two loaves, repeat with the second half of the dough and place on the second pan.)

Make the topping: In a small bowl, whisk 1 large egg with 2 tablespoons water. Using a pastry brush, lightly brush the top of the loaf thoroughly, reaching all of the way down the sides without dripping onto the pan. Reserve the remaining egg mixture. Set the challah aside in a warm place, uncovered, until it looks puffed but not doubled, about 35 minutes. (If making two loaves, brush the second loaf the same way.)

Preheat the oven to 350°F. If baking two loaves, position racks in the center and top third of the oven.

Brush the loaf (or loaves) a second time, making sure to coat the exposed creases in the braids. If desired, sprinkle the loaf (or each loaf) evenly with 1½ teaspoons poppy seeds or sesame seeds. Bake until golden brown and the loaf sounds hollow when tapped on the bottom, 35 to 40 minutes. Let cool completely on a wire rack before serving.

Single Batch Makes 1 loaf

Double Batch Makes 2 loaves

MAKE AHEAD

The dough can be refrigerated for up to 48 hours before shaping, rising, and baking. This is especially helpful if you want to bake the challah on Friday night but are not home in the afternoon to make the dough. The baked challah can be cooled, wrapped tightly in plastic wrap and an overwrap of aluminum foil, and frozen for up to 2 months. Thaw at room temperature, then place in a 300°F oven until warmed through.

EQUIPMENT

Follow the suggestions for the cinnamon rolls but replace the baking dishes with two half sheet pans.

BIG BATCH NOTES

If baking two loaves, do not put them on the same sheet pan, as they will begin to crowd each other as they rise. Instead, put each loaf on its own pan, position the oven racks in the center and top third of the oven, and then switch the pans between the racks and rotate them from back to front about halfway through baking.

LISA DONOVAN

buttermilk chess slab pie

WHILE A PASTRY chef at City House in Nashville, Tennessee, Lisa Donovan's favorite days were the Sunday Suppers, when they welcomed the whole city to the table. The chefs were able to divert from the regular menu to play around with fun ideas and, in general, have fun cooking for large groups of people. She was so inspired that she expanded the idea to create the Buttermilk Road Sunday Supper Series, a pop-up restaurant that celebrates the tradition of the community-family Sunday feasts.

Buttermilk is also the key ingredient in Lisa's signature chess pie, a dessert she developed as the pastry chef at Husk, a popular Nashville restaurant celebrating southern foodways and ingredients. Unlike fruit desserts that depend on the short, seasonal arrival of the summer's peaches or berries, this smooth, rich, butter-yellow chess pie can be made year-round, whenever a simple but celebratory dessert deserves to decorate the table. Eggs, sugar, melted butter, and tangy buttermilk are whisked with lemon and vanilla, poured into a pie shell, and baked to form a rich custard in flaky, golden brown pastry.

Lisa's chess pies became so popular that, even when cooking at home, one pie was never enough for her family and friends. This slab pie version became her big batch solution. Baked in a half sheet pan instead of the usual round pie pan and cut into squares, a slab pie is a great dessert for transporting to a family reunion or birthday party. It also works for any day that needs a sweet pick-me-up. And if you should be so lucky to have a square or two remaining at the end of the party, the only thing better than fresh pie for dessert, as any pie eater will tell you, is leftover pie for breakfast.

Makes 18 to 24 servings
(one 18-by-13-inch pie)

MAKE AHEAD

The dough can be refrigerated for up to 2 days or frozen for up to 1 month; if frozen, thaw overnight in the refrigerator. The pie tastes best when served the day it is baked.

BIG BATCH NOTES

The pie serves 18 to 24 which makes it a big batch recipe. If you should want more servings, bake a second pie, making it and baking it separately from the first.

INGREDIENTS

Crust

All-purpose flour	4 cups
Kosher salt	1 Tbsp
Unsalted butter, preferably high-fat European style such as Plugra, chilled	1 lb
Ice water, or as needed	½ cup

Filling

Lemons	2
Sugar	6 cups
All-purpose flour	1 cup
Kosher salt	2 tsp
Large eggs	12
Buttermilk	3 cups
Unsalted butter, melted and cooled	1 cup
Vanilla bean, split lengthwise	1

Make the crust: Fill a 4-cup capacity measuring cup full of ice and top off with water. Set aside. In a large bowl, toss together the flour and salt to mix well. Cut half of the butter into ½-inch cubes and the other half into 1-inch cubes. Scatter the butter cubes over the dry ingredients, making sure they are not sticking together. Use your hands to begin working the butter into the flour; you want to incorporate all of the butter into the flour without overworking it. Every piece of butter should be coated with some flour before you begin to add the water, and there should be no whole cubes of butter. Doing this deftly is key; if your butter starts to feel too warm at any time, slip the bowl into the freezer or refrigerator to cool off.

Drizzle about ¼ cup of the ice water over the butter-flour mixture. Using only your hands as paddles—do not use your fingers or do any kneading—toss the water into the flour mixture until it is fully absorbed. Add a little more water and continue to paddle with your hands. Continue adding water and paddling the mixture with your hands until it begins to form into a ball; you will likely add a total of about ½ cup ice water, depending on the day's humidity. When the mixture has become dough and feels moist but not wet or sticky, give it a few strong kneading turns in the bowl to work it all together. The dough should feel tacky and supple and be neither sticky nor moist. Form into a thick disk and wrap in plastic wrap. Let chill and rest in the refrigerator for at least 30 minutes before rolling.

Position racks in the center and bottom third of the oven and preheat the oven to 400°F. Cover the center area of the bottom rack with aluminum foil to catch any drips from the pie.

Remove the dough from the refrigerator and let stand for 5 minutes to lessen, but not lose, its chill. Lightly flour a work surface and a rolling pin and transfer the dough to the floured surface. Roll out the dough into a 19-by-13-inch rectangle, flouring the work surface and pin as needed to prevent the dough from sticking. Carefully transfer the dough to an 11-by-17-inch sheet pan (jelly-roll pan), pressing it gently onto the bottom and sides, and decoratively crimp the edges. Place the crust in the freezer while you prepare the filling.

Make the filling: Grate the zest from the lemons into a small bowl, then halve the lemons and squeeze the juice into the same bowl. In a large bowl, whisk together the sugar, flour, and salt. In a second large bowl (preferably one with a spout), whisk together the eggs and buttermilk, blending well. Gradually whisk the sugar mixture into the egg mixture, mixing well, then slowly whisk in the butter. Using the tip of a knife, scrape the seeds from the vanilla bean into the mixture, then add the lemon juice and zest and whisk to combine.

Open the oven door, pull out the center rack, and set the pie crust on the center rack. Carefully pour the filling into the crust, slide the rack into the oven, close the oven door, and reduce the oven temperature to 350°F. Bake for 40 to 45 minutes, then check the pie; the crust should be golden brown and the center should jiggle only slightly. If the pie is not set, reduce the oven temperature to 325°F and continue baking, checking every 5 to 10 minutes, until set.

Transfer the pie to a wire rack and let cool completely, then cut into squares and serve.

EMILY LUCHETTI

lemon-blueberry trifle

THE NAME "TRIFLE" belies the generous nature of this beautiful dessert that originated in eighteenth-century England and is traditionally served at Christmas. But star pastry chef Emily Luchetti, whose goal in creating desserts is "to make them fun, straightforward and flavorful—[dishes] designed to please, delight, and just make life rosier"—looked beyond the calendar, recognizing instead the natural seasonal versatility of the trifle, as this trio of trifles illustrates.

Made up of layers of cake, custard cream, fruit, and sometimes whipped cream, trifles are particularly ideal for big groups because they feed many, can be prepared in advance, look impressive, and, thanks to their vertical structure, fit easily in the refrigerator. Perhaps the sole problem with making a party trifle ahead of time is that someone might secretly dig into it before the big event.

A few years ago, Emily was throwing a holiday party for twenty-five people. Knowing her husband's weakness for nibbling on desserts, she wrapped the trifle dish in aluminum foil and labeled it "beef stock," hoping to throw him off the scent. On the night of the party, he was so surprised to see her pull out the foil-swaddled dish, revealing the ruse, that he now checks every item in the refrigerator, regardless of what the label says.

Because this trifle's lemon and blueberry layers are so striking, you'll want to serve it from a classic trifle dish, a large, clear glass bowl, or even a wide glass vase. You can also make individual trifles using wineglasses, small tumblers, or ice cream glasses. If you want to add a liqueur to your trifle, brush it onto the cooled sponge cakes before assembly.

INGREDIENTS

Sponge Cake

Unsalted butter, at room temperature, for preparing pans	
All-purpose flour	2½ cups
Baking powder	1 Tbsp plus 2 tsp
Kosher salt	¼ tsp

continued on following page

continued on following page

Makes 20 servings

MAKE AHEAD

The cakes can be stored at room temperature for up to 1 day or frozen for up to 1 week. To freeze, bake, unmold, and slice the cake as directed. Wrap each piece of cake in waxed or parchment paper, place in zippered plastic freezer bags, and freeze. Thaw at room temperature before using. The lemon curd and fruit compote can be refrigerated for up to 1 day. The assembled trifle must be refrigerated for at least 4 hours and no longer than 8 hours before serving.

BIG BATCH NOTES

This recipe will easily serve twenty. If you make two trifles, do not double the cake recipe, as the amount of batter is more than can be mixed or baked at once. Make two separate recipes. The other components—compote, lemon cream, whipped cream—can be doubled.

INGREDIENTS

Large eggs, separated	10
Sugar	2½ cups
Boiling water	½ cup plus 2 Tbsp
Vanilla extract	2 tsp
Finely grated lemon zest	2 tsp

Lemon Cream

Large eggs	2
Large egg yolks	6
Sugar	¾ cup
Fresh lemon juice	¾ cup
Heavy cream	1¾ cups

Blueberry Compote

Blueberries	3 pints (about 6 cups)
Sugar	½ cup
Fresh lemon juice	1 tsp

Make the sponge cake: Position racks in the top third and center of the oven and preheat the oven to 350°F. Butter the bottoms of two half sheet pans avoiding the sides, then line the bottoms with parchment paper.

Sift together the flour, baking powder, and salt into a bowl and set aside. In a stand mixer fitted with the whisk attachment, combine the egg yolks and sugar and whip on high speed until thick and pale yellow, about 2 minutes. Reduce the speed to medium-low, add the boiling water and vanilla, and beat until well mixed, scraping down the sides of the bowl as needed. Increase the speed to high and again whip until the mixture is thick, about 2 minutes. Reduce the speed to low, add the flour mixture and lemon zest, and beat until well mixed. Transfer the batter to a large bowl.

Clean and dry the mixer bowl and whisk attachment and reassemble the mixer. Add the egg whites to the bowl and whip on high speed until soft, billowing peaks form. They should be smooth and not at all clumpy. Scoop half of the whipped whites onto the batter and fold in gently, being careful not to overmix. Then fold in the remaining half, again being careful not to overmix.

Divide the batter between the two prepared pans, spreading it evenly.

Bake until golden brown and the cakes spring back when lightly touched, about 15 minutes. Let cool completely in the pans on wire racks.

lemon-blueberry trifle   251

Make the lemon cream: In a large bowl, whisk together the eggs, egg yolks, and sugar until blended. Whisk in the lemon juice.

Pour the lemon mixture into a heavy nonreactive (stainless-steel or enameled cast-iron) saucepan, place over low heat, and cook, stirring constantly with a heat-resistant spatula, until the mixture has thickened, about 8 minutes. Switch to a whisk and whisk until smooth. Remove from the heat and strain through a fine-mesh sieve into a clean bowl. Cover with plastic wrap, pressing the wrap directly onto the lemon mixture to prevent a skin from forming. Refrigerate until cold, about 1 hour.

In the stand mixer fitted with the whisk attachment, beat the cream on medium-high speed until soft peaks form. Using a rubber spatula, fold the whipped cream into the cold lemon cream mixture just until combined. Cover and refrigerate until needed.

Make the blueberry compote: In a saucepan, combine the blueberries, sugar, and lemon juice over medium heat and cook, stirring occasionally, until the berries begin to release their juice and become soft, about 5 minutes. Remove from the heat. Puree half of the blueberry mixture in a food processor and stir the puree back into the berries remaining in the saucepan. Let the compote cool to room temperature.

Unmold and cut the cake: One at a time, run a thin knife around the edge of each cake pan to loosen the cake sides, then invert the cake onto a large cutting board. Lift off the pan and peel off the parchment.

The cake can be cut into rectangles or rounds, depending on the vessel you are using for the trifle. To cut into rectangles, using a serrated knife, cut each cake into quarters and then split each quarter in half horizontally. To cut into rounds, use the edge of the upturned trifle bowl (or other round vessel you will be using) as a template, and mark out four rounds on the cakes. Use a small knife to cut out each round. Depending on the size of the bowl, the rounds may not be complete. Don't worry, as you will have plenty of trimmings to make complete layers in the bowl.

Assemble the trifle: Spread a thin layer of blueberry compote on the bottom of a 5-quart trifle dish or glass bowl. Top with a layer of the cake, cutting to fit if needed. Top the cake with another layer of the blueberry compote and then with a layer of the lemon cream. Repeat the layers until the bowl is full. Cover the trifle and refrigerate for at least 4 hours and no longer than 8 hours before serving.

STRAWBERRY-PEACH TRIFLE

Make the sponge cake, bake, unmold, and cut as directed.

Make the strawberry layer: In a heavy saucepan, combine 4 pints strawberries, hulled and quartered, and 1 cup sugar over medium heat and cook, stirring frequently, until the mixture has a jam-like consistency, about 15 minutes. Let cool to room temperature. To make the peach layer, peel, pit, and chop 4 pounds peaches, transfer to a bowl, and stir in ¼ cup sugar. Check for sweetness and add up to 2 tablespoons more sugar if needed. (The strawberries can be refrigerated for up to 1 day. The peaches are best if used within 1 hour.)

Make the cream filling: In the stand mixer fitted with the whisk attachment, combine 3 cups heavy cream, 3 cups sour cream, and ½ cup sugar. Split a vanilla bean in half lengthwise and, using the tip of a knife, scrape the seeds into the mixture. Beat on medium speed until soft peaks form.

Assemble the trifle: Spread a thin layer of strawberries on the bottom of a 5-quart trifle dish or glass bowl. Top with a layer of the cake, cutting to fit if needed. Top the cake with another layer of the strawberries and then a layer of peaches. Spoon a layer of the cream over the peaches. Repeat the layers in the same order—cake, strawberries, peaches, cream—ending with the cream. Cover and refrigerate for at least 4 hours and no longer than 8 hours before serving.

ROASTED PINEAPPLE–COCONUT TRIFLE

Make the sponge cake, bake, unmold, and cut as directed.

Prepare the pineapple and toast the coconut: See notes at right.

Make the cream filling: Make the same cream used in the Strawberry-Peach Trifle.

Assemble the trifle: Arrange a single layer of the pineapple rings on the bottom of a 5-quart trifle dish or glass bowl. Top with a layer of the cake, cutting to fit if needed. Top the cake with another layer of pineapple rings and then a layer of pineapple puree. Spoon a layer of the cream over the puree and top with the toasted coconut. Repeat the layers in the same order—cake, pineapple rings, pineapple puree, cream, coconut—ending with the coconut. Cover and refrigerate for at least 4 hours and no longer than 8 hours before serving.

ROASTED PINEAPPLE PURÉE

Preheat the oven to 400°F and line two half sheet pans with parchment paper. Peel and core 2 pineapples and cut into rings ¼-inch thick. In a large bowl, toss together the pineapple and ½ cup firmly packed brown sugar, coating evenly, then transfer the pineapple in a single layer to the prepared pans. Bake until caramelized, 8 to 10 minutes. Puree half of the pineapple in a food processor. Let the pineapple puree and rings cool. (The roasted pineapple can be refrigerated for up to 1 day.)

TOASTED COCONUT

With the oven still at 400°F, spread 2 cups unsweetened shredded dried coconut on a half sheet pan and toast, stirring once or twice, until golden brown, about 5 minutes. Let cool. (The toasted coconut can be stored at room temperature for up to 1 day.)

JODI LIANO

cookie exchange

JODI LIANO, FOUNDER of San Francisco Cooking School, hosts an annual cookie exchange at her San Francisco Bay Area home during the holiday season. It's a tradition that is common in many communities, as families and friends get together to share batches of their favorite treats, often using recipes passed down through generations.

Jodi suggests asking each guest to bring three or four dozen cookies, bars, or candies to swap. Ideally, each recipe comes with a great story to share with the rest of the party. At the end of the evening, everyone goes home with a collection of new cookies. Recipe cards are optional but much appreciated.

Jodi has just two firm rules about cookie exchanges: no store-bought cookies and no chocolate-chip cookies! Here are three of Jodi's favorite recipes: an airy chocolate candy, chai-spiced cookies, and crunchy caramel-chocolate bars. She recommends offering a light dinner, like a soup or a hearty salad, so guests can avoid a sugar overload.

CHOCOLATE HONEYCOMB CANDY

Even though this isn't a cookie, it is a true crowd-pleaser at Jodi's cookie exchange. As candy recipes go, it is a good one for beginners. Use either milk or dark chocolate to coat the finished candy, which has a toffee-like flavor and a foamy, airy texture.

INGREDIENTS

Vegetable oil, plus more for preparing the pan	1 tsp
Dark corn syrup	1 cup
Sugar	1 cup
Baking soda	2¾ tsp
Vanilla extract	½ tsp
Kosher salt	pinch
Dark or milk chocolate, coarsely chopped	4 oz

Makes about 2 quarts of candy

MAKE AHEAD

The candy can be stored in an airtight container (preferably tin rather than plastic) at room temperature for up to 4 days.

EQUIPMENT

Silicone baking mat or parchment paper; candy thermometer.

BIG BATCH

If you want a larger quantity, make two separate batches, as it is difficult to spread a large batch properly before it begins to harden.

Line a sheet pan with parchment paper and lightly oil the paper, or line the pan with a silicone baking mat.

In a heavy saucepan, combine the corn syrup and sugar over medium-high heat and cook, stirring often, until the sugar dissolves. Attach a candy thermometer to the side of the saucepan and continue to cook without stirring, using a pastry brush dipped in cold water to brush down the sides of the pan as needed to wash away any stray sugar crystals, until the mixture reaches 300°F (hard-crack stage). Remove the pan from the heat and carefully put the thermometer in the sink.

Sprinkle the baking soda into the pan and add the vanilla and salt. Immediately and gently stir the mixture with a heat-resistant spatula to mix well, then carefully pour the mixture in an even layer onto the prepared pan. Spread gently with the spatula; too much pressure on the honeycomb will deflate it. Place the pan on a wire rack and let the candy harden and cool to room temperature.

Pour water to a depth of about 2 inches into a saucepan. Place the chocolate and oil in a heatproof bowl that will fit snugly in the rim of the pan without touching the water. Bring the water to a gentle boil, rest the bowl on the rim of the pan, and heat, stirring, until the chocolate melts and the mixture is smooth. Remove the bowl from the pan and let the chocolate rest until there is no steam coming off of it but it is still liquid, about 2 minutes.

Pour the chocolate onto the cooled candy. Then, using an offset spatula, spread the chocolate evenly over the surface. Let stand until the chocolate is set, 1 to 3 hours, depending on the temperature of your kitchen. Break the candy into roughly 2-inch pieces.

CHAI SPICED MELT-AWAY COOKIES

These spicy, tender, powdery cookies are similar to Mexican wedding cookies or sandies but with a hint of the warm spices found in a cup of chai. They are particularly well suited to big batch cooking as they don't spread during baking. That means you can fit more than the usual amount on a sheet pan, to yield lots of cookies in record time.

INGREDIENTS	SINGLE BATCH	DOUBLE BATCH
Unsalted butter, at room temperature	1 cup	2 cups
Confectioners' sugar, sifted, plus more for dusting	½ cup	1 cup
Vanilla extract	2 tsp	4 tsp
Finely grated orange zest	1 tsp	2 tsp
Cake flour	2¼ cups	4½ cups
Ground allspice	¾ tsp	1½ tsp
Ground cardamom	¾ tsp	1½ tsp
Ground cinnamon	½ tsp	1 tsp
Kosher salt	¼ tsp	½ tsp

Preheat the oven to 350°F. If baking a double batch, position two racks in the center of the oven. Line one half sheet pan with parchment paper, or line two pans if making a double batch.

In a large bowl, combine the butter, confectioners' sugar, vanilla, and orange zest and mix thoroughly with a wooden spoon. (You can use a stand mixer or handheld mixer on low speed, mixing for about 1 minute. Do not overmix.) Sift together the flour, allspice, cardamom, cinnamon, and salt into a bowl. Add the flour mixture to the butter mixture and mix just until a smooth dough forms.

Single Batch **Makes about 3 dozen**

Double Batch **Makes about 6 dozen**

MAKE AHEAD

The cookies can be stored in airtight tin containers at room temperature for up to 10 days. (Do not store the cookies in plastic containers, as they will soften.) They can also be frozen in ziplock plastic freezer bags for up to 1 month. Thaw the cookies at room temperature and coat with additional confectioners' sugar before serving.

BIG BATCH NOTES

Shape all of the balls at once and place them in a cool place or in the refrigerator until ready to bake. Because the cookies bake quickly, you can bake one sheet at a time, eliminating the need to rotate the pans halfway through baking. If you have only one pan and are baking a double batch, be sure to let the pan cool completely before placing more dough on it for baking.

Using about 1 tablespoon for each cookie, roll the dough into balls. Place the balls on the prepared pans, placing them close together (the cookies do not spread).

Bake the cookies until just set but not browned, 8 to 10 minutes. If baking two pans, switch the pans between the racks and rotate them from back to front about halfway through baking. Remove from the oven and, while still warm, either gently toss the cookies in additional confectioners' sugar or sift the sugar over them. Transfer to wire racks and let cool completely.

CARAMELITAS

Bar cookies are one of the easiest ways to feed a crowd, as they can be cut into any size you like. These chewy, caramel-rich bars call for homemade caramel sauce, but you can use store-bought as a time-saver. If making a single batch, you will have leftover caramel, which can be used as dessert topping.

INGREDIENTS	SINGLE BATCH	DOUBLE BATCH
Unsalted butter, melted and cooled, plus more at room temperature for the baking pan(s)	¾ cup	1½ cups
Old-fashioned rolled oats or quick-cooking oats	1¾ cups	3½ cups
All-purpose flour	1½ cups	3 cups
Firmly packed light brown sugar	¾ cup	1½cups
Baking soda	½ tsp	1 tsp
Kosher salt	¼ tsp	½ tsp
Unsalted butter, melted	¾ cup	1½ cups
Semisweet or bittersweet chocolate, coarsely chopped	12 oz	1½ lb
Chopped walnuts or pecans	1 cup	2 cups
Caramel Layer		
Granulated sugar	1 cup	
Water	⅓ cup	
Unsalted butter, cut into 1-Tbsp pieces	¼ cup	
Heavy cream, heated to steaming	1 cup	

Preheat the oven to 350°F. Butter a 9-by-13-inch baking pan, then line the bottom of the pan with parchment paper. If making a double batch, butter and line two 9-by-13-inch baking pans.

In a large bowl, combine the oats, flour, brown sugar, baking soda, and salt and stir to mix well. Pour in the melted butter and stir to coat evenly. Measure out 1 cup of the oat mixture if making a single batch or 2 cups if making a double batch and set aside. Press the remaining oat mixture onto the bottom of the prepared baking pan, or divide evenly between two pans if making a double batch.

Bake until golden brown, 12 to 15 minutes. Remove from the oven and sprinkle the chocolate and nuts evenly over the surface.

Make the caramel layer: In a heavy saucepan, combine the sugar and water over medium heat and stir just until the sugar dissolves. Increase the heat to medium-high and bring to a boil. Cook, without stirring, swirling the saucepan occasionally and washing down any crystals that appear on the sides of the pan with a brush dipped in cold water, until the syrup caramelizes and turns a deep amber. Remove from the heat and slowly and carefully stir in the butter and cream (the sauce will sputter and bubble up), mixing well. If making a single batch, measure out 1 cup of the caramel. Transfer the remaining caramel to an airtight container and reserve for another use. It will keep refrigerated for up to 2 weeks.

Drizzle the caramel evenly over the nuts and chocolate, stopping within ¼ inch of the pan edges. Sprinkle the reserved oat mixture evenly over the surface.

Bake until the topping is golden brown, 18 to 22 minutes. Let cool completely in the pan(s) on wire racks. Cut into bars to serve.

ALICE MEDRICH

ultimate butter cake

WHETHER YOU'RE HOSTING a birthday party or a graduation, welcoming a new neighbor, or bringing cupcakes to a bake sale, this is the go-to cake recipe for all your needs. Baking expert, cooking teacher, and cookbook author Alice Medrich has created the ultimate yellow cake recipe, and it just happens to be gluten-free. This recipe, which calls for rice and oat flours, is adapted from *Flavor Flours*, Alice's award-winning cookbook that explores in depth baking with gluten-free flours.

This sunny yellow cake has the iconic buttery, vanilla-scented flavors that everyone loves. And the baker will love it, too, because it is an easy one-bowl batter that gives excellent results with little effort. You can use this batter to make a layer cake, cupcakes, or an easy-to-transport Bundt cake. There's also an orange variation, as well as one infused with nutmeg and drizzled with bourbon glaze.

Makes 8 to 10 servings (One 9-inch double layer cake or 8-inch triple layer cake)

MAKE AHEAD

The chocolate frosting will keep in the refrigerator for up to 5 days and the cream cheese frosting will keep for up to 3 days. Store the frostings in airtight containers and bring to room temperature before using. The cake can be frosted up to a few hours in advance and left at room temperature, or refrigerated, and then brought back to room temperature before serving.

INGREDIENTS

Unsalted butter, at room temperature, plus more for the pan	1 cup
White rice flour or Thai white rice flour (see *Ingredient Notes*, page 262)	2⅔ cups (400 g) or 4 cups (400 g)
Gluten-free oat flour (see *Ingredient Notes*, page 262)	½ cup (50 g)
Sugar	2 cups minus 3 Tbsp
Fine sea salt	¾ tsp
Plain yogurt, any percent butterfat	1 cup
Large eggs, at room temperature	4
Vanilla extract	2 tsp
Baking powder	2 tsp
Baking soda	1 tsp
Xanthan gum (see *Ingredient Notes*, page 262)	½ tsp
Chocolate Frosting (page 262) or Cream Cheese Frosting (page 263)	1 recipe

Position a rack in the lower third of the oven and preheat the oven to 350°F. Butter two 9-by-2-inch round cake pans or three 8-by-2-inch round cake pans and line the bottoms of the pans with parchment paper.

261

INGREDIENT NOTES

American brands of white rice flour (including Authentic Foods Superfine rice flour) are not as finely milled as the Thai rice flour (Erawan Brand) found in Asian groceries or online. You may use 400 grams of either type in this recipe, but note that it takes 4 cups—rather than 2⅔ cups— of Thai rice flour to equal the 400 grams called for. If you opt for Thai rice flour, be sure that it is regular rice flour in the red labeled package rather than glutinous or sweet rice flour which comes in the green labeled package.

If you or your guests are avoiding gluten, be sure the oat flour is labeled "gluten-free." While oats naturally contain no gluten, gluten-free oats are processed in separate facilities to avoid cross-contamination with other grains.

In a stand mixer fitted with the paddle attachment, combine the rice flour, oat flour, sugar, butter, and salt and mix on medium speed until the mixture is the texture of brown sugar, about 1 minute. Add the yogurt, eggs, vanilla, baking powder, baking soda, and xantham gum and beat on medium-high speed until the batter is very smooth and fluffy, 2 to 3 minutes.

Scrape the batter into the prepared pans, dividing it evenly, and smooth the tops. Bake until a wooden toothpick inserted into the center comes out clean and dry, 25 to 30 minutes for 9-inch cakes and 22 to 25 minutes for 8-inch cakes. Let the cakes cool completely in the pans on wire racks.

Slide a thin knife or a small metal spatula around the edge of each pan to loosen the cake sides, then invert each cake onto a rack, lift off the pan, and peel off the parchment. Turn the cakes right side up.

For a two-layer cake, place a cake layer on a serving platter, spread one-fourth of the frosting on top, and top with the second layer. For a three-layer cake, spread one-fifth of the frosting on the first layer, top with the second layer, spread with one-fifth of the frosting, and top with the third layer. Spread a very thin layer of frosting over the top and sides of the cake just to smooth the surface and glue on any crumbs. Chill to set the frosting, about 30 minutes. Stir the remaining frosting until smooth (warm it slightly if necessary) and spread it over the top and sides of the cake as luxuriously as you like.

Serve the cake at room temperature, cut into wedges.

FROSTINGS AND VARIATIONS

Chocolate Frosting

Put 1 cup heavy cream and 17½ ounces (500 g) milk or dark chocolate into a stainless-steel bowl. Pour water to a depth of 1 inch into a wide skillet, bring to a simmer, and turn off the heat. Set the bowl of chocolate in the water and let rest for 15 minutes, gently shaking the bowl several times to submerge the chocolate in the cream. When the chocolate is melted, start whisking at one edge of the bowl and continue whisking until all of the chocolate is incorporated and the mixture is smooth. Add 1 cup room-temperature unsalted butter, cut into chunks, and whisk once or twice to break them up. Let the mixture rest for 5 minutes to finish melting the butter before whisking the frosting smooth. Set aside until cool and thickened enough to spread. Makes about 4 cups.

Cream Cheese Frosting

Warm 1 pound cream cheese and 1 pound unsalted butter in a microwave oven on low until soft but not melted. Transfer to a bowl, add 3 cups confectioners' sugar and 1 teaspoon vanilla extract, and beat with a wooden spoon until smooth. Makes about 4 cups.

Orange Butter Cake

Substitute 4 teaspoons finely grated orange zest and ¼ cup fresh orange juice for the vanilla extract, add them with the yogurt and eggs, and bake in two layer pans. Spread the cooled layers with apricot jam (warmed if too stiff to spread), sprinkle with powdered sugar, and serve with lightly sweetened whipped cream.

Cupcakes

Line two 12-cup muffin pans with paper liners. Make the butter cake or orange butter cake batter as directed and fill the cups about two-thirds full. Bake until a toothpick inserted near the center of a cupcake comes out almost clean, 20 to 25 minutes. Let cool completely in the pans on wire racks, then remove from the pans and frost as desired. Top each frosted cupcake with candied rose petals or violets if you like.

Bundt Cake

Butter a 10- or 12-cup Bundt pan or spray with vegetable oil cooking spray. Make the butter cake or orange cake batter as directed, scrape the batter into the prepared pan, and smooth the top. Bake until a toothpick inserted in the center comes out clean and dry, 45 to 50 minutes. Let cool completely in the pan on a wire rack. To unmold the cake, rap all sides of the pan against the countertop, then invert onto the rack and lift off the pan.

Holiday Bundt Cake with Bourbon Glaze

Add 2 teaspoons freshly grated nutmeg to the butter cake batter with the baking powder and bake as directed for the Bundt cake. When the cake is cool and unmolded, in a bowl, stir together 1 cup confectioners' sugar and ¼ cup bourbon (or brandy or rum, if you prefer) until smooth to make a glaze. Pour the glaze over the cake, letting the excess drip down the sides.

texas sheet cake

A CROSS BETWEEN a chocolate cake and a brownie, this cake is more than just an easy-to-make, Texas-size dessert. A large, flat cake that can be cut into many pieces and is easily transportable, the sheet cake is a practical and delicious addition to birthday parties, picnics, and potlucks. Unlike most cakes, which must cool completely before they can be frosted, this Lone Star State beauty gets its moist texture from a smooth icing that is poured directly onto the warm cake and then spread evenly. As the icing soaks into the cake, it creates a rich top reminiscent of fudge.

This recipe comes from cookbook author, graphic designer, stylist, and self-taught baker Irvin Lin, who writes *Eat the Love*, a popular baking blog, and is the author of *Marbled, Swirled, and Layered*. Irvin, who was born in the Midwest, says that Texas sheet cake was a potluck favorite in the landlocked states in which he grew up. He is also known for his annual dessert parties and ice cream socials, where he gathers people together around a bounty of sweets. When Irvin moved to San Francisco some years back, he baked this recipe for a DIY dessert party held at 18 Reasons, to everyone's delight.

Single Batch **Makes 20 servings**

Double Batch **Makes 40 servings**

MAKE AHEAD

The baked and iced cake in its pan can be covered in plastic wrap and refrigerated for up to 3 days; bring to room temperature before serving. Or overwrap the cake with aluminum foil and freeze for up to 3 months, then thaw the cake at room temperature.

INGREDIENTS	SINGLE BATCH	DOUBLE BATCH
Cake		
All-purpose flour	2 cups	4 cups
Granulated sugar	1½ cups	3 cups
Firmly packed dark brown sugar	¼ cup	½ cup
Baking soda	½ tsp	1 tsp
Large eggs, at room temperature	2	4
Large egg yolks, at room temperature	2	4
Full-fat sour cream	¼ cup	½ cup
Vanilla extract	2 tsp	4 tsp
Bittersweet chocolate, chopped into ¼-inch chunks	8 oz	1 lb
Vegetable oil	¾ cup	1½ cups
Freshly brewed hot strong coffee	¾ cup	1½ cups

continued on following page

BIG BATCH NOTES

The double batch can be made in a stand mixer and divided between two half sheet pans. Bake on the top third and center racks in the oven. To ensure the cakes bake evenly, be sure to switch the pans between the racks and rotate the pans from back to front a little bit more than halfway through the bake time.

INGREDIENT NOTES

There are two types of unsweetened cocoa powder, natural and Dutch processed. Natural cocoa is roasted and pulverized cacao beans. Hershey's in the familiar brown can is the best-known brand; they also make a "special dark" cocoa with a red label that works well here. Dutch-processed cocoa powder is similar but has been treated with alkali to reduce the acidity of the cacao, giving the powder a mellower flavor and a darker, slightly reddish color. For the best results, always use the type specified in a recipe.

INGREDIENTS	SINGLE BATCH	DOUBLE BATCH
Dutch-processed cocoa powder (see *Ingredient Notes*)	½ cup	1 cup
Unsalted butter, cut into ½-inch cubes	¼ cup	½ cup
Kosher salt	½ tsp	1 tsp
Topping		
Unsalted butter, cut into ½-inch cubes	½ cup	1 cup
Heavy cream	½ cup	1 cup
Dutch-processed cocoa powder	½ cup	1 cup
Kosher salt	¼ tsp	½ tsp
Light corn syrup	1 Tbsp	2 Tbsp
Confectioners' sugar, sifted	3 cups	6 cups
Vanilla extract	1 Tbsp	2 Tbsp
Pecan halves, coarsely chopped	1½ cups	3 cups

Make the cake: Preheat the oven to 350°F. For a double batch, position racks in the center and top third of the oven. If making a single batch, spray one half sheet pan with cooking spray. If making a double batch, spray two half sheet pans.

In a large bowl, whisk together the flour, granulated and brown sugars, and baking soda, mixing well. In a medium bowl, whisk together the eggs, egg yolks, sour cream, and vanilla until well blended.

In a saucepan, combine the chocolate, oil, coffee, cocoa powder, butter, and salt over medium heat, stirring constantly, until the chocolate melts and the mixture is smooth, 3 to 5 minutes. Remove from the heat, pour into the dry ingredients, and stir with a large heat-resistant spatula until well mixed. Add the sour cream mixture and stir until smooth. Spread evenly in the prepared pan(s).

Bake the cake(s) until a wooden toothpick inserted into the center comes out clean, 18 to 20 minutes. If baking a double batch, switch the pans between the racks and rotate them from back to front about halfway through baking. Be careful not to overbake.

Make the topping about 10 minutes before the cake(s) is ready: In a saucepan, combine the butter, cream, cocoa, salt, and corn syrup over medium heat and cook, stirring constantly with a whisk, until the butter melts and the mixture is smooth. Remove from the heat. Add the confectioners' sugar and vanilla and whisk until smooth.

Remove the cake(s) from the oven. Pour the topping over the hot cake(s) and spread evenly with a small offset spatula (or butter knife) to the edges. Sprinkle the pecans over the still warm topping and gently press down on them to set them in the icing. Let the cake(s) cool to room temperature, about 1 hour, then move the cake(s), uncovered, to the refrigerator for 1 hour to set the icing fully.

Just before serving, bring the cake(s) to room temperature and cut into squares or rectangles with a sharp knife warmed in hot water and wiped dry before each cut.

JEN CASTLE AND BLAKE SPALDING

ice cream social

EVERY YEAR ON the Fourth of July, Jen Castle and Blake Spalding, chef-owners of Hell's Backbone Grill, host a free ice cream social for everyone in their small town of Boulder, Utah. Locals young and old come together to dress up scoops of home-made ice cream with hot fudge sauce, candied almonds, creamy *cajeta* (goat's milk caramel), and other irresistible toppings.

Following their Buddhist principles, Castle and Spalding started the annual ice cream social as a way to bring the residents of Boulder together. Now, this sweet community gathering has evolved into a much-loved, volunteer-run event with music, entertainment, and an all-ages talent show.

Hosting an ice cream social is a simple, joyful way to celebrate just about anything during the summer. And while Jen and Blake love to make ice cream, the real fun is in the toppings. Fresh fruit, whipped cream, toasted nuts, sprinkles, gooey sauces—get as creative as you want! I suggest buying a few crowd-pleasing flavors of ice cream from your favorite ice cream shop or grocery store and then letting your family and friends mix and match the toppings as they like.

Here are three of the homemade toppings Jen and Blake make for their annual get-together. Each one is an updated version of an old-fashioned soda fountain classic and will transform any serving of ice cream into a special sundae. The mildly tangy Mexican caramel sauce is made from condensed goat's milk, the hot fudge sauce gets a southwestern accent with the addition of piñon nuts, and the almonds are candied in the oven with a dusting of cinnamon. See page 271 for ideas on how to put together your own ice cream social.

Single Batch **Makes 3 cups**

Double Batch **Makes 6 cups**

CAJETA

This traditional Mexican caramel sauce is thick and luscious. If you are lucky enough to have some left over, it is also wonderful spread on toast, drizzled on pancakes or waffles, or used as a dip for fresh fruit.

INGREDIENTS	SINGLE BATCH	DOUBLE BATCH
Sugar	4 cups	8 cups
Water	1 cup	2 cups
Unsalted butter	⅓ cup	⅔ cup
Kosher salt	½ tsp	1 tsp
Canned unsweetened evaporated goat's milk or unsweetened evaporated cow's milk (see *Ingredient Notes*)	1 cup	2 cups

In a heavy saucepan, combine the sugar and water and bring to a boil over high heat, swirling the mixture occasionally to dissolve the sugar. Once the sugar has dissolved, boil the mixture, swirling the pan occasionally (do not stir) and using a pastry brush dipped in cold water to brush down the sides of the pan as needed to wash away any stray sugar crystals, until the mixture is a medium amber and has a honey-like consistency. If the mixture appears to be browning too fast, reduce the heat to medium.

Remove the pan from the heat and stir in the butter and salt. Slowly pour in the goat's milk while whisking vigorously until smooth. The mixture will bubble furiously when you begin adding the milk, but the bubbling will subside once you begin whisking. Let cool slightly before serving, then serve hot, warm, or at room temperature.

PIÑON HOT FUDGE SAUCE

Ground pine nuts lend a buttery flavor and pleasing texture to this rich fudge sauce. Jen and Blake use piñon nuts, which grow in the high desert of the Southwest, but the more common European pine nut, from the Italian stone pine, can be substituted.

INGREDIENTS	SINGLE BATCH	DOUBLE BATCH
Shelled piñon or pine nuts	1½ cups	3 cups
Sugar	½ cup	1 cup
Dutch-processed cocoa powder (see *Ingredient Notes*, page 266)	¼ cup	½ cup
Kosher salt	¼ tsp	½ tsp
Hot water	¾ cup	1½ cups
Heavy cream	1¼ cups	2½ cups
Light corn syrup	1 cup	2 cups
Distilled white vinegar	1 Tbsp	2 Tbsp
Semisweet chocolate chips	⅓ cup	⅔ cup
Unsweetened chocolate, coarsely chopped	2 oz	4 oz
Unsalted butter, cut into 1-Tbsp pieces	4 Tbsp	½ cup
Vanilla extract	1 Tbsp	2 Tbsp

MAKE AHEAD

The sauce can be stored in an airtight container in the refrigerator for up to 2 weeks. It will crystallize when refrigerated; to reheat, bring to a simmer over medium-low heat, whisking often, then simmer for 5 minutes, whisking until smooth.

BIG BATCH NOTES

Use a large, tall saucepan when making the sauce, as the goat's milk will bubble up when it is added to the hot caramel.

INGREDIENT NOTES

Look for canned evaporated goat's milk in the canned milk section of your supermarket. Meyenberg, which produces canned goat's milk is a widely distributed, high-quality brand. If using evaporated cow's milk, be sure to use unsweetened.

Single Batch **Makes 4 cups**

Double Batch **Makes 8 cups**

MAKE AHEAD

The sauce can be stored in the refrigerator for up to 1 week or in the freezer for up to 1 month. Reheat gently over medium-low heat if refrigerated. If frozen, hold the container of sauce under hot running water until the sauce is thawed enough to transfer it to a saucepan, then heat gently over low heat, stirring occasionally, until warmed through.

Pulse the nuts in a food processor until coarsely ground (the texture of couscous). Transfer to a small bowl.

Sift together the sugar, cocoa, and salt into a heavy saucepan. Add the hot water and stir to combine. Place over medium heat and bring to a simmer, whisking often until smooth. Add the cream, corn syrup, vinegar, and chocolate chips, increase the heat to medium-high, and bring to a boil. Continue to boil, swirling the mixture occasionally, until slightly reduced, 8 to 10 minutes. The mixture will be thin and sticky.

Remove from the heat and add the unsweetened chocolate, butter, vanilla, and ground nuts. Stir until the chocolate and butter are melted and all of the ingredients are evenly blended. Serve warm.

CINNAMON ALMONDS

Single Batch **Makes 3½ lightly packed cups**

Double Batch **Makes 7 lightly packed cups**

MAKE AHEAD

The almonds can be stored in an airtight container at room temperature for up to 6 weeks.

BIG BATCH NOTES

To ensure the nuts toast evenly, divide the almond mixture between two half sheet pans and switch the pans between the racks and rotate them from back to front about halfway through toasting.

If you've never tried your hand at candied nuts, this simple stir-and-bake method will boost your confidence.

INGREDIENTS	SINGLE BATCH	DOUBLE BATCH
Sliced natural almonds	2 cups	4 cups
Sugar	¾ cup	1½ cups
Water	¼ cup	½ cup
Ground cinnamon	1 Tbsp	2 Tbsp

Preheat the oven to 325°F. Line a half sheet pan with parchment paper.

Combine the almonds, sugar, water, and cinnamon in a large bowl and stir to mix well. Turn the mixture out onto the prepared pan and spread evenly. Bake for 10 minutes. Using a heat-resistant spatula or a wide metal spatula (such as a pancake turner), stir and flip the almonds (the mixture will be thick), and then once again spread the mixture into a thin, even layer. You want to keep the mixture from clumping together or it will not turn into a nice shatter candy after it has finished baking. Continue baking until the sugar is browned and bubbling, about 10 minutes more.

Let the almond mixture cool completely on the pan on a wire rack, then crumble into fine shards.

HOW TO HOST AN ICE CREAM SOCIAL

You will need about ½ pint store-bought or home-made ice cream and, depending on your guests, 4 to 6 tablespoons of toppings for each serving. Here are some key components:

o **At least two neutral ice cream flavors**, such as vanilla and chocolate (although a nut flavor can be good, too). Purchase the ice cream in large containers (some wholesale clubs sell 3- to 5-gallon containers) so they retain cold longer outside the freezer.

o **Crunchy topping** chopped nuts, spiced nuts, toasted coconut

o **Chunky topping** chopped toffee or peanut butter cups, crumbled pretzels or cookies, diced brownies

o **Colorful topping** sprinkles, nonpareils, chopped M&M'S

o **Saucy topping** caramel, butterscotch, marshmallow, lemon curd

o **Chocolate topping** hot fudge and/or chocolate syrup

o **Fruit topping** fresh berries or sliced fruits, fruit puree, jam

o **Whipped cream** keep the bowl chilled on ice

Basic Supplies

o If possible, large chest freezer to store the ice cream before the event

o Large ice cream coolers to hold the ice cream on the serving table (especially critical on a hot day)

o Metal ice cream scoops and a container to hold them

o Large selection of serving bowls and spoons for the various sauces and toppings

o Single-serving bowls and spoons (compostable if available) and napkins

A buffet is the best serving option. Lay out the supplies on a long table or counter, with the bowls at one end and the spoons and napkins at the other end, so guests have less to hold as they assemble their bowls. Between them, put out the ice cream, allowing it to soften slightly for about 10 minutes (less time on a hot day) before serving, and the toppings. Depending on the temperature of the day and the size of the crowd, you may want to put the ice cream containers in ice-filled coolers. Have the ice cream scoops in a container of warm water nearby.

orange and almond cake

CLAUDIA RODEN, AN acclaimed cookbook author, was born in Cairo, Egypt, and then lived in Paris and London. She is the author of many books on Middle Eastern and Mediterranean cooking, including *The Book of Jewish Food*.

This unusual, supermoist orange cake has been a mainstay in Claudia's dessert repertoire since the late 1960s. She received the recipe from a distant relative, but it wasn't until many years later, when researching for her book *The Food of Spain*, that she discovered that it comes from southern Spain, where the streets were lined with oranges.

The cake features ground almonds in place of wheat flour, making it naturally wheat- and gluten-free. With its Jewish origins, this recipe is an ideal choice for the weeklong holiday of Passover, when no wheat or certain other grains that are leavened can be eaten.

The ingredients—just eggs, sugar, almonds, baking powder, and whole oranges—are simple. The secret lies in how you handle the oranges. Instead of peeling and juicing them, you boil them whole for a couple of hours until soft, then puree them, peels and all. This juicy puree gives the finished cake an almost pudding-like texture. Claudia likes to serve the cake with dollops of whipped cream infused with orange blossom water and a tiny bit of sugar.

Single Batch
Makes 8 to 10 servings
(One 9-inch cake)

Double Batch
Makes 16 to 20 servings
(Two 9-inch cakes)

MAKE AHEAD

The cakes can be baked up to 1 day in advance, cooled, tightly covered with plastic wrap, and refrigerated.

INGREDIENTS	SINGLE BATCH	DOUBLE BATCH
Large navel oranges	2	4
Unsalted butter, at room temperature, for the pans		
Ground almonds or almond flour, plus more for the pans	1½ cups	3 cups
Large eggs	6	12
Sugar	1 cup	2 cups
Baking powder	1 tsp	2 tsp
Whipped cream, for serving (optional)		

One or two 9-inch round spring-form pans.

If using standard cake pans, after the cakes have cooled, invert the cakes onto the rack, lift off the pans, and turn the cakes right-side up and place on serving platters.

BIG BATCH NOTES

Be sure to rotate the cakes 180 degrees in the oven halfway through baking so they will bake evenly.

In a large saucepan, combine the unpeeled oranges with water to cover, bring to a boil over high heat, reduce the heat to medium, and simmer until soft, about 2 hours. Drain, let cool, and cut each orange into a few pieces and remove any seeds. Transfer the pieces to a food processor and process until a puree forms. You should have 1 cup for a single batch and 2 cups for a double batch.

Preheat the oven to 400°F. Butter and flour one 9-inch springform pan if making a single batch or two 9-inch round springform pans if making a double batch.

In a large bowl, whisk the eggs until blended. Add the ground almonds, sugar, and baking powder and stir to mix thoroughly, then stir in the orange puree, again mixing well. Pour the batter into the prepared pan if making a single batch. If making a double batch, divide the batter evenly between the prepared pans.

Bake the cake(s), rotating the pans 180 degrees about halfway through baking, for about 1 hour. Test for doneness by inserting a toothpick into the center. This is a very moist cake, so some wetness in the center is normal. If when you remove the tooth-pick it is very wet, bake the cake(s) for another 10 minutes and test again.

Let the cake(s) cool completely in the pans on wire racks. Unlatch the sides and lift them off, then carefully slide the cake(s) off the pan bottoms onto serving platters. Cut into wedges and serve with whipped cream, if desired.

KATIE WORKMAN

bake sale brownies

BAKE SALES ARE the sweetest way to fund-raise for a good cause. You can bake to send a school debate team to a state championship, to raise money for a local homeless shelter, or to send relief to families devastated by a hurricane or flood. Sometimes the cause is global; other times, it is right next door. Bake sales can be homegrown and exclusively local, or they can span the country and raise millions for their causes.

Author Katie Workman regularly makes these double-plus-good brownies for local school bake sales. Feeding people is an important part of Katie's life, as a mother of two and as the author of *Dinner Solved!* and *The Mom 100: Recipes, Stories, and Real-Cook Solutions*, both written to help busy families come together around the dining table. Katie is also on the board of New York's City Harvest, a leading food rescue nonprofit, and is a longtime active supporter of Share Our Strength, which fights nationally against childhood hunger.

Single Batch **Makes 24 Brownies**

Double Batch **Makes 48 brownies**

MAKE AHEAD

The pans of brownies can be covered with plastic wrap and stored at room temperature for up to 1 day. To freeze them, overwrap the plastic-wrapped pans with aluminum foil and freeze for up to 1 month. Thaw at room temperature and cut before serving.

INGREDIENTS	SINGLE BATCH	DOUBLE BATCH
Unsalted butter, plus more at room temperature for the pan	1 cup	2 cups
Unsweetened chocolate, coarsely chopped	3 oz	6 oz
Dutch-processed cocoa powder (see *Ingredient Notes*, page 266)	½ cup	1 cup
Sugar	2½ cup	5 cups
Kosher salt	½ tsp	1 tsp
Vanilla extract	1 Tbsp	1½ Tbsp
Large eggs, at room temperature	3	6
All-purpose flour	1½ cups	3 cups

Preheat the oven to 350°F. Generously butter a 9-by-13-inch baking pan or two 9-by-13-inch baking pans if making a double batch.

In a large saucepan, combine the butter and chocolate over low heat, stirring almost constantly, until the ingredients are melted and smooth. Remove from the heat and set aside to cool slightly.

BIG BATCH NOTES

Be sure to rotate the pans from back to front halfway through baking to ensure the brownies bake evenly.

In a large bowl, stir together the cocoa powder, sugar, and salt, mixing well. Add the chocolate mixture and vanilla and stir until smooth. Beat in the eggs, one at a time, mixing quickly after each addition so the egg does not have the chance to cook at all before it is well blended. Add the flour and stir until well mixed.

Scrape the thick batter into the prepared pan(s), dividing it evenly and smoothing the top with a spatula if making a double batch. Bake, rotating the pans from back to front about halfway through baking, until the edges just begin to pull away from the sides of the pan and a wooden toothpick inserted into the center comes out clean, 25 to 30 minutes.

Let the brownies cool completely in the pans on wire racks. Cut into squares to serve.

ICE CREAM SANDWICHES

Makes 12 sandwiches

Ice cream sandwiches made with chewy brownies are a great treat. We found that it was easier to cut through that top layer brownie before freezing.

1 single batch recipe brownie batter (see page 277)
2 to 3 pints ice cream (any flavor), slightly softened

Preheat oven to 350. Butter two 9 x 13-inch pans. Line each one with parchment paper draping the parchment over the sides to create handles. Prepare the brownie batter (page 277). Divide and pour it into the two prepared pans. Bake on different racks for 12 to 15 minutes, until a toothpick inserted into the center of each pan comes out with just a few crumbs. (Do not over bake). Transfer to a wire cooling rack and let cool completely, at least 30 minutes.

Place a layer of ice cream on top of one of the brownies (still in it's pan). Use a spatula to press it down and smooth the top. Meanwhile use the parchment handles to lift the second pan of brownies out of its tray. Remove the parchment and place it on top of the frozen ice cream layer and press down a little. Using a serrated knife, lightly cut the top layer of brownie into squares approximately 4 x 4 inches. Do not cut all the way through the ice cream layer. Return the pan to the freezer to set up for at least an hour.

Remove from the freezer. Run a knife around the brownie stack to make sure it's not stuck, and use the parchment handles to transfer the whole sandwich block to a cutting board. Using the cuts on the top brownie layer as a guide, cut completely through to form brownie sandwich squares. If you have difficulty cutting, dip the serrated knife in hot water.

Put them back in the freezer for at least 30 minutes to finish setting up. They will keep in an airtight container in the freezer for up to 2 weeks.

frog hollow farm fruit crisp

"FARMER AL" COURCHESNE was doing his usual rounds, dropping off flats of his famed Frog Hollow Farm peaches, when he met (and fell in love with) Becky, a pastry chef at a busy Oakland, California, restaurant. Soon they were married, and Becky joined Al at the farm in nearby Brentwood, among the peach and plum trees.

Bay Area cooks and restaurant chefs prized Frog Hollow Farm's luscious organic fruits, but there was always the problem of what to do with the farm's surfeit of less-than-perfect produce. Becky convinced Al to build a large commercial kitchen on the property, and when it was finished, she began developing recipes for preserves, chutneys, and fruit pastries of all kinds. Soon, Frog Hollow Farm was turning nearly all of its extra fruit into delicious jams, jellies, tarts, cookies, scones, and galettes and selling them at their café in the San Francisco Ferry Building.

With its nutty-crunchy cinnamon topping over a warm fruit filling, this crisp has long been Becky's favorite easy family dessert. As she says, "It doesn't require a lot of fuss and is always a crowd-pleaser. It can be made with almost any fruit you have on hand, in any season. It's perfect for using up those wrinkled apples or overripe peaches. You can also combine fruits; for this apple version, you might add pears and even throw in some cranberries if you've got them and a little orange zest."

This recipe makes 12 cups of topping, and you won't need all of it for this recipe, so store the rest in the freezer. It will keep for months, which means you can whip up a crisp whenever you've got extra fruit on hand. Becky uses a 5-quart ceramic casserole dish for her crisp, although she fills the dish only three-quarters full. Overfilling means the topping may brown before the fruit is thoroughly cooked. For the nuts, Becky suggests using almonds in the spring and summer, since they pair so beautifully with stone fruits, followed by pecans or walnuts in the fall. Hazelnuts will work too, as long as they are toasted and skinned.

Single Batch **Makes 12 servings**

Double Batch **Makes 24 servings**

MAKE AHEAD

The topping can be refrigerated for up to 2 days or frozen for up to 1 month. The topping can be used directly from the freezer.

One or two 4- to 5-quart baking
dishes or pans.

BIG BATCH NOTES

You will need a very large bowl
for mixing the filling. Although
you can make the double batch
in a large hotel pan (12 by 20 by
4 inches), you will have much more
control over the baking if you use
two large baking dishes.

INGREDIENTS	SINGLE BATCH	DOUBLE BATCH
Topping		
All-purpose flour	1¾ cups	3½ cups
Lightly packed light brown sugar	¾ cup	1½ cups
Granulated sugar	2½ Tbsp	⅓ cup
Ground cinnamon	1 tsp	2 tsp
Kosher salt	1 tsp	2 tsp
Unsalted butter, cut into ½-inch cubes and chilled	¾ cup	1½ cups
Walnuts, pecans, or almonds, lightly toasted and roughly chopped	1 cup	2 cups
Filling		
Firm, tart apples, such as Pink Lady or Granny Smith, peeled, cored, and cut into 1-inch cubes	4 to 4½ lb	8 to 9 lb
Granulated sugar	1 cup	2 cups
All-purpose flour	⅓ cup	⅔ cup
Vanilla extract	1 tsp	2 tsp

Whipped cream, crème fraîche, or vanilla ice cream,
for serving

Make the topping: In a stand mixer fitted with the paddle attachment, combine the
flour, brown and granulated sugars, cinnamon, and salt and mix on low speed until
combined. Add the butter and mix on medium-low speed until the mixture resembles
coarse crumbs with some pea-size pieces of butter (similar to pie dough). The mixture
will look and seem powdery. Add the walnuts and mix just until evenly distributed.
(You can also do this step by hand, stirring together the dry ingredients and then
working in the butter with a fork.) Refrigerate until ready to use or, if you're not using
the topping right away, store it in the freezer until ready to use.

Make the filling: Preheat the oven to 375°F. Have ready one 4- to 5-quart baking dish
or pan if making a single batch or two dishes or pans if making a double batch.

Place the apple chunks in a large bowl and add the sugar, flour, and vanilla. Toss well
to coat the apples evenly with the other ingredients. Pour the fruit into the baking
dish or divide evenly between the two baking dishes. Pat down the fruit to compact it
a bit, then top with about 2 cups of the topping (if making a double batch, sprinkle 2
cups of the topping over each baking dish), covering the fruit so just a few pieces are
poking through.

Bake until the apples are soft and the topping has browned, about 1¼ hours. Begin checking after 1 hour. Stick a knife into the center, and if you feel resistance, the crisp needs more time. If the topping is looking too dark and the filling isn't yet cooked, lay a piece of aluminum foil over the crisp and continue baking until the filling is tender, checking every 15 minutes.

Remove from the oven. The crisp is best when allowed to sit for 45 minutes to 1 hour before serving, so it is still warm but not hot. Serve with whipped cream.

NANCIE MCDERMOTT

old-school southern coconut custard pie

Single Batch **Serves 8 to 10**
(One 9-inch pie)

Double Batch **Serves 16 to 20**
(Two 9-inch pies)

MAKE AHEAD

The dough can be refrigerated for up to 2 days or frozen for up to 2 months; if frozen, thaw the dough overnight in the refrigerator. The custard filling can be refrigerated for up to 1 day. Although this pie is sturdier than a cream pie, it is still best eaten shortly after it is made. If you don't plan to serve it right away, refrigerate it until serving.

FOOD WRITER, COOKING teacher, television personality, and North Carolina native Nancie McDermott loves everything that comes out of the Southern kitchen, but she's got a special penchant for the South's best baked goods. She has written over a dozen cookbooks, including two regional dessert books, *Southern Cakes* and *Southern Pies*, working with some of the region's best bakers—both home cooks and professionals—to discover the most authentic recipes and the richly detailed stories of how, when, and where they come to the table.

In describing her coconut custard pie, Nancie says, "This is a traditional Southern pie. With its blind-baked crust, stove-top custard filling, and perfectly browned meringue, this pie takes time, attention, and skill. It's meant to impress. Celebrate. Show off. Delight. It's a pie to bring to a family reunion or to a covered-dish luncheon outside in the summer when the congregation gathers and those who have moved away come back."

The crowning glory of this pie is its lofty meringue topping. To make a perfect meringue, says Nancie, the egg whites must be beaten into "glorious, ethereal clouds, then baked just enough to dazzle without burning." A great meringue can take some practice, but it's a skill well worth mastering, with the baker's careful attention rewarded by the joy this pie inspires at the table.

With plenty of coconut folded into the luscious custard filling, this is a true coconut lover's pie. And if that's not enough, even more coconut is scattered over the puffy meringue topping. A final baking browns the coconut to a toasty crunch and contributes to the pie making a showstopping appearance on any festive table. If you don't want to fuss with the meringue and final dusting of coconut, this pie is also delicious topped with mounds of whipped cream.

INGREDIENTS	SINGLE BATCH	DOUBLE BATCH
Crust		
All-purpose flour	1¼ cups	2 ½ cups
Sugar	1½ tsp	1 Tbsp
Kosher salt	½ tsp	1 tsp
Unsalted butter, chilled and cut into ½-inch cubes	6 Tbsp	¾ cup
Ice water	4 to 6 Tbsp	½ cup to ¾ cup
Filling		
Large egg yolks	3	6
Sugar	¾ cup	1½ cups
All-purpose flour	⅓ cup	⅔ cup
Kosher salt	⅛ tsp	¼ tsp
Whole milk	2 cups	4 cups
Unsweetened or sweetened shredded or flaked coconut	1 cup	2 cups
Unsalted butter	3 Tbsp	6 Tbsp
Vanilla extract	1 tsp	2 tsp
Meringue		
Large egg whites	3	6
Sugar	5 Tbsp	½ cup plus 2 Tbsp
Unsweetened or sweetened shredded or flaked coconut	¼ cup	½ cup

EQUIPMENT

One or two 9-inch pie plates.

BIG BATCH NOTES

If making a double batch, bake the crusts side by side on the center rack of the oven. If they do not fit on the same rack, bake them on the top third and center racks and swap their positions halfway during baking to ensure even browning. Prepare the filling and meringue topping as directed and divide them evenly between the two crusts.

Make the crust: In a food processor, combine the flour, sugar, and salt and pulse a few times until mixed. Scatter the butter over the flour mixture and process for 15 seconds, then pulse just until the flour mixture and butter come together in a rough mass, with pea-size bits of butter still visible in the flour mixture.

With the motor running, pour in the smaller amount of ice water and process just until the dough begins to form a shaggy ball. Add more ice water only if the mixture does not clump together. Lightly flour a work surface and dump the dough out onto the floured surface. Quickly gather up the dough into a mass, shape into a disk about 6 inches in diameter, and wrap in plastic wrap. If making a double batch, divide the dough in half, shape into two 6-inch disks, and wrap each disk in plastic wrap. Refrigerate for at least 30 minutes.

Preheat the oven to 375°F. If baking a double batch and your oven rack will not accommodate the crusts side by side, position racks in the top third and center of the oven.

On a well-floured work surface, roll out a dough disk into a 12-inch round, rolling from the center to the edge and turning and flouring the dough as needed to make sure it doesn't stick. Fold the dough round in half, carefully transfer it to a 9-inch pie plate unfold the round, and center it in the plate. Press the dough gently onto the bottom and sides of the pie plate, then trim away the excess dough, leaving about a ¾-inch overhang. Fold the overhang under and pinch lightly so it stands up against the rim, then flute the edge with the thumb and index finger of one hand. If making a double batch, repeat with the remaining dough disk

Line the prepared pie crust(s) with parchment paper and fill with pie weights, dried beans, or raw rice. Bake the crust(s) until very lightly browned at the edges and somewhat dry to the touch, 10 to 12 minutes. (If baking two crusts on two racks, switch them between the racks about halfway through baking.) Remove the pie plate(s) from the oven, carefully lift out the parchment and weights, and then return the pie plates to the oven. Continue to bake the crust(s) until dry to the touch and nicely browned, 10 to 12 minutes longer. Let cool to room temperature on a wire rack.

Make the custard filling: In a bowl, whisk the egg yolks until blended. In a saucepan, whisk together the sugar, flour, and salt, then whisk in the milk until well mixed. Place the saucepan over medium heat and cook, stirring and scraping the sides and bottom of the pan often with a whisk or heat-resistant spatula, until the mixture comes almost to a boil, is steaming, and has thickened into a smooth, velvety sauce, 6 to 8 minutes.

Remove from the heat, scoop out about ½ cup of the hot, thick milk mixture with a measuring cup, and set it aside. While whisking constantly, slowly pour the remaining hot milk mixture into the egg yolks. Pour the bowl of warm egg yolk–milk mixture back into the saucepan, then return the pan to medium heat and cook, stirring constantly, until the mixture thickens and comes to a gentle, noisy bubbling. Let the mixture boil for about 1 minute.

Remove from the heat, add the coconut, butter, and vanilla, and stir until the butter has melted and all of the ingredients are evenly mixed. Transfer to a bowl and cover with plastic wrap, pressing the wrap directly onto the surface of the custard to prevent a skin from forming. Let cool to room temperature.

Spoon the cooled custard into the prepared pie crust. If making a double batch, divide the custard evenly between the crusts. Refrigerate the pies while you prepare the meringue.

Make the meringue: Preheat the oven to 350°F. In a bowl with a handheld mixer, or in a stand mixer fitted with the whisk attachment, beat the egg whites on medium speed until foamy. Increase the speed to high and gradually add the sugar, about 2 tablespoons at a time, and continue to beat until the egg whites swell up into plump, shiny, soft clouds that hold firm, curly peaks.

Scoop the meringue on top of the cooled custard filling, spreading it all the way to the crust and mounding it slightly in the center of the pie. Create swoops and swirls in the meringue for decorative effect. Sprinkle the coconut evenly over the meringue. If making a double batch, divide the meringue and coconut evenly between the two pies.

Bake the pie(s) until the meringue is a beautiful golden brown, 10 to 15 minutes. (If making a double batch and the pies do not fit side by side, bake the pies one at a time.) Let cool on a wire rack or a folded kitchen towel to room temperature. Serve at room temperature or, if desired, refrigerate and serve chilled.

old-school southern coconut custard pie   287

SHAKIRAH SIMLEY

big batch peach jam can

MAKING JAM IS one of Shakirah Simley's favorite ways to capture the sweetness of every season. During her five years at Bi-Rite as community programs manager, cooking teacher, and "canner in residence," she found it was a perfect way to make the most of local, seasonal fruit and a great way to gather together with friends to share in a jam can: the pitting, chopping, and putting up of fruit. What was once a hot-weather chore becomes an afternoon of sticky, juicy, communal fun.

One year Shakirah "adopted" an organic Elberta peach tree at Masumoto Family Farm, where third-generation Fresno, California farmer David Mas Masumoto, author of the award-winning memoir *Epitaph for a Peach: Four Seasons on My Family Farm*, tends eighty acres of organic nectarines, peaches, and raisin grapes. Over two summer weekends, Shakirah's harvest team picked over three hundred pounds of peaches from their tree, then went back to the 18 Reasons kitchen to turn the fruit into dozens and dozens of jars brimming with golden peach jam.

Before Shakirah joined Bi-Rite, she ran her own small-batch preserving company called Slow Jams, where she quickly learned that late-season fruits are sweeter and make the best jam. When making peach jam, choose peaches that are fragrant, thin skinned, and are heavy for their size. For this recipe, there's no need to peel the peaches. That way you won't waste too much of the beautiful fruit and the peels add color. Shakirah recommends using the preserves in galettes, on ice cream, or atop buttered toast.

Makes 20 to 24 half-pint jars

MAKE AHEAD

Jam, by its very nature, is a cook's make-ahead dream. Properly sealed and stored, the jars will keep for up to 1 year. The fruit can be prepped up to 36 hours in advance and stored in resealable bags in the refrigerator.

INGREDIENTS

Yellow peaches	20 lb
Sugar	6 lb
Large lemons, zest finely grated and then juiced	3 to 4 (enough to yield 1 cup juice)
Maldon sea salt or flake salt (optional)	2 teaspoons

EQUIPMENT

One to two stainless steel, heavy-bottomed large pots for cooking the jam; twenty-four half-pint glass canning jars and two-part canning lids; canning tongs; saucepan and regular tongs for sterilizing the lids; canning funnel and ladle for filling the jars. A water-bath canner or steam canner is handy for the boiling-water bath, though a large pot and a wire rack that fits in the bottom will work, too. If you opt for the large pot, the same pot can be used for sterilizing the jars.

BIG BATCH NOTES

The best advice for a successful jam can is to have everything you need on hand and ready to go.

Wash the jars, flat lids, and screw bands in hot, soapy water, rinse well, and set aside until ready to use. Place a saucer or small plate in the freezer to chill. Pit the peaches and cut them into ¼-inch dice (do not peel).

Put all of the peaches in a large, wide, heavy-bottomed stainless steel pot and add 3 cups water to cover the bottom of the pot. The water will help prevent the fruit from scorching. Place the pot over medium heat and cook, stirring occasionally, until the fruit is tender, slightly foamy, and the liquid has increased, about 15 to 20 minutes. The peaches should be softened and slightly submerged in liquid.

Evenly sprinkle the sugar over the fruit mixture, then stir the sugar into the fruit, distributing it evenly and dissolving it completely. Once the sugar has dissolved, cook the fruit, stirring often, until the mixture has reduced by about half and has reached a consistent boil with even, thick bubbling, 25 to 30 minutes. The timing will depend on the size of your stove's burner and the intensity of its heat.

While the fruit is cooking, bring the water in the pans with the jars and lids to a full simmer, then turn down the heat to low.

When the peach mixture is about ready, stir in the lemon zest and juice and the salt (if using). To check the jam for doneness and thickness, remove the chilled saucer from the freezer. Place a teaspoon of the hot jam on the saucer. If it congeals enough that you can nudge it with your finger into a soft lump, it's ready. If it remains liquid and runs all over the saucer, the jam needs to cook longer. Wipe off the saucer and return it to the freezer. Continue cooking the jam for another few minutes or so, then test again.

Using a large spoon, skim off the foam from the surface of the jam. Using canning tongs, remove jars from the hot water and drain briefly on a kitchen towel. Using a ladle and a canning funnel, ladle the hot jam into the hot, sterilized jars, leaving ½-inch headspace (between the jam and jar rim). Use a chopstick to remove air bubbles from each jar, then wipe the rims clean. Retrieve the flat lids and rings from the hot water with tongs, top each jar with a lid, centering it on the rim, and then add a ring band. Screw the band down until you meet resistance, then increase to fingertip tight. Repeat until all of the jam is in jars.

To process the jars in a boiling-water bath, place a wire rack on the bottom of a large pot (or line the bottom with a kitchen towel) and fill the pot with water to a depth of about 4 inches. Bring the water to a simmer; at the same time, bring a kettle filled with water to a boil. When the water is simmering, using the canning tongs, lower as many jars as will fit comfortably into the pot, spacing them about 1 inch apart. Add as much of the boiling water as needed to cover the jars by at least 1 inch. Cover the pot, bring the water to a full rolling boil, and boil for 10 minutes. Turn off the heat and, using the tongs, transfer the jars from the pot to a work surface lined with a kitchen towel, spacing them about 1 inch apart. Repeat with the remaining jars. Let the jars cool upright, undisturbed, for 8 to 12 hours.

To test if the seal on a jar is good, press on the center of the lid with a fingertip. If the lid remains concave when you remove your finger, the seal is good. If it springs upward, the seal is not good. Store any jars that did not seal properly in the refrigerator and use within 3 weeks. Store jars with a good seal in a cool, dark, dry place and eat within 1 year.

SHAKIRAH'S RECIPE TIP

Put the leftover peach pits in a sterilized quart jar and add good-quality vodka (at least 40 percent alcohol) to cover completely. Cap tightly and let sit at cool room temperature for 1 month in a cool, dry dark place. Use as a peach *noyaux* (French-style liqueur) in drinks or as an almond-flavored extract in baking.

big batch peach jam can   291

chef biographies

CATHY BARROW is a cookbook author and food writer. Her popular blog was a way to document her forays into food preservation but soon included stories of her day-to-day life in the Washington, D.C., area and beyond, as she cooked, traveled, gardened, and shared lots of meals and memories in the kitchen. She writes for several national publications and is the author of two cookbooks, *Mrs. Wheelbarrow's Practical Pantry* and *Pie Squared*.

NOAH BERNAMOFF AND RAE COHEN are the owners of New York City's Mile End deli and authors of *The Mile End Cookbook: Redefining Jewish Comfort Food from Hash to Hamantaschen.* Inspired by their Jewish-Montreal roots, the couple brought a new twist to the iconic New York deli scene.

GEORGEANNE BRENNAN is the author of many cookbooks, including *My Culinary Journey: The Food and Fêtes of Provence, La Vie Rustic, A Pig in Provence,* and others. She splits her time between Northern California and Provence, France, where she gardens, forages, teaches cooking classes, and operates La Vie Rustic, an online marketplace offering artisanal salt blends, seeds, and beans.

VIOLA BUITONI knows pasta. She grew up in Perugia, Italy, in a family of pasta makers (the name behind the Buitoni pasta brand). Today, Viola leads cooking tours of Italy and teaches cooking classes at the Italian Consulate of San Francisco, 18 Reasons, and other venues.

ANNA WATSON CARL is a blogger, food writer, and the author of *The Yellow Table: A Celebration of Everyday Gatherings,* a collection of recipes, stories, tips, and tricks for feeding friends and family. Her articles have appeared in *Travel + Leisure, Food52,* and other publications. For Anna's book tour, she traveled around the country, hosting dinner parties in settings ranging from fields to lavish formal dining tables.

JOE CARROLL is the author of *Feeding the Fire: Recipes and Strategies for Better Barbecue and Grilling,* a primer on barbecue, and the owner of the award-winning restaurants Spuyten Duyvil, Fette Sau, and St. Anselm in Brooklyn, New York.

JENNIFER CASTLE AND BLAKE SPALDING are the chef-owners of Hell's Backbone Grill in Boulder, Utah. Every July Fourth they host a free ice cream social for their community, driven by volunteers and generous donations.

ASHLEY CHRISTENSEN is a James Beard Award–winning restaurateur in Raleigh, North Carolina, and is the author of *Poole's: Recipes and Stories from a Modern Diner.* She is the founder of Stir the Pot, a charity that unites chefs to funnel cash into the documentary arm of the Southern Foodways Alliance, as well as an active philanthropist involved in many nonprofit organizations.

FRANICS FORD COPPOLA is a film director, producer, screenwriter, and the owner of a winery and restaurant in Northern California. In 2001, Francis and others started North Beach Citizens, a neighborhood organization devoted to helping homeless and low-income residents in San Francisco's North Beach, where his film company, American Zoetrope, is based. Each year, he gathers the community in the basement of a local church for a family-style feast that raises money to support the organization's programs.

BECKY COURCHESNE is a pastry chef, a passionate cook, and the mastermind behind a line of famous organic conserves, marmalades, jellies, and chutneys, made with Frog Hollow Farm fruit grown right in Brentwood, California.

LISA DONOVAN is a pastry chef and writer living in Nashville, who is known for her wonderful Southern pastry— serving her Church Cakes and pies to finish fine dining experiences. Lisa is currently writing and producing content for cookbooks, working on her own writing—both in food and in the arts— and opening a collaborative space with her husband, artist John Donovan, in north Nashville's growing arts district.

CHARLOTTE DRUCKMAN is a journalist and food writer whose work has appeared in various publications, including the *Washington Post, Wall Street Journal, The New York Times, Food & Wine,* and *ELLE.* Her first cookbook *Stir, Sizzle, Bake* was released in 2016 and her follow-up—*Kitchen Remix*—arrives in 2018 (Clarkson Potter). She is also the author of *Skirt Steak: Women Chefs on Standing the Heat & Staying in the Kitchen* and co-author of chef Anita Lo's cookbook *Cooking Without Borders.* Bonus: She's the proud co-founder of Food52's Tournament of Cookbooks (aka "The Piglet"), and lives in New York City.

BRETT AND ELAN EMERSON are the owners of Contigo, a San Francisco restaurant that celebrates both sustainability and communal dining. Brett and Elan describe Contigo as their "love letter to Barcelona," a city where they spent cherished time learning the art of paella making, as well as other Spanish and Catalan specialties.

ANYA FERNALD is the CEO of the Belcampo company, a farm-to-table business that raises organic sustainable meat. She is also the founder of Eat Real, an annual Oakland, California, food festival that brings farmers, regional food producers, and hungry attendees together, and the author of *Home Cooked: Essential Recipes for a New Way to Cook,* a collection of essential weeknight and entertaining recipes.

MARIA FINN is an author and journalist who writes about food and other subjects and is passionate about sustainable seafood. She has written four books, including *The Whole Fish.*

JOHN INGLE is a chef, saxophonist, bay swimmer, and manager of San Francisco's iconic Dolphin Club. While his music is out there, his food is local and traditional, drawing on the cornucopia of ingredients of the Bay Area's small farms, ranches, and the sea.

ANGELO GARRO is the founder of Omnivore Salt (an artisanal salt line), an avid food forager, and a slow food advocate. He makes architectural wrought iron in his Renaissance Forge in San Francisco, where he also loves to cook and entertain. Angelo is famous among his friends for his large, festive, food-filled gatherings.

JOYCE GOLDSTEIN is a chef, mentor, philanthropist, and author. She was the chef-owner of the groundbreaking restaurant Square One, in San Francisco, and continues to be widely recognized for her work in the restaurant industry. She has authored many books, among them *The New Mediterranean Jewish Table, Inside the California Food Revolution,* and *Italian Slow and Savory.*

PHYLLIS GRANT is a food writer and the voice behind the popular blog Dash and Bella, where she chronicles recipes and stories from cooking with her two children. She writes for Food52 and was included in the *Best Food Writing of 2017.*

KATHY GUNST is the author of *Soup Swap: Comforting Recipes to Make and Share* and 13 other cookbooks, including *Notes from a Maine Kitchen; Relax, Company's Coming!;* and several branded titles for Stonewall Kitchen. Kathy has been hosting soup swaps in her home in Maine and around the country for more than five years. She teaches cooking classes in Maine and beyond and is the "resident chef" on NPR's *Here and Now.*

IHSAN AND VALERIE GURDAL are the owners of Formaggio Kitchen in Boston and Cambridge, Massachusetts, and New York City. Throughout the year, they organize gatherings for staff and friends.

SANDRA GUTIERREZ is the author of *Empanadas: The Hand-Held Pies of Latin America* and *Latin American Street Food,* among other cookbooks. Sandra grew up in Latin America, where she learned about the regional foods and discovered her love for making and eating empanadas. As a recognized expert in Latin cuisines, she has taught cooking classes throughout the country.

GONZALO GUZMÁN is the chef at Nopalito, which serves authentic regional Mexican cuisine in San Francisco, California. He is the author of the cookbook *Nopalito: A Mexican Kitchen.*

TANYA HOLLAND is the chef and owner of Brown Sugar Kitchen and B-Side BBQ in Oakland, California, and is the author of *Brown Sugar Kitchen: New-Style, Down-Home Recipes from Sweet West Oakland* and *New Soul Cooking: Updating a Cuisine Rich in Flavor and Tradition.* Tanya is a frequent guest on national television programs and works with many organizations that help others, including Share Our Strength's "No Kid Hungry" campaign and community food banks around the country.

TRACI DES JARDINS is a San Francisco restaurateur, a two-time James Beard Award winner, and is known as one of the top female chefs in the nation. Throughout her career, Traci has been a deeply dedicated philanthropist, supporting Share Our Strength, La Cocina, Citymeals on Wheels, AmFar, and other organizations that fight hunger and help those in need.

SARA JENKINS is the former owner of the late sandwich shop Porchetta and the current owner of Porsena in New York City and Nina June restaurant in Maine. She is also the author of *The Four Seasons of Pasta* and *Olive and Oranges.*

PABLEAUX JOHNSON is a writer and international photographer based in New Orleans. He's the founder of the Red Beans Road Show, a restaurant pop-up series that takes the New Orleans Monday-night tradition of red beans and rice on the road. Pableaux has partnered with chefs from all over the country, and his road show regularly sells out.

SUZANNE JONATH is the author's mother and has been hosting an annual Hannukah "latke-and-vodka" party for many years.

DENNIS LEE is the head chef of Namu Gaji, a popular Asian restaurant with a strong Korean influence in San Francisco, California. Dennis and his two brothers own and operate the restaurant and a one-acre farm that supplies much of the produce for the kitchen.

JODI LIANO is the founder of San Francisco Cooking School, where she is also an instructor. The school offers chef and pastry certificate courses, as well as weeklong and one-night classes teaching specialty cuisines and techniques. She has worked as a recipe tester and developer for the Food Network, *Bon Appétit*, and Williams-Sonoma.

IRVIN LIN is the author of *Marbled, Swirled, and Layered* and the founder of Eat The Love. He's renowned for his dessert parties and ice cream socials, where he gathers people together around a bounty of sweets.

EMILY LUCHETTI is the author of many award-winning cookbooks on pastry, including *A Passion for Desserts* and *The Fearless Baker*. Emily has been honored for her work as executive pastry chef at many of the best restaurants in San Francisco, including Park Tavern and Farallon. She is the founder of Dessertworthy, a movement that aims to empower people to make healthier choices around dessert.

TROY MACLARTY is a biologist-turned-chef. Trained in the kitchen of Chez Panisse and inspired by his travels throughout India, Troy opened Bolly-wood Theater in Portland, Oregon, a colorful, lively restaurant decorated as an homage to Indian cinema with a menu that features his own contemporary, West Coast interpretation of Indian street foods.

DEBORAH MADISON is a chef, cooking teacher, and award-winning cookbook author. She has written many books, including *Vegetable Literacy, The New Vegetarian Cooking for Everyone,* and most recently, *In My Kitchen.* Deborah founded Greens Restaurant in San Francisco, one of the earliest farm-driven, vegetarian restaurants in the country. She is active in the slow food movement, has served on the board of the Seed Savers Exchange, and was codirector of the Monte del Sol Edible Kitchen Garden program in Santa Fe, New Mexico.

DOMENICA MARCHETTI is a food writer, recipe developer, and cooking teacher who specializes in Italian cooking. Growing up in a large Italian family, she spent much of her time gathering in kitchens around food, and she still loves to cook big dinners for her family. She is the author of many books, including *Big Night In, The Glorious Pasta of Italy, The Glorious Vegetables of Italy, Preserving Italy,* and *Rustic Italian Cookbook*, as well as a host of culinary tours through Italy.

NANCIE MCDERMOTT is a food writer, cooking teacher, television personality, and the author of 14 cookbooks, including *Fruit, Southern Soups and Stews,* and *Southern Pies.* She is a member of the International Association of Culinary Professionals, Les Dames d'Escoffier, and Women Chefs and Restaurateurs, and is active in the North Carolina Triangle Chapter of Slow Food and the Southern Foodways Alliance.

MICHELLE MCKENZIE is the former program director for 18 Reasons and the author of *Dandelion and Quince: Exploring the Wide World of Unusual Vegetables, Fruits, and Herbs,* which encourages home cooks to explore the world of vegetables.

ALICE MEDRICH is a pastry chef, teacher, one of the country's foremost experts on chocolate and chocolate desserts, and an award-winning cookbook author. She has written nearly a dozen books, among them *Flavor Flours, Pure Dessert, Seriously Bittersweet,* and *Sinfully Easy Delicious Desserts.*

PREETI MISTRY is the chef-owner of Navi Kitchen and the now-closed Juhu Beach Club in Oakland, California, where she served her own versions of the street food she enjoyed as a kid on family trips to Mumbai. She is the author of *The Juhu Beach Club Cookbook.* Before opening her restaurant, Preeti was an executive chef at Google and a contestant on season six of Bravo's *Top Chef.*

SAM MOGANNAM runs his family-owned Bi-Rite Market, a beloved San Francisco neighborhood institution since 1964. Sam began working in the shop as a kid, helping stock the shelves of what was then just an everyday grocery store alongside his dad, brother, and uncle. Along with transforming the market into a specialty food emporium offering regional produce and artisanal products, Sam has installed an open kitchen where he develops recipes for the store's high-quality prepared food. Sam is the author of the cookbook *Bi-Rite Market's Eat Good Food,* serves as a mentor to budding food entrepreneurs, and is a passionate supporter of the local food community.

RUSSELL MOORE and ALLISON HOPELAIN own Camino, a restaurant in Oakland, California, with a menu focused on rustic, sustainable, wood-fired international cuisine. They also authored *This Is Camino*, a cookbook that reveals some of the secrets behind their tremendously popular wood-fired food.

GABI MOSKOWITZ is the blogger behind the blog BrokeAss Gourmet, which inspired a spin-off television show, *Young & Hungry* on ABC Family. Gabi is the author of *The BrokeAss Gourmet Cookbook, Hot Mess Kitchen,* and *Recipes for Your Delicious, Disasterous Life.*

ANDREA NGUYEN is an expert on Asian cooking and the author of the blog Viet World Kitchen as well as many books, including *Asian Dumplings, Asian Tofu, Into the Vietnamese Kitchen, The Banh Mi Handbook,* and *The Pho Cookbook*. She teaches cooking classes, has appeared on national television and radio programs, and is a freelance columnist and consultant.

YOTAM OTTOLENGHI is an Israeli-born British chef who has authored many internationally best-selling and award-winning cookbooks, including *Jerusalem, Plenty,* and *Nopi*. His food has transformed the way home cooks and chefs alike approach cooking, both with vegetables and in the Mediterranean style. He is the co-owner of several successful London restaurants and delis.

MELISSA PERELLO is the chef-owner of Frances and Octavia restaurants in San Francisco, California. She and her restaurants have won a number of awards, including a Michelin star.

GAYLE PIRIE and JOHN CLARK are the chef-owners of Foreign Cinema, a beloved San Francisco restaurant that opened in 1999 and still enchants visitors to this day. The couple wrote two books including *The Foreign Cinema Cookbook*. They love to host big dinners, celebrations, and fundraisers for local non-profits and community organizations. Andrew Dovel is a longtime chef de cuisine at the restaurant who enjoys making big batch dinners.

CAROLYN PHILLIPS is a lauded cookbook author and Chinese food expert. She lived in Taiwan for many years and she writes under the moniker Madame Huang where she explores the world of Chinese cuisine. Her books include *All Under Heaven* and *The Dim Sum Food Guide.*

BINITA PRADHAN is the founder and chef at Bini's Kitchen, a San Francisco–based catering company and take-out window serving Nepalese cuisine. Bini learned how to cook *momos*, Nepalese dumplings with a spice-spiked filling, from her mother, and now she brings the traditions and flavors from the foothills of the Himalayas to the Bay Area.

RYAN PREWITT is the chef-owner of Pêche Seafood Grill in New Orleans, which earned him the titles of Best Chef, South and Best New Restaurant by the James Beard Foundation. Ryan is a member of The Fatback Collective, a group of southern chefs, farmers, and other food industry professionals who build community and support local entrepreneurs.

ELISABETH PRUEITT is the cofounder of the beloved San Francisco–based Tartine Bakery and Tartine Manufactory. She is also the author of two cookbooks, *Tartine* (with Chad Robertson) and *Tartine All Day*. Elisabeth helped found the nonprofit Conductive Education Center of San Francisco, which benefits families with children with motor disorders.

CLAUDIA RODEN is a longtime, award-winning cookbook author and cultural anthropologist specializing in the culinary histories of North Africa, the Mediterranean, and the Middle East. She has authored over a dozen cookbooks, including *Invitation to Mediterranean Cooking, The Book of Jewish Food,* and *Claudia Roden's Simple Mediterranean Cookery.*

RICK RODGERS has received IACP and Gourmand Awards for his cookbook writing, and *Bon Appétit*'s Food and Entertaining Award for his work as a culinary teacher. He has written over 40 books with his own byline, and co-authored, ghost written, or edited over 30 more for celebrities, restaurants, bakeries, and chefs around the world.

SONOKO SAKAI is an onigiri expert and the author of *Rice Craft*, a comprehensive guide to making the iconic Japanese rice balls. Sonoko, who was raised in Tokyo and now lives in Los Angeles, travels around the country to teach cooking classes and spread the joy of easy, healthy, fun onigiri. She is also a soba expert and teaches workshops on making the noodles.

STEVE SANDO is the owner of Rancho Gordo, a highly regarded source for heirloom beans, chiles, grains, herbs and spices, hot sauce, and more based in Napa, California. Steve works with farmers in Central California, Oregon, Washington, New Mexico, and Latin America to bring his customers only the best-quality products. He is also an avid cook, and the author of many books including *Supper at Rancho Gordo* and *The Rancho Gordo Vegetarian Kitchen.*

LIZA SHAW is a restaurant consultant, helping new chefs open and run their restaurants. She was the owner of the beloved (now-closed) Merigan Sub Shop as well as a partner and executive chef at A16, both in San Francisco.

SHAKIRAH SIMLEY is a writer, master food preserver, and community organizer living in San Francisco. In 2008, she founded Slow Jams, a small-scale Bay Area–based jam company that sources urban fruit. She is a 2017 Fellow for the Stone Barns Center for Food and Agriculture, former Community Director for Bi-Rite and its family of businesses, and is the co-founder of Nourish|Resist, a multiracial organizing collaborative dedicated to using food spaces and people as tools for collective resistance. She received her M.A. from the University of Gastronomic Sciences via a Fulbright scholarship, and was honored as one of Zagat's "30 under 30."

JAMES SYHABOUT is the owner and chef of San Francisco's Hawker Fare, which serves the Isan Thai and Laotian food that he's been cooking with his mother since he was ten years old. He trained at the California Culinary Academy and went on to open The Dock, Old Kan Beer & Co., and the Michelin-starred Commis. James is the author of *Hawker Fare: Simple Recipes for Thai Isan & Lao Home Cooking*.

BRYANT TERRY is an educator, social activist, the author of four cookbooks, including *Afro-Vegan* and *The Inspired Vegetarian*, and a popular Bay Area DJ. He teaches vegetarian and vegan cooking classes, develops vegetarian and vegan menus for institutions and special events, and is a recognized speaker on food justice issues. He has received the James Beard Leadership Award and was named one of the most creative people in business by *Fast Company* magazine.

PIERRE THIAM is the author of two cookbooks about Senegalese food, *Yolele!: Recipes from the Heart of Senegal* and *Senegal: Modern Senegalese Recipes from the Source to the Bowl*, both inspired by his Senegalese upbringing. Pierre is a respected authority on the rich culinary history of Africa and its diaspora.

MARGO TRUE is the food editor at *Sunset* magazine. Before *Sunset*, she was the executive editor at *Saveur* and senior editor and writer at *Gourmet*. She has received three James Beard journalism awards for her food writing.

DANA VELDEN is a food writer and cookbook author who helps host the Oakland, California, chapter of Empty Bowls, an international project to fight hunger. She is a contributing writer to The Kitchn, a popular culinary website, and is the author of *Finding Yourself in the Kitchen*.

ALICIA VILLANUEVA is the owner and chef of Alicia's Tamales Los Mayas and has been making tamales since she was a young girl growing up in Mexico. Alicia brought her world-class and deliciously authentic tamales to the Bay Area by way of La Cocina, a nonprofit food-business incubator in San Francisco's Mission District. Alicia's Tamales Los Mayas prides itself on its mission to provide sustainable, local, organic food made by hand.

ROBB WALSH is a Texas food expert, cookbook author, and James Beard Award–winning journalist. Robb is the founder of the nonprofit organization Foodways Texas, which preserves and promotes Texas food culture. He chronicled his chili expertise in *The Chili Cookbook*, one of over a dozen cookbooks he has written. He's also a partner at the El Real Tex-Mex Cafe in Houston.

ALICE WATERS is a chef, author, food activist, and the founder and owner of Chez Panisse Restaurant in Berkeley, California. She has been a champion of local, sustainable agriculture for over four decades. She founded the Edible Schoolyard Project in 1995, a Berkeley-based program that introduces middle school students to the experience of growing, harvesting, preparing, and sharing food from an organic farm. She is the author of multiple books include *Coming to My Senses, My Pantry*, and *Chez Panisse Cafe Cookbook*.

MERRY "CORKY" WHITE is a food anthropologist at Boston University and the author of *Cooking for Crowds*. Her book, which was illustrated by Edward Koren, was recently reprinted in 2013 for its 40th anniversary.

KATIE WORKMAN was the founding editor in chief of Cookstr.com, originated the popular Cookstr weekly newsletter, and is the author of two family-focused cookbooks, *Dinner Solved!* and *The Mom 100 Cookbook*. She generously devotes her time to Share Our Strength, City Harvest, and other organizations focused on ending hunger.

permissions

acknowledgments

After many years of working on this book, I can't think of anyone in my life who hasn't been a helpful part of it in some way. All books are collaborations and this book is a collaboration of so many wonderful people.

First and foremost, I want to thank the big-hearted chefs and cooks who generously contributed their recipes. People who cook for other people are the loveliest people of all.

Thank you to Publisher Craig Cohen and Editorial Director, Will Luckman and the team at powerHouse Books for their deep commitment to this project and making meaningful beautiful books.

A huge thanks to the wonderful community at 18 Reasons, for all that they do to bring people together. For their kind partnership and work, I am grateful to executive director Sara Nelson, program manager Theresa Salcedo, past program manager Michelle McKenzie, and executive Chef Mike Weller as well as the amazing volunteers. A special thanks to Chef Mike for his big spirit and wonderful Feed Your People recipe testing dinners. Thanks to the amazing board of directors who supported this endeavor.

I wish to thank photographer Molly DeCoudreaux for her amazing, gorgeous photography and ability to capture the generous spirit of both the food and the people; for her incredible drive and commitment to this project; her patience, passion, and partnership in this project.

I also wish to thank Debbie Berne for her marvelous design, art direction, and attention to detail. She designs with an editorial eye, a project director's problem solving finesse, and incredible kindness.

I also wish to thank Emma Rudolph, a wonderfully talented editor and project manager whose editorial acumen, stealth focus, and sense of humor was essential for maintaining the editorial integrity of the book and getting us to the finish line.

Thanks also to writer/editor Jessica Battilana for her lovely prose and for her help focusing the overall structure of the book, testing recipes, and bringing a number of terrific chefs into the project.

Special thanks to Rick Rodgers for always keeping it real for real cooks. In addition to writing the front matter, his big batch expertise was essential in guiding the recipe format. I am grateful for his experience and commitment to excellence.

Thank you to Davia Nelson and the Kitchen Sisters for helping me like a sister.

A huge thanks to Sharon Silva, a superb editor and long time friend.

Thank you to my agent and friend Danielle Svetcov and the Levine Greenberg Agency who stood by the project throughout.

A big thanks to Michael Barnard of Rakestraw Books whose dual knowledge of big batch cooking and cookbooks was essential to this project. A super special thank you to Celia Sack whose store Omnivore Books is a haven of inspiration as is she.

Thank you to the recipe testers Eric Lundy, who also cooked many a Feed Your People pop-up dinner, and to Kevyn Allard whose astute feedback was extremely helpful. Thank you to Jodi Liano and her students at the San Francisco Cooking School: Brie Almena, Nathalie Arch, Marni Berger, Hannah Furgerson, Anne Jung, Meredith Tan, and Debbie Wong, and a very special thanks to Sofia Yokosawa.

For their editorial assistance I wish to thank editor Amanda Dix who started on the project, had a baby and came back to proofread the book 2 years later and to Laura Rothman who also started and came back to finish after a stint doing pastry at Chez Panisse. Thanks also to Analena Barrette, Mandy Ferreira, Megan McCrea, Lisa McGuiness, Katje Richstatter. Thanks to Jennifer Flaxman and Mitra Parineh who believed in this project from the start. Thank you to Stephanie Rosenbaum Klaussen for her research and writing on the headnotes. Thanks to Dean Burrell for his managing editorial expertise and to Laurel Leigh for helping me launch the project.

For their artistic vision and gorgeous styling thank you to Ethel Brennan, Glenn Jenkins, and Ali Zeigler. Thanks to Carol Hacker for additional props. For the food styling expertise, thank you to Emily Caneer, Betty Ann Chung, Fanny Pan, Pesha Perlsweig, and Abby Stolfo. Thank you to photography assistants Erin Conger, Candiss Koenitzer, and Bebe Carminito.

Thank you to Kate Chase for her strategic content and marketing direction. Thank you to permissions manager Mary Jo Courchese. Thank you to Jesse Kleinsaser for his marketing acumen and beautiful newsletters.

For their help with the Kickstarter campaign a special thanks Lisa Q. Fetterman (who is such a inspiration in all ways), to filmmakers Alana and Eric Lowe for doing such a lovely film, publicity maven Andrea Burnett and to Darcy Lee of Heartfelt. Thank you to Anya Fernald for cooking the Kickstarter launch dinner and for supporting the project in all ways, and to Peter Temkin and Anna Watson Carl for cooking Feed Your People dinners. For donating to the campaign, thank you to Rancho Gordo and Belcampo Meat Company. Thank you to Lisa Hazen for creating the website. Thank you to Bruce Cole, Davina Baum, Max Garrone, Susan Fassberg, Dorka Keehn , Erica Lenkert, Rachel Levin, David McElroy, Nion McEvoy, Gabi Moskowitz, Amanda Rose, Deborah Scharfetter, and Susie Wyshak for the extra support and advice.

A thank you to the community of friends in the media and food worlds who offered extra input and encouragement along the way: Stacy Adinmando, Meredith Arthur, Nick Balla, Alex Beckstead, Courtney Burns, Julie Chai, Charlotte Druckman, Helena Eichlin, Mira Evnine, Nikki Henderson, Diane Jacobs, Vicky Kalish, Peggy Knickerbocker, Kim Laidlaw, Donata Maggipinto, Mani Niall, Nadine Nelson, Jen Newens, Tori Ritchie, Erin Scott, Emily Kaiser Thelin, Ted Weinstein, Sacha Skon, Naomi Starkman, and Larissa Zimberoff.

So many wonderful community organizations that helped and inspired. Thank you to Caleb Zigas and Jessica Mataka at La Cocina, Karen Heisler and Krystin Rubin at Mission Pie, Jason Rose and Sam Mogannam at Bi-Rite, Kathryn Thomansen and the Eat Retreat community, the marvelous Food Gals, Llano Secco, and the wonderful women of Les Dames Escoffier.

For their invaluable support thank you to MJ Bogatin, Elise Cannon, Catherine Huchting, Kim Kawamura, Jessica Strand, and Molly Sullivan.

And finally thanks to my family: Arthur Jonath, Suzanne Jonath, Michael Jonath, Sylvie Jonath, Monique Jonath, Sarah Jonath, Nicole Avril, Dan Gelfand, Hugo Gelfand, Beverly Zoller, Leah Zoller, and Jason Greenhalgh, and to my lovies Miel Lappin and Todd Lappin. You guys feed my soul everyday.

Thank you to all of the great people who donated to the Kickstarter. You are the reason this book exists. Thank you all so much.

Taylor Acker, Rachel Adams, Stacy Adimando, Adam Alexander, Victoria Anakushina, Joshua Archer, Adrienne Arieffe, Vicky Aronson, Meredith Skrzypek Arthur, Lisa Baggerman Hazen, Kate Bakker, Marcia Bana Tonetto, Michael Barnard, Chris Barrett, Vanessa Barrington, Jessica Battilana, Lionel Bawden, Laura Beaudrow, Jen Bekman, Larry Bellnap, Valerie Bellnap, Jack Bennett, Shoshana Berger, Elizabeth Berliner, Debbie Berne, Sasha Bernstein, Shujan Bertrand, Melissa Bianco, Muhammad Amin Bin Suhaimi, Dwight Bishop, Destin Lane Block, Laura Brainin-Rodriguez, Ann Bramson, Mary Anne Brennan, Leland Brewster, Calvin Bridges-Avalos, Michele Bronson, Lena Brook, Matt Brown, Ruth Brown, William Brown, Mikyla Bruder, Erik Budde, Andrea Burnett, Christina Burns, Shona Burns, Peter Caldwell, Elise Cannon, David Cardinal, Anna Watson Carl, Glenda Carpio, Julie Chai, Tina Chan, Jodie Chase, Kate Chase, Harold Check, Ariella Chezar, Belinda Chin, Richard Chlopan, Rana Cho, Chocolate Cookie School, Caroline Chow, Kate Chynoweth, Harvey Clark, Renee Clark, Sarah Clegg, Tanner Cobb, Brianna Coffino, Bruce Cole, Chris Colin, Betsy Cordes, Susan Coss, Susan Coyle, Karen Cross, McKinzie Crossland, Debbie Deal, Rachel Dearborn, Allison DeLauer, Natalie DeNormandie, Michael DePinto, Alex Dolle, Maxine Dolle, Alexandre Domingue, Thad Doria, Charlotte Druckman, John Drummond, Lorrie Duval, Jeska Dzwigalski, Helena Echlin, Chas Edwards, Sally Ekus, Cheryl Eng, Sylvia Erickson, Mira Evnine, Susan Fassberg, Virginia Felch, Anya Fernald, Russ and Anne Fernald, Lisa Q. Fetterman, Maria Finn, Jennifer Flaxman, Food and Farm Film Fest, Christopher Ford, Betsy Foster, Jennifer Friedland, Simon S. Fung, Susan Gaffney-Evans, Steph Galinson, Sara Gallagher, Lori Gannon, Angelo Garro, Max Garrone, Christine Gasparac, Pamela Geismar, Daniel Gelfand, Dan Geller, Alessandra Ghini, Anna Ghosh, Kathleen Gilligan, Sara Gillingham, David Golden, Dayna Goldfine, Jennifer Granick, Phyllis Grant, Erica Greene, Hollie Greene, Cory Greenberg, Amber Gregory, Shandon Griffin, Jennifer Grillo, Grocer's Daughter, Carly Guthrie, Phillip Hahn, Henry Hall, Meesha Halm, Shelley Handler, Bronwen Hanna-Korpi, Liz Hardaway Sjodin, Sarah Harmeyer, Everett Harper, Grace Hawthorne, Margret Hefner, Kristen Herndon, Alexandrea Hickey, Tamara Hicks, Shawnette Hill, Carl Hlavenka, Lori Hokeness, Martha Holmberg, AnnaMarie Hoos, Norah Hoover, Martha Hopkins, JD Hovland, Jasmin Huang, Jon Huang, Julie Hunkins, Gina Hyams, Ali-Breeze Jackson King, Maike Jacobs, Carl Jahn, Michelle Jarvis, Adam Jay, Glenn Jenkins, Brooke Johnson, Arthur Jonath, Michael Jonath, Alexandra Jones, Carey Jones, Nate Jordan, Romy Jue, Whitman Kam, Sari Kamin, Monica Kamio, Amy Kaneko, Noah Karesh, Joel Karp, Paul Katz, Bill Kaufman, Kim Kawamura, Katya Kazbek, Dorka Keehn, Sky Kelsey, Ryan King, Steven Kirsh, Joyce Klassen, Pei-Ru Ko, Katherine Kodama, Jessica Koga, Erin Kunkel, Kim Laidlaw, Nghi Lam, Leticia Landa, Debra Lande, Madeleine Landry, Deane Lappin, Michael Lappin, Todd Lappin, Angela Lau, Laura Lazzaroni, Kate Leahy, William LeBlond, Darcy Lee, John Lee, Bradley Leons, Laurel Leigh, Erika Lenkert, Alain Lesaffre, Scott Leverette, Rachel Levin, Emily Lewis, Jodi Liano, Tami Linde, Peter Linde, Catherine Lipsetz Dauer, Monica Lo, Christina Loff, Lokables LLC, Diane Long, Loteria Films, Eric Lowe, Anita Lowe, Natalie Ma, Leslie Mackereth, Ian Maddox, Donata Maggipinto, Olivia Maki, Sarah Malarkey, Tiffany Marcheterre, Domenica Marchetti, Gregory Margolis, Kitty Margolis, Ed Marquand, Diana Martin, Liz Martin, Anne Marxer, Robbin Mashbein, Dawn Masiero, Jacob McCarty, Marisa McClellan, Karin McClune, Morgan-Sean McCright, David McElroy, Nion McEvoy, Lisa McGuinness, Betsy McNair, Colum McNamara, Timothy S. McNamara, Donna Friedman Meir, Emily Miller, Grace Ellen Miller, Jim Miller, Sam Mogannam, Hilary Mohs, Cathy Crane Moley, Tom Moore, Genevieve Morgan, Gabi Moskowitz, Matthew Moy, Anne Zieleniewski Murphy, Sigmund Naah, Janice Nasser, Patty Nelson, Peter Nelson, Jennifer Newens, Andrea Nguyen, Ben Nichols, Susan Norris, Ruth Nott, Jen Nurse, Adam O'Donnell, Evonne Okafor, Hannah Onstad, Nathaniel Osborn, Claudia Ossa, Lorena Oswald, Chris Palia, Biana Pardini, Ron Pardini, Mitra Parineh, Kira Parker, Philip Paternite, Penelope Perez, Peter Perez, Sandy Peterson, Woody Peterson, Tammy Petro, Abigail Phillips, Aubrie Pick, Marc Pierre, Simon Platt, Helen Plett, Elizabeth and McKee Poland, Amy Portello Nelson, Natalie Compagni Portis, Phillip S. Powell, Rachel Pringle, Andrew Prodroumou, Hannah Rahill, Christina Ramirez, Natalie Ramirez, Mary Beth Ray, Susan Reich, Chris Reilly, Cheri Rendler, Jenni Ricci, Paul Richmond, Liz Rico, Catherine Riggs, Victoria Ritchie, Deena Rosen, Geoffrey Rosen, Cliff Ross, Ned Rote, Ryan Roth, Clair Roulin, Krystin Rubin, Caroline Russell, Lindsay Sablosky, Jill Santopietro, Celeste Schaefer Snyder, Jay Schaefer, Deborah Scharfetter, Deborah Schumacher, Gretchen Scoble, Erin Scott, Eileen Serra, Hank Shaw, Roger Shaw, Sandra Shepard, Kathleen Sieler, Barbara Sigismund, Shakirah Simley, Vera Simon-Nobes, Leanna Simons, Dawn Solis, Rebecca Spector, Allison Stern, Kathy Strahs, Andrew and Michal Strickman, Michael Strong, Cora Stuhr, Jake Su, Deidre Megan Sullivan, Molly Sullivan, Danielle Svetkov, Kiri Tannenbaum, Neo Ce Tao, Lisa Taw, Jessica Taylor, Olivia Terenzio, Bryant Terry, Anna Theil, Emily Kaiser Thelin, Dan Thompson, ThredWave, Ted Tilles, Bryan Ting, Steven Toews, Kathryn Tomajan, Laura Tomas, Emily Torgrimson, Ellen Towell, Adam and Stevette Treco, Madeleine Trembley-Perrot, Margo True, Mike Valdez, Justin Varney, Carmen Vega, Tracy Vernon, Jennifer Vetter, Lisa Vipond, Sune Vourela, Bela Waidelich, Kathleen Wall, Merritt Watts, Andy Weiner, Ted Weinstein, Susan Wels, Ben Wenk, John West, Aaron White, Roger Whittaker, Kelsey Wilcox, Sky Williamson, Charles Willson, Cynthia Wong, Katie Workman, Darcy Wright, Gretchen Wustrack, Kim Wylie, Jason Yahinsky, Lesley Yarborough, Marco Yergovich, Alexandra Zeigler, Roy Zemlicka, Ellen Ziegler, Caleb Zigas, Annelies Zijderveld, Larissa Zimberoff, Beverley Zoller, Leah Zoller, Kara Zuaro, Karen Zuercher.

table of equivalents

LIQUID/DRY MEASUREMENTS

U.S.	Metric
¼ teaspoon	1.25 milliliters
½ teaspoon	2.5 milliliters
1 teaspoon	5 milliliters
1 Tablespoon (3 teaspoons)	15 milliliters
1 fluid ounce (2 Tablespoons)	30 milliliters
¼ cup (4 Tablespoons)	60 milliliters
⅓ cup (5 Tablespoons + 1 teasp)	80 milliliters
½ cup (8 Tablespoons)	120 milliliters
¾ cup (12 Tablespoons)	180 milliliters
1 cup (16 Tablespoons; 8 fl. oz.)	240 milliliters
1 pint (2 cups; 16 fl. oz.)	480 milliliters
1 quart (4 cups, 32 fl. oz.)	960 milliliters
1 gallon (4 quarts)	3.8 liters
1 ounce (by weight)	28 grams
1 pound	450 grams
2.2 pounds	1 kilogram

LENGTHS

U.S.	Metric
⅛ inch	3 millimeters
¼ inch	6 millimeters
½ inch	12 millimeters
1 inch	2.5 centimeters

OVEN TEMPERATURES

Fahrenheit	Celsius	Gas
250	120	½
275	140	1
300	150	2
325	160	3
350	180	4
375	190	5
400	200	6
425	220	7
450	230	8
475	240	9
500	260	10

index

stir-frying, 129
storage
    containers, 12
    tips, 9–10
Strawberry-Peach Trifle, 253
Syhabout, James, 174, 296

T

Tabbouleh, Green, with Farro and
    Herbs, 207–8
Tamales, Alicia's, 25–29
Tart, Cherry Tomato, with Anchovies
    and Garlic Confit, 229–31
Terry, Bryant, 221, 296
Texas Sheet Cake, 265–67
Thai Curry Chicken Wings (Phat
    Garlee Peek Gai), 174–75
Thiam, Pierre, 159, 296
Timpano, Big Night, 103–9
tofu
    Steamed Shiitake and Vegetable
    Dumplings, 32–33
tomatillos, 28
    Grandma Salazar's Chile Verde,
    73–74
    Tomatillo Salsa Cruda, 147
tomatoes
    Big Pan Seafood Paella, 121–25
    Black Bean Soup, 67–68
    Bollywood Theater Spicy Shrimp
    Curry, 178–79
    Cherry Tomato Tart with
    Anchovies and Garlic Confit,
    229–31
    Chickpea Curry Soup, 85–86
    El Real's Chili con Carne, 69–70
    Grilled Clambake, 189–90
    Herbed Baked Fish with Pearl
    Couscous, 198–99
    Le Polpette della Mama, 93–95
    Marinara Sauce, 154
    Minestrone, 53–55

Mom's Guju Chili, 80–81
Nepalese Momos, 37–39
Old-School Chicken Parm,
    153–57
Pico de Gallo, 21
Ratatouille, 205–6
Santa Maria–Style Beans, 173
Tomato-Almond Pesto, 113
Tomato-Basil Sauce, 198–99
Tomato-Cilantro Sauce, 38
tortillas, warming, 145, 146
trifles
    Lemon-Blueberry Trifle, 249–52
    Roasted Pineapple–Coconut
    Trifle, 253
    Strawberry-Peach Trifle, 253
True, Margo, 198, 296
tuna
    Call-It-What-You-Will Cobb Salad,
    217–19
    Italian White Bean Salad with
    Tuna, 233–34
turkey
    Nepalese Momos, 37–39

V

vegetables
    Pickled Vegetables (Verduras en
    Escabeche), 147
    stir-fried, 129
    See also individual vegetables
Velden, Dana, 85, 296
Villanueva, Alicia, 25, 296
volunteering, 13

W

Waffles, Cornmeal, 163–67
walnuts
    Caramelitas, 258–59
    Frog Hollow Farm Fruit Crisp,
    281–83

Walsh, Robb, 69, 296
warming equipment, 11–12
Waters, Alice, 53, 54, 296
White, Merry "Corky," 57, 296
Wine-Braised Brisket, 133–34
Workman, Katie, 277, 296

Y

Yassa Ginaar (Senegalese Grilled
    Chicken with Lime-Onion
    Sauce), 159–61

Z

zucchini
    Minestrone, 53–55
    Ratatouille, 205–6

For my parents
for teaching me the joys of gathering
around the table

Feed Your People: Big-batch, big-hearted cooking and recipes to gather around

Compilation and Text Copyright © 2018 by Leslie Jonath
Photographs Copyright © 2018 by Molly DeCoudreaux

Pages 298–299 constitute a continuation of the copyright page.

Published in the United States by powerHouse Books,
a division of powerHouse Cultural Entertainment, Inc.
32 Adams Street, Brooklyn, NY 11201-1021
e-mail: info@powerHouseBooks.com
website: www.powerHouseBooks.com

First edition, 2018

Library of Congress Control Number: 2018933940

ISBN 978-1-57687-804-0

Printed in China through Asia Pacific Offset

Created by Connected Dots Media, LLC
www.connecteddotsmedia.com
Designed by Debbie Berne

10 9 8 7 6 5 4 3 2 1